Praise for *Successfully Navigating Your Parents' Senior Years*

"When it comes to family caregiving, why start from scratch? Star Bradbury's book *Successfully Navigating Your Parents' Senior Years* reflects her years of experience as director of assisted-living and memory-care facilities. Her insider knowledge and know-how play particular importance when dealing with dementia and what can be done ahead of time. For example, readers gain insights on planning for the high costs of managing memory care, financially and otherwise. Taking care of parents when one of them has dementia is also addressed in this book. Tips on what to do when plans are clearly failing are another consideration of this book. This book will save readers time, money, and precious energy. I especially like the author's sensitive treatment of the death and dying process beginning with her essay titled, "What is a good death?" We are never prepared for the departure of our parents and reading this book will hold the reader's hand through the entire caregiving journey."

—**Joy Loverde, author of *Who Will Take Care of Me When I'm Old* and *The Complete Eldercare Planner***

"*Successfully Navigating Your Parents' Senior Years* is an exceptionally comprehensive compendium of the problems, pitfalls, opportunities, and solutions people face when helping the elderly navigate the aging and dying process. From downsizing, drivers' licenses, pre-need guardianship papers, tax relief for shower grab bars, robotic companionship, meal deliveries, retirement communities, long term care, slow medicine, Medicare, Medicaid, death doulas, funerals, green burials, and writing an obituary, Star covers it all, and she covers it well."

—**Samuel Harrington, MD, author of *At Peace: Choosing a Good Death After a Long Life***

"A golden guidebook, *Successfully Navigating Your Parents' Senior Years* comes from Star Bradbury's decades of enriched experiences with thousands of elders and their adult children while educating, working with, and helping them to plan ahead for later life. Her delightful conversational warmth carries you gently through fully delineated details and critical questions as she handholds and explores with you the challenges of planning for and conversing with elder loved ones about retirement, health transitions and healthcare, home settings and services, legal and financial issues, end-of-life issues, and so much more. Her superb guidebook builds your knowledge base, communication skills, and confidence toward planning and achieving the best choices for you, your aging parents, and other loved ones to age optimally and successfully."

—**Leilani Mangerian Doty, PhD, former director of the University of Florida Cognitive and Memory Disorder Clinic**

"Star Bradbury beautifully combines her knowledge, experience, and compassion into a must-have guide to help aging parents enjoy their senior years in the healthiest, safest, and most dignified way. This is the compass we have needed—from a navigator we can trust."

—**Dr. Claudia Cometa, owner of Peace Advocacy Group**

"As an elder law attorney, I plan to give Star's book to all my clients. Walking through the aging process with the fictional Spencer family is so useful as they show us how to apply the principles behind successful aging addressed in the book. They are like so many of my clients! The wide range of issues—discussing how we want to die, how to use long-term care insurance, how to prevent exploitation, and finally how to pay for it all! It's a handbook on how we can help our loved ones walk through the sunset chapter of their lives with grace and independence. I am giving the book to my own daughters as well! This is what aging gracefully can look like . . ."

—Shannon Miller, certified elder law attorney and former president of the Academy of Florida Elder Law Attorneys

"Older persons in their 70s and 80s face a heightened risk of experiencing health, money, and housing problems. They have difficulties performing everyday activities and getting their personal affairs in order. Help from family members is often crucial. But their loved ones often have little experience asking the right questions, finding the most appropriate information, and judging the most effective actions. Star Bradbury's new book to the rescue! Building on a lifetime of personal and professional experience, each of her chapters will be an invaluable resource for older persons and their families seeking the best courses of action."

—Stephen M. Golant, PhD, professor at the University of Florida and author of *Aging in the Right Place*

"At last, a comprehensive approach to helping you navigate the complex stage of life faced by your aging parents. Star's excellent publication provides thoughtful, expert guidance and is a must read for those with aging parents. We are honored to be included as a recommended resource."

—Marci Lobel-Esrig, founder, CEO, and general counsel for SilverBills

"Star Bradbury has written an excellently paced guide with a focused, detailed timetable for long-term care planning. Her years of work related and personal experience helping guide seniors' families gives her a clear view of the information needed to plan ahead, have meaningful discussions and access relevant resources. It is not unusual to postpone difficult and challenging life-changing decisions, but *Successfully Navigating Your Parents Senior Years* will give you the confidence needed to take the first step forward. Check it out—well worth it!"

—Flory Antiga-Stephens, LCSW, case manager for the Senior Healthcare Center at Melrose

"As a certified geriatric care manager, I'm aware that most people don't know how many options and resources are out there for seniors. *Successfully Navigating Your Parents' Senior Years* will leave you fully informed, with confidence and clear expectations for what the future will bring."

—Cindy Flowers, certified geriatric care manager and Florida Aging Life Care Association chapter president

"In my ministry and as the beloved elders in my family age, I have frequently longed for a resource like this. Here Star offers her considerable wisdom and expertise, to fill the gap and lead the way, empowering readers with the information they need to ask good questions, have difficult conversations, and make thoughtful plans. Aging is inevitable (if we are lucky!), but this book equips us to move into our later years (and those of our loved ones) with hope and care—no luck required."
—**Rev. Bromleigh McCleneghan, writer and coordinating minister at the United Church of Gainesville**

"The perfect handbook for any caregiver! Star Bradbury is a compassionate, reliable guide through the stressful realities of aging and the minutiae of senior living, with sage advice, adaptable plans, and resources for parents and children alike. Having worked with Star over the years, I can attest to her knowledge on the critical information needed to age successfully."
—**Kristen Griffis, chief executive officer of Elder Options**

"A fantastic and badly needed road map—one which incorporates a rare blend of wisdom and experience with the modern technologies that can help simplify a complex journey."

—**Todd Rovak, Carefull app cofounder**

Successfully Navigating Your Parents' Senior Years

Successfully Navigating Your Parents' Senior Years

Critical Information to
Maximize Their Independence
and Make Sure They
Get the Care They Need

STAR BRADBURY

BenBella Books, Inc.
Dallas, TX

BenBella Books, Inc.
10440 N. Central Expressway
Suite 800
Dallas, TX 75231
benbellabooks.com
Send feedback to feedback@benbellabooks.com

BenBella is a federally registered trademark.

Printed in the United States of America
10 9 8 7 6 5 4 3 2 1

Library of Congress Control Number: 2022038263
ISBN 9781637742471 (trade paperback)
ISBN 9781637742488 (electronic)

Editing by Leah Wilson and Joe Rhatigan
Copyediting by Scott Calamar
Proofreading by Madeline Grigg and Lisa Story
Indexing by WordCo.
Text design and composition by PerfecType, Nashville, TN
Cover design by Brigid Pearson
Printed by Lake Book Manufacturing

Dedicated to the millions of caregivers—families, healthcare workers, and my fellow aging life care professionals, who show up every day to make a positive difference in the life of an elder, and to my husband, who was both patient and supportive of me for the years it took to write this book.

Contents

Part 3: When Your Parents Need More Help and Care

Part 4: A Prepared Exit Plan

Introduction

The phone rings in the middle of the night. It is your mother's neighbor calling to say that your mom fell and was just taken to the hospital. Maybe your aunt is calling to say your dad is having major surgery tomorrow, and you know you cannot get there. Your sister calls crying and tells you Mom was just diagnosed with dementia. You live in another state, another country, or just many hours away. Now begins your journey into the confusing world of senior healthcare, full of complex information, decisions, and options.

In my twenty-five years working in senior living, I heard a common refrain: "I wish there was a book that would help me navigate this time in my parents' lives." It can be overwhelming, no matter how accomplished or educated one is. The average person does not know the difference between assisted living and skilled care, or the difference between home care and home healthcare, much less what a life care community is. The truth is, "You don't know what you don't know." The result? We make poor decisions based on limited knowledge.

Parents really would prefer not to have to rely on help from their children, and adult children are stressed out with too much on their plates already. Parents are living longer and even the baby boomers are stressed. You might be in your forties or fifties, coping with aging parents in their sixties and seventies, or just as easily be in your sixties or seventies dealing with parents in their nineties! This challenge is not going away anytime soon for a vast majority of our population, and I understand that you need help now!

Having been the director of an assisted-living and memory care facility and having worked in a life care community for eighteen years, I have expertise that I can share with you that will make a critical difference for you and your family and help you make informed, educated decisions. Looking back on my own life, I wish I had the knowledge I have now—knowledge I share with you in this book! I have consulted with thousands of families and helped them develop a flexible plan focused on *successful aging*. What choices can you and your parents make together that will maximize their health, safety, and independence, now and in the future? What can you do before the next pandemic, the next medical emergency, to be better prepared? There is *much you can do now* to aim for a positive outcome and help your parents and loved ones age successfully. My book gives you a step-by-step guide and includes resources, checklists, and helpful websites at the end of the book. Also, throughout the book, we will be following the Spencers, an imaginary family, as they go through both the expected and the unexpected. You will learn from these scenarios how to apply my core principles to a variety of decisions they face. Some will be obvious, but some may surprise you.

• • •

The key to being prepared for change is to expect it: to anticipate it as best as one can, when it comes to aging parents and yourself. There are literally hundreds of things you can do before a crisis that will allow you to respond without panic. Whether it is gathering critical medical or financial information before a dementia diagnosis or emergency, or learning now about senior living options or home care, you will be educated and confident moving forward. Developing a family plan that works for everyone requires flexibility, patience, compassion, and knowledge. Educate yourself now to be prepared for the future and avoid some of the pitfalls I've both made and witnessed.

♀ What if you knew the red flags to look for that could mean dementia is in your parent's future? Learn about *pre-need guardianships* and *preparing financially for dementia.*

♀ What if you had a list of the critical financial documents to gather before a death or a debilitating stroke or dementia? *Documents like life insurance, long-term care insurance, birth certificates, deeds, home insurance, and much more.*

♀ Did you know falls are the leading cause of death in the elderly, and most falls happen in and around the home? *A simple grab bar can prevent a deadly fall! Learn how to make your parents' home ideal to "age in place."*

♀ What if you knew how to hire the best in-home care or find the right retirement community or assisted living or skilled nursing care? *Learn the critical questions to ask and the agencies that monitor them.*

As you journey through your parents' aging process, there will be multiple opportunities for you to advise, support, and perhaps make decisions that will affect their lives and yours. These choices can range from big to little or legal to mundane, but all have potential consequences, and one small piece of new knowledge can make a big difference. And to be clear, some adult children really do want Mom and Dad to live with them and some parents love the idea! If this is your plan, you can still apply everything in this book to make sure your plan works! If not, then my book will provide you with a wealth of new information to educate you and your family about options you may not even realize exist. (For example, check out what a life care community is on page 131.)

My mother once bought me a sweatshirt that said, "Growing Old Is Not for Sissies." I did not appreciate it at the time. I've come to see that growing older gracefully takes courage, wisdom, and humility. But even the most capable seniors need their adult children or someone to be there for support, guidance, and when necessary, a warrior in their defense (think emergency room). Those seniors with involved adult children almost always fare better than those with no help or support system.

I have lost all four of my parents (including stepparents), in-laws, a dear sister, sister-in-law, and many close friends. My personal experiences left me asking myself if I had done everything possible to help, especially with my parents. I began to understand that much can be done before a crisis to be better prepared. Working in senior living, I came to accept that losing favorite residents who had become friends was part of life. Each death was painful and a deep loss, and each death taught me something special and different about both myself and life. But it gave me the wisdom to share with you, dear readers—information that will help you make informed decisions for both you and your parents.

With decades in senior living, plus my personal experiences, I have learned what works and what doesn't when it comes to successful aging. My hope is that this book will help educate you and your family, give you some peace of mind, and empower and prepare you to help your parents age successfully and to face the challenges that are part of this journey.

Star Bradbury

Part 1

Develop a Plan

Planning is bringing the future into the present so that you can do something about it now.

Alan Lakein

Developing a plan of action isn't about telling your parents what to do. Nor is it when your parents demand one course of action, especially if you are part of this plan and it doesn't work for you. Ideally, this is a team effort, with lots of back-and-forth communication, mindful and respectful of each other's wishes. This section gives you important information on when to start planning with your parents, plus the principles needed to help guide the discussion, along with important critical medical and financial information. Finally, can you tell if your parents need help already? Chapter 4, "Do Your Parents Need Help Now?" gives you an overview of what to watch out for when deciding if your parents need help sooner rather than later, especially when it comes to memory loss and confusion, and the importance of getting a proper diagnosis.

Chapter 1

Get the Ball Rolling

My good friend Stephanie was an only child. Her mom had passed away when she was only sixteen, and she was very close to her dad. But he was stubborn, very independent, and resisted any help as he grew older. Every time Stephanie brought up the topic of living wills and appointing her or anyone as his healthcare surrogate, he said he did not want to discuss it. But the last thing he wanted was to "be a vegetable" or kept around when he "couldn't be useful anymore." Then, he had a massive stroke and was rushed to the hospital. Without a living will, the doctors were compelled to put him on a respirator and intubate him. He lasted for many months in this condition—an awful experience for Stephanie, and one that could have been avoided.

As an *aging life care specialist*, I talk with families every day who have no idea how to navigate the confusing world of senior healthcare and senior living. And why should they? When you get the call that Mom was just diagnosed with dementia or Dad just had a stroke and can't live alone anymore, you likely do not know where to turn for answers. Plus, these events always occur in the midst of our already busy lives. No wonder caregivers are overwhelmed!

In my twenty-five years of experience working with families in senior living, time and again I see both parents and adult children making piecemeal decisions with little or no thought to the long-term impact on what I call successful aging: *the ability to live a healthy, independent lifestyle for as long as possible by planning ahead for the inevitable changes that come with aging.*

Adult children are reluctant to have these conversations with parents and often avoid the topic. Parents don't want to worry their adult children, so they, too, avoid the subject. And sometimes, if truth be told, they don't want their "kids" telling them what to do or "taking control."

But it doesn't have to be this way! With a little preparation, you and your family can face the future with the confidence of having had discussions about the options on the table. As you look at the length of time you might be helping your aging parents, understand it could easily be over twenty-five years. If you are forty now, and your parents are sixty-five or seventy, they could easily live until ninety, as this is the fastest-growing demographic in the United States today. A plan for parents in their sixties will be drastically different than a plan for parents in their eighties or nineties. What can you do to meet the ever-changing dynamics of aging parents? The key is fearlessly opening the door to having these kinds of difficult conversations all along the way and working together to develop a plan that works for your family.

If you are quietly muttering things like "This will never work in my family," keep reading, as I promise I will discuss techniques to begin these kinds of conversations, even with difficult families. The key to a good plan is accepting it will likely have to change as life throws you curveballs. And of course, remembering we are not in control. We can leave that to a higher power!

It is not a guessing game about **if** a parent's health will fail, or **if** they will eventually no longer be able to live independently, it is **when**. The statistics don't lie, and more parents will need long-term care or will develop dementia than will die in their sleep. It is estimated that 70 percent of seniors over the age of sixty-five are going to need some kind of long-term care services, according to national organization USAging.

When to Start Planning: The Go-Go, Slow-Go, and No-Go Years

When parents first retire, their adult children often are surprised at how busy their parents are! "You're traveling again?" or "I can't keep up with your schedule" are phrases heard often. Having worked in senior living settings for so many years, retirees jokingly used to tell me, "You'll be surprised you ever had time to work!"

I call these the "go-go" years. (I credit my friend Tony Kendzior for these terms.) These go-go years are the ideal period after one retires when you are literally on the go, your health allows for this, and perhaps your pocketbook as well. But after this period come the slow-go years followed by the no-go years. The mistake is for you or your parents to assume that the go-go years go on forever. Looking ahead to the fragile no-go years, where one will likely need help of some kind, means talking openly and honestly about how to prepare for this during the go-go years. There is no promise you won't skip slow-go and move straight to no-go. That is why a plan is critical sooner rather than later.

Please do not think that sitting down with your sixty-something parents is too soon to begin this kind of planning. If I could wave a magic wand and make just one wish, it would be that these kinds of conversations started early. I understand how hard it is to begin these conversations, but I promise you that the majority of parents will appreciate your concern. Maybe you will be one of the lucky ones whose parents actually do have a plan. It will be wonderful to find this out by initiating the discussion! And if not, then you are simply expressing your love and concern by asking gentle inquisitive questions to begin with. Understand that these conversations evolve over time into more difficult topics like end-of-life wishes.

Principle #1: Maximize and Prolong Your Parents' Independence

Adult children know that the goal of most parents is to raise their children to be independent and able to function on their own in the world. But I challenge readers to think in terms of applying this concept in reverse: *How can I help maximize and prolong my parents' independence as they age?*

All parents will agree that they want to maintain their independence for as long as possible, and this is what adult children want as well! This is the key to opening discussions. Use Principle #1 as a framework for all decisions for as long as you can. Not only will your parents feel empowered, but they may be less likely to resist creating a plan with you.

For example, maybe your parents want to age in place. If their home is multilevel with staircases, staying in that home may actually impede their ability to remain independent! If there are no full bathrooms on the ground floor, and Mom falls and breaks a hip, then what? Maybe the answer is to downsize. Great! But only consider one-story homes!

What if one of your parents is already widowed, and you can see they are becoming more socially isolated and withdrawn? Does staying in their home sound like a good plan? Maybe it is, if they have a strong support system and lots of friends or family nearby who are able and willing to spend time with them.

There is no one right answer. Every family and situation is different. After some practice, you will find that using this principle will help you and your parents stay focused on looking at the bigger picture: maintaining independence for the longest possible time and staying flexible as you go.

Principle #2: Apply the JITSP Concept ("Just in Time" Senior Planning)

Another key to successful planning is to break down your plan into manageable increments. It does not make sense to waste your or your parents' time trying to foresee the future and make a ten-year plan. I can't claim authorship of applying the JIT or "just in time" concept to making a plan for seniors. I first read about this in a study developed years ago in Minnesota that focused on helping solo seniors develop a workable plan for aging well.

What can we learn from a concept usually applied to the manufacturing world? Reduced to its simplest component, the "just in time" method is an inventory strategy where materials are only ordered and received as they are needed in the production process. Part of this approach includes "continuous improvement." This allows for everyone involved in this process (including factory workers) to make suggestions to the current process and continually improve it.

With aging parents, you're looking at the near-term future, three to five years, and not trying to meet demands in a future that may or may not ever arise. Caregivers need to stop imagining worst-case scenarios for themselves or their parents when they peer into the future. From my own experience, this will only drain you and create more fear and anxiety. Stick with looking at present needs and those you can anticipate in the next few years. Think of your inventory in this situation as applying to both your financial resources and your emotional resources! How much can you expend and for how long? How long can you honestly manage to have Dad living with you as his dementia increases? Never make quick decisions that won't work in the long run, especially financially.

Developing the Plan

It is easy to feel overwhelmed when trying to formulate a plan that will meet the challenges that usually come along with aging parents. And if you are an adult "kid" trying to manage running your own family, working, plus worrying about your own parents, it is no wonder you are overwhelmed. You may be in your own retirement years as well, with parents in their nineties, wondering if they will outlive you! If you are in the role of caregiver or long-distance caregiver, I understand you are stressed. What can you do now to develop a plan no matter what your circumstances? If your parents are still on the young side, you want to develop a plan before they need care, before the inevitable crisis. The same principles apply, albeit differently, if your parents are in their late eighties or their nineties.

Be One of the Team

I suggest that as you enter these kinds of conversations, you emphasize that you want to be part of the process of developing a plan. Be wary of coming across as being in charge unless the situation calls for this. As "one of the team," you want to help them make a three- to five-year plan that will ensure, to the greatest degree possible, that they will age successfully. Go back to Principle #1 by starting with the right question: "How can I help maximize and prolong my parents' independence as they age?"

This is the constant framework you use as you develop this JITSP three- to five-year plan. Making their independence the focus of any conversation will give you a higher degree of success as there will be no argument on this from most parents. The more involved your parents are, the more likely they will achieve the outcome they are hoping for, and the less stressful it will be for you!

Shared Responsibility

It is my experience that often there is one family member who takes the lead. But their willingness does not mean they need to do this by themselves. If you have multiple siblings, my suggestion is that everyone does their part in some way so no one family member is burdened with all the research, planning, coordinating, or hands-on care. You'll find numerous helpful websites I've compiled at starbradbury.com/resources that will provide free help, information, and counseling, whether you are an only child or not.

Providing a Framework: The Five Pillars of Aging Successfully

As you and your family develop a plan that will work for both short and long term, I'd like to provide you with a broad framework that will be helpful. When I sit down with a "solo senior" or a couple that wants to develop a plan to age successfully, I tell them they need to look at the following basic areas:

- Do I want to "age in place" or move, and if so, where? What options will help me stay independent longer?
- Do I have all the critical medical documents known as advance directives, such as a living will or healthcare surrogate form? Does the family have copies? My doctors?
- Do I have all the legal and financial documents I need, such as a will, power of attorney, trust, and more?
- Do I know how I will pay for long-term care if I need it? This could be care in my home or in assisted or skilled-care facilities.
- What will keep me engaged and connected to my community? Do I have a purpose and a passion? What do I want my legacy to be?

I'm in This Alone!

If you are reading this and saying, "I have no siblings, it is only me," here is my suggestion: You simply cannot procrastinate on planning ahead. Even if your parent won't plan, you can—especially if you already know the burden will fall to you. Enlist as much support and help as possible. Build your own support team, as you will need it. Help your parent(s) be prepared by suggesting a list of who else, besides you, will be part of their support team. If you have a friend who has been through this already, meet with them and take notes. Join online chat groups like Daughterhood, founded by Anne Tumlinson, to help struggling caregivers. There are numerous Facebook caregiver support groups, and they are an important part of coping with the stress of caregiving for many people. It is imperative that you already have the names of friends and neighbors to call in an emergency, names of home care and home healthcare agencies, and various senior living options that could work if your parent could suddenly no longer live alone. Make sure to carefully read Part Three, "When Your Parents Need More Help and Care."

Keep in mind, this is the conversation I have with someone already in their sixties or seventies. All of these topics are woven into the context of this book, and you will find they will be woven into your conversations with your parents as well. This framework works hand in hand with Principle #1, focused on maintaining their independence and Principal #2, Just in Time Senior Planning. As they say, timing is everything, so choose your timing carefully.

For instance, my father and stepmother lived in New York City. Many years ago, when they were both still alive, I made the mistake of bringing up financial questions with both of them, and I was far too direct. I received a nasty letter when I returned home telling me their finances were none of my business. I believe that had I sat down and approached the conversation with open-ended questions like the ones I list below, the outcome would have been quite different. We patched things up, but I learned an important lesson!

The First Basic Questions

Open the conversation by clearly stating you want to talk about their future plans, if this is appropriate. If a crisis is unfolding, then you will ask more serious questions and already be discussing available options. But initially, you can cite friends that are coping with a current emergency involving their parents, and you can explain that you want to be more prepared. Take the approach that *you are the one who is concerned* because not knowing means you will be guessing, and you would like to be able to help.

Start with three or four basic questions.

- What kind of lifestyle do you want as you age?
- Are you thinking about relocating when you retire and if so, where?
- Do you want to stay in your home as you get older?
- Are you considering any retirement communities?

None of the above questions are threatening, and all of these have open-ended answers. The goal is to get the ball rolling, not create a plan after the first conversation! My advice? You genuinely need to hear what their thoughts and wishes are before weighing in at all. Keep in mind that developing even "Plan A" will likely take numerous conversations and may be months in the making.

Starting with these kinds of questions will give you the chance to find out if your parents are looking ahead realistically. Have they thought about leaving a rural area for a more urban setting (which is the current trend)? Moving closer to "one of the kids"? Staying put in their home?

If they are not living close to any family, you should feel safe asking if they believe they are prepared for the unexpected. Ask them:

- Do you feel you have a strong supportive community/network where you live now to get the help you might need?
- Who could you call for help in the event of an emergency? Could you share this information with us?
- How is your "professional team," including your doctors, dentists, accountants, and advisors? Are they all retiring soon? Will they be available when you need them?

Some of the data coming out of Covid is the devastation of loneliness on seniors. Even more than family, the degree of connectedness to a community is a determining factor in aging well. When I do any kind of assessment as a consultant, one of the first things I ask about is the strength of their social network. This is the best predictor of aging successfully over any other data!

It is important for you to know the answers to these questions, especially if you do not live nearby. If your mom or dad can't give you the names of at least four to five friends they can call in an emergency, they do not have a strong enough support system. If all their friends are the same age as they are, in their eighties, let's say, this is not a strong list. If you know your parents are isolated or do not have many friends, I advise you to encourage them to either move closer to you or another sibling if possible, or into a retirement community where they will make new friends and be able to receive more services as they age. Chapter 14, "Managing Your Parents' Care Long

Distance," provides many helpful tips on building a network of support for both you and your parent.

Dealing with Stubbornness?

You may find yourself treading carefully if a parent is in serious denial about their need for care already. As the conversation allows, you may add a few more questions that delve even deeper, especially if they have already told you they want to stay in their home. Ask them:

- Have you thought about making some modifications to your home such as a walk-in shower or adding safety bars?
- Have you given any thought to moving closer to me or another family member?
- I worry about what will happen if one of you has a serious health issue . . . have you thought about what you would do?
- For a single parent: What is the plan if your health fails and you need help?
- Are you worried about your finances?

If Mom is already using a walker, you might tactfully say something like, "Mom, I worry about you. If you could not go up and down the stairs to get to your bedroom and bathroom, what would you do?" This is an opener to discuss the possibility of downsizing to a one-story home, relocating closer to family, or considering a community that provides some services.

Planning Together: The Spencers Show Us How

Let's meet the imaginary Spencer family.

Josie and her husband, Dan, live in North Carolina. Josie, in her mid-forties, is a professional, and they have two children, ages ten and thirteen. Her parents, Sally and Bob Spencer, live in New Jersey and are in their mid-seventies. She has an excellent relationship with them, and they are in relatively good health.

Josie is concerned because she knows she cannot drop everything because of her full time job and get to New Jersey quickly if either one of her parents has a major health event. She knows that Dan will be supportive, but he works full-time as well in a demanding job. Dad (Bob) had open-heart surgery in his mid-sixties, but he seems to have recovered. Both Mom and Dad are retired, active, and still traveling—in their go-go years. Josie has two siblings, John and Wendy.

Josie decides she needs to be proactive and calls a family meeting. She sits down with both her parents, her husband, and her siblings and asks them if they could have an open conversation about their plans for the next three to five years. (I advise not doing this on the fly; make an appointment with all the parties involved. A Zoom meeting will work best to include far-flung family members.)

Beginning the dialogue allows for all parties involved to communicate their thoughts and maybe bring up topics no one has considered. Josie gets to express that she feels unprepared to deal with any kind of medical emergency should something happen to one of them. She would like her parents to consider moving closer to her in a few years. Sally says she has been thinking about this but was afraid to bring it up. She and Bob are relieved to know this is an option they can consider.

Bob tells the family he knows they are doing great now, but he has wondered how difficult it would be for Sally to deal with the house if he dies first. Nor does he want to be a burden on Josie or her siblings, and he shares that he would like to live near them, not with them.

Josie's brother, John, states that he and his wife, Sophia, are also open to them moving closer to him in Denver. Wendy, who lives in California, is a single schoolteacher, and she offers to help when she can. They agree to keep this conversation going, ask a lot of questions to start with, and build a plan together. They set a Zoom time/date for their next meeting in a month's time.

After their first meeting, Josie and Dan continue to apply the JITSP approach. Josie asks if they could all look at making a three- to five-year plan *together* and break things down to smaller time frames. Josie and her siblings ask the basic questions and find out that their parents like the idea of relocating from New Jersey. They talk about the options and decide the following:

- Josie's parents, Sally and Bob, agree they will consider moving in four years before they turn seventy-nine, unless they move sooner due to health reasons.
- Bob and Sally will look at adding some basic safety features in their bathroom to make it safer for a later time when they will still be in their home (see Chapter 6, "Aging-in-Place Considerations").
- Josie, John, and Wendy will help investigate both Denver (where John lives) and Raleigh, North Carolina (where Josie and Dan live), as potential places to live.
- They will compare the two cities: the cultural environment, the cost of real estate, available retirement communities, available top-notch healthcare, and the cost of long-term care.
- They set another meeting for the following month.

After a year, Bob and Sally have decided they want to move to Raleigh as the weather is milder, and the area offers excellent healthcare and medical and cultural activities to choose from. They start the downsizing process very slowly, so they won't be stressed out! The plan is to tackle a closet a month and begin getting rid of things they won't bring with them to Raleigh.

Adjusting for Curveballs

But remember the unexpected curveballs life throws at you? The following year, Josie's dad, Bob, has a mini-stroke at seventy-six that leaves him with some weakness on one side and a limp. While he recovers quickly, Bob and Sally are worried. Josie and the family agree to meet this new challenge by implementing the plan to move to Raleigh sooner, not in three years. The initial plan allowed them to kick into gear and know their direction, but the

JITSP allowed them to meet this new challenge by applying the "continuous improvement" approach. They decide it is realistic to make the move in nine months to a year.

And keeping Principle #1 in mind, the family is looking at what decisions they can make that will maximize their parents' independence:

- Moving sooner allows them to be closer to Josie and Dan, a strong and willing support system that will be critical to this plan's success.
- If Dad passes away before Mom in the next few years, Mom will already have made a difficult move, and vice versa.
- They can sell the house in New Jersey without it being a crisis or a death that might force a quick sale.
- They have already looked at some real estate and retirement communities that might work.
- The family has already discussed this option and they are prepared to implement this plan!

All these decisions allow for less stress in the long run. Responsibilities can be divided, and the plan can develop over time. The family can continue to look at what the best options might be for Bob and Sally with the change in Bob's health. As the story unfolds, we will see how the two principles in this chapter will be applied to making the right decision about hiring help in their home, using technology to keep them safe, and choosing the right community.

Make These Principles Your Foundation

As you look at your own situation, I suggest that you create a list of questions that apply to your family. Do you already have all the critical medical and financial documents you need or is it time to start gathering them? Let's say your parents want to consider moving to a retirement community. Start visiting these communities now; many have long waiting lists and it can take years to get the apartment or home you want! Investigate your options, just like the Spencers.

Should your parents or loved one stay in their home, and can you help them make their home safer? Give them the benefit of the doubt and respect their choices whenever possible. Sometimes this just might mean allowing them to fail before stepping in. We can all learn from our mistakes, and if they choose to age in place and then fail, it will be time to rethink the plan.

Hopefully, you are using the "continuous improvement" approach of the JITSP and anticipating what they need next. When a plan you have in place is clearly failing, it is time to regroup, rethink, and come up with new options. Maybe Mom is living alone and refused to move, until now. Look at the options in her town and yours. I advise all my clients to have *more than one plan*. Remember, it is not "if" your parents will need help, it is "when." Stay ahead of the crisis by thinking ahead and knowing your options when a predictable crisis unfolds.

If Mom is struggling already, it may mean bringing her closer to you. If she understands that with your help, support, and frequent oversight (because she is now near you) she will stay independent and healthier longer, she may agree. No one wants to be alone when they are sick or failing, and being closer will allow both of you to benefit. As a client of mine so aptly said: "I can't make Dad happy, but I can be sure he is safe and his needs are being met."

Adapting to the changes all of us have to face will teach us to be resilient. What worked before, or we thought would work in a year or two, has to be upended if our assumptions were off. But if you keep coming back to the original framework of fostering independence and staying flexible, you can handle this. Think of this book as the foundation that will guide you as you navigate this journey of helping your parents age successfully. Accept that you simply cannot anticipate every possible outcome and your plan will not be perfect. But one thing is certain: it is better than no plan at all!

Chapter 2

Critical Medical Information

One night many years ago, I received one of those dreaded midnight calls. My father had been transported to the hospital, and the situation was very serious. My sister and I arrived to discover that he was already on a respirator. Since it was a holiday weekend, we could not reach his regular doctor. He was brought to a small hospital near his nursing home, not his regular hospital. My stepmother was beside herself. We all knew he did not want to be placed on a respirator to be kept alive, but we discovered that once you are on a respirator, it is not that easy to have it removed.

When we asked the doctor to remove him from the respirator, he refused. It was a hospital with a religious affiliation, and without a living will, he was reluctant to make a decision that might allow my father to die. In his late eighties, my father was in terrible health, had advanced Parkinson's, worsening dementia, and had been in and out of the hospital with a persistent infection that had become severely septic. We knew he didn't want to continue, something he had shared with us many times. At least as a family, we all agreed. However, the hospital all but called us murderers. It was only through persistence and faith in my father's wishes that my sister and I found an alternative hospital and stood our ground against the entire administration of the hospital he was in. We had to sign a liability release and pay to privately transport him to a hospital that offered hospice care. Fortunately, my stepmother supported these decisions. My father was lovingly cared for during the last few weeks of his life with hospice care, and he died without pain, not on a respirator, and with dignity. This was over twenty-five years ago, and while I believe things have improved, these issues still exist. We knew we were carrying out my father's wishes because we had asked him.

Don't Wait for a Crisis! Start "the Conversation"!

While I recognize that all the preparation in the world cannot prevent medical emergencies, there is much you can do before one happens. Having an open and up-front conversation early on is critical. As I said in Chapter 1, I do not believe that age sixty is too early! Explain to your parents that if something happened to them suddenly or while they were traveling (something a bit easier to relate to), you would be in a better position to assist them should they need it. Anyone can accept that they could find themselves in some kind of situation beyond their control or one that is totally unexpected!

What if they died together in an accident? What if one was injured and the other unable to communicate? Your need for information is more plausible than just saying "I am worried about you," although parents do not usually want to worry their adult children.

The younger your parents are, the more likely they will be to cooperate. You might think the opposite is true given that at an older age the scenarios you propose are more likely to happen. But my experience is the exact opposite. One can blame our human tendency to procrastinate combined with the reluctance to face our own mortality. Sometimes I suspect that some magical thinking comes into play . . . *if I don't do a living will, I won't die!* I was told by a good friend of mine that there is a superstition in her community: If I complete a living will, I'll hasten my death! My experience is that this comes from a universal fear of death.

So why is it that 92 percent of seniors agree that it is important to discuss their end-of-life wishes but only 32 percent have had what has come to be known as "the Conversation"?

As difficult a topic as this is, you need to overcome your reluctance to talk about failing health or end-of-life issues. For adult children accustomed to having competent, healthy parents, it may seem very uncomfortable to initiate this discussion. But life can change fast and unpredictably. For instance, during the Covid pandemic, many families were caught off guard, having procrastinated about addressing this topic. Please accept that most

---

The Conversation Project

I highly recommend a website called "The Conversation Project"—theconversationproject.org. They offer a free Conversation Starter Guide and Kit that offers a step-by-step approach to initiating this discussion. It poses questions such as:

- If I am diagnosed with a serious illness that could shorten my life, I would prefer to . . . (fill in the blank)
- If you were seriously ill or near the end of your life, how much medical treatment would you feel was right for you?
- Where do you prefer to be toward the end of life?

Under each question are options such as "I strongly prefer to spend my last days in a healthcare facility," or "I strongly prefer to spend my last days at home." I have used this with many families, and it has been the best tool I have found to help. All materials are easy to download, offered in twenty-five different languages, and they are free.

parents are well aware of their own mortality and will welcome your interest in discussing this with them.

When Is Fear an Appropriate Tactic?

If requesting, cajoling, and modeling has not worked, then I give you permission to resort to fear! Seriously, sit down with your parents and watch the terrifying video made by Dr. Zubin Damania, aka ZDoggMD, at zdoggmd .com/end-of-life, that tells it like it is . . . what really happens when a person shows up without a living will in the hospital ER. It's not pretty. Not having advance directives (see below) requires doctors to follow hospital protocol and procedures that Dr. Damania says "forces them to torture people until they die."

Twenty-five percent of elderly people die in the ICU without a living will. Medically, doctors are then required to move forward with the most aggressive care and are obligated to try and save the patient's life, even if such attempts are futile. But don't blame the doctors! They have a sworn Hippocratic oath and liability issues to consider.

When anyone tells me they don't want to burden their families with making these types of decisions, or, worse, they don't trust anyone in their family to make these decisions, I tell them what the standard protocol is when they arrive at a hospital without a living will, aside from the dramatic ER description given by Dr. ZDogg. All hospitals have dealt with this exact scenario, so they have written ethics procedures that generally require them to follow a specific order of who to contact first to make a life-or-death decision:

- Spouse
- Legal guardian
- Adult children
- Siblings
- Friends
- Neighbors

You can see that no matter what, your family will be contacted. They can refuse, and the hospital will continue down this list. If there is literally no one, then they contact a licensed clinical social worker, *a perfect stranger*, who has no knowledge of your values or your end-of-life wishes, to make this difficult decision. Nobody wants this to happen.

Advance Directives: What Are They?

I believe that most of my readers are familiar with the terms "living will," "healthcare surrogate," or "medical power of attorney," often collectively referred to as "advance directives." However, I also know there is still a great deal of confusion surrounding exactly what these forms are and what they mean to you and your parents. If I was asked which forms are the most critical to address with your parents concerning medical issues, there is no doubt in my mind I would say advance directives.

Simply put, advance directives allow one to share their wishes for end-of-life care. It is the vehicle that families, doctors, and hospitals rely on so they know what kind of medical treatment you would choose when you are no longer able to express this for yourself.

By completing a living will, you are communicating your personal wishes for care to be provided or care to be withdrawn, based on the options you selected on the form.

A living will is a legal document that basically outlines your preferences for medical care when you have become incapacitated. It is not the same thing as a last will and testament, which details how you want your assets to be distributed. This is strictly for medical treatment or withdrawal. Most living wills use very specific language about treatments you want or do not want such as hydration, tube feeding, mechanical ventilation, and cardiopulmonary resuscitation. It also allows for you to choose what is called "palliative care" or "comfort care," which may include pain management or minimum hydration.

When you choose a healthcare surrogate, healthcare proxy, healthcare agent, or medical power of attorney (all interchangeable terms that mean the same thing), you are asking this person to advocate for your wishes because you no longer can. They will be your spokesperson, your representative when the time comes to tell the doctor and the hospital that you do or do not want further treatment. They will be confident about their choices because the living will directs and informs them, as did, hopefully, the many conversations you have had with this special person. Do not confuse the term "medical power of attorney" with a "power of attorney" (POA)—they are completely different documents of equal importance. A *medical* POA is only for making medical decisions when you can no longer make those decisions for yourself. A power of attorney authorizes someone to represent or act on your behalf in legal matters, financial matters, business matters, and more. In essence, you are granting this person the authority to act as if they were you! They are known as your "agent." There are many types of POAs. More information on this is provided in Chapter 3, "Financial Information: What You Don't Know Will Hurt You."

There are no right or wrong answers here. By planning ahead, you can clearly state what medical care you want or do not want and avoid unnecessary suffering. Most important? It lifts the burden of asking caregivers to guess your wishes during moments of crisis or grief.

Who Needs Advance Directives?

Every adult should have one *regardless of age.* If you ask your parents whether they have filled out any advance directives (both a living will and a healthcare surrogate/proxy form) and they say "no," tell them you are doing one for yourself. Then talk with them about your own end-of-life wishes. What if there were medical interventions they disapproved of? What if they don't want artificial tube feeding? Or what if they do? This is not about agreeing or disagreeing about accepting or refusing treatment, this is about completing the documents, so stay focused on this during your conversations!

Suggest organizing a family gathering to share your parents' wishes and discuss what is important to them. Make sure your parents proof the document, sign, and date it. Email copies of the directives to all siblings and any other family members who should have this information. Make sure to include any physicians and attorneys involved. I also suggest sending actual paper copies, so they remain on file. When the time comes, you do not want to have to defend yourself by saying, "But I talked with Dad and he told me he didn't want to be on a respirator," if you are the only person he told, and no one can find the email you sent ten years ago. Over time, if this document is changed, make sure to repeat this updating/sharing process.

Types of Living Wills

Any living will is aimed at accomplishing the same thing: creating clear directives for your healthcare proxy or surrogate, your doctor, and your family, when you are no longer able to speak for yourself. Let your parent choose the living will that works best for them. In fact, offering your parent a choice may even encourage them to fill one out. There are too many versions of living wills to count, but here are two general types:

- Those typically put together by an attorney as part of estate planning are usually pared down, minimal, and may not be broad in scope. Hospitals and doctors prefer them because they are short and easy to understand, and convenient to scan and upload.
- Some living wills, like "The Five Wishes Living Will," or the "Healthcare Directive," provided by the national not-for-profit organization Honoring Choices, are free online documents that give a person room to describe their end-of-life preferences in more detail. They are known as more family- and user-friendly. They allow you to clearly list exactly what medical treatments you would or would not want if you are unable to voice your own decisions and elaborate more extensively on your end-of-life wishes.
- Consider writing your own supplement to your living will that specifically addresses dementia. Under what circumstances, with a diagnosis of dementia, would you want treatment to stop?

Consider a Video Summary of the Living Will

One of the best ideas I heard recently is for your loved one to make a video summary of the living will. They should keep it to about three or four minutes long and cover the basics on treatments they do or do not want. Make sure they start by saying their full legal name, birthdate, date of the video, and where they keep copies of their original living will and who they have appointed as healthcare proxy/medical power of attorney. With smartphones now able to take first-rate videos, the recordings easily can be uploaded as medical records to any hospital, becoming a critical part of anyone's end-of-life wishes. However, a video is not a substitute for the actual document. Keep in mind: in a true emergency-room type of situation, no doctor is going to search for the video. However, it will help eliminate family disagreements!

Choosing a Healthcare Surrogate (HCS)

Most couples list each other as their HCS, but it is important to list at least one alternate or backup. This is a burden parents often do not wish to place on their children, especially if the siblings are not apt to agree with each other about the situation. If you are asked to be anyone's healthcare surrogate, you should be honored that they have faith that you will carry out their wishes, perhaps in the face of opposition from other family members. Ideally, a healthcare surrogate should be in the same town or close enough to get to you or the hospital, but it is not required. And while this seems obvious, an HCS needs to be someone trusted by you or your parent to carry out your wishes *no matter what*. Are they a strong personality who can interact confidently with a hospital and doctors?

If you really feel you will not be able to function in this capacity, then don't accept the responsibility. Be honest with your mom and dad and tell them you just don't think you can do it. Believe me; they would rather know this *before* the time comes for you to make the call. My younger son told me, when I asked, that he could not do this. I chose my husband first, and my best friend, who lives nearby, as my backup. I decided that asking my out-of-state children was not a good plan. I can tell you that most states prefer your healthcare surrogate to reside in the same state, and in the same town, if possible.

What Are the Rules in Your State?

It is always a good idea to check the rules in your state, but almost all states accept any living will. Legally, most people will execute advance directives in the state they legally claim as their primary residence. If they spend summers far away from their healthcare surrogate, they may want to have a second or third person listed who lives in this alternate location. Local hospitals and hospices will also provide free documents. Look for workshops offered in your area by local senior centers or hospice organizations that provide supportive decision-making and trained counselors to assist you or your parents! As a facilitator myself, I have seen half the class leave without executing a living will. Do not underestimate some people's reluctance to execute one. If your parents have done so, count your blessings!

Who Are the Appropriate Legal Witnesses?

Most states require two witnesses for both the living will and your HCS forms, so be sure to check the witnessing requirements in your state. Some attorneys advise that no blood relations whatsoever be a witness, or anyone who could benefit from your death financially. Also, it is not a good idea to have anyone from your life- or health-insurance companies sign. This eliminates any possible conflict-of-interest allegations. Some states require these documents to be notarized, not just witnessed, so again, be sure to check. Choose a neutral person who is not related to you.

Review Advance Directives

It is generally a good idea for you and your parents to review these kinds of documents every few years or after a major life event such as a divorce, incapacitation, or a death. Make this part of applying Principle #2, JITSP, Just in Time Senior Planning! Are the persons listed still available, capable, and willing? Has someone passed away or become ill themselves? Remember, these documents are critical and will be of no help to anyone if they don't have copies when needed or if the people listed as surrogates are no longer around! Make sure to review these documents with your parents on a regular basis! Keep copies with you when you are traveling and ask your parents to do the same. Ask your parents to carry wallet-size ID cards indicating they have advance directives and where they can be found. If your parents have divorced, remarried, or become widowed, this is also the time to update advance directives. No one wants an ex-husband or ex-wife making life-and-death decisions!

Do Not Resuscitate Order (DNR)

A "do not resuscitate" order is altogether different from an advance directive. A DNR is a legal order written either in the hospital or, often, provided by a patient's primary care physician. Hospitals and doctors do not like patients to have a DNR unless the patient is terminal and is predicted to have a finite amount of time left to live—in fact, many doctors will not fill out a DNR for their patient except under these circumstances. The DNR does not allow a patient to undergo CPR or advanced cardiac life support (ACLS) if their heart stops or they stop breathing. Sometimes a DNR is called a "no code" since the term "code" is used in hospitals to alert the resuscitation team, as in a "code blue." Hence a "no code" means no resuscitation. Some people find this term alarming or offensive. There are new terms I have heard called "allow natural death" (AND) or Physician Orders for Life-Sustaining Treatment (POLST), and both are more accurate since they describe what is really happening.

It is important to remember that a DNR/AND/POLST does not affect treatments such as chemotherapy, antibiotics, etc. Also, a DNR is not an advance directive or living will and does not replace these documents. A physician must sign and order a DNR based on the patient's wishes, whereas a living will is written by the patient. The healthcare surrogate or agent may request a DNR if they have been appointed through the living will.

However, understand that a DNR does not mean that emergency medical services (EMS) will honor it. Years ago, I was the administrative director of an assisted-living facility (ALF), and one of the residents fell unconscious to the floor and stopped breathing. Our staff began CPR immediately and we called 911. We checked his chart and found he had a DNR, but the facility rule was to continue administering CPR. In a matter of minutes, the ambulance arrived, and we told one of the EMTs about the patient's DNR. "Yes, ma'am, I see the man's DNR, but it is my job to transport this gentleman to the hospital alive if possible. We will continue with the CPR and let the hospital staff make this call." Who can blame them? If a family doesn't agree, it only takes one member to suc them or the facility. So DNRs usually only work if one of the following is true:

- ♥ The doctor who wrote the order is the one treating the patient when they arrive in the hospital.
- ♥ The DNR is on file with the hospital, and it is the correct, current state form.
- ♥ You have a copy with you when you arrive at the hospital with the patient.
- ♥ You are the Healthcare Surrogate and can reassure any doctor that you understand what a DNR is and support this choice in full.

If you know your parent is terminal, find the courage to talk with your mom or dad and ask them how they feel about a DNR. You will have great peace of mind if you know exactly how they feel before they can no longer tell you.

My mother spent the last year of her life in skilled nursing care. My stepfather, Bill, spent hours with her every day. As fate would have it, they were in the middle of a conversation when she had a massive stroke with Bill at her side. When the paramedics arrived, Bill told them she had a

DNR, and he refused to allow them to resuscitate her. He was adamant, and they acquiesced. It would never have happened had he not been there. He knew what she wanted, and he was sure enough of her wishes to follow through in a moment of extreme fear and shock. That is what I call courage. Don't ever underestimate the immense responsibility of being a loved one's healthcare surrogate. You are given the great task of carrying out the wishes of your parent, not *your* wishes. As hard as it may be, if your parent is ready to go and they have told you this through advanced directives and conversations, then your job is to carry out their wishes. If they have asked you to handle this role, then they had a good reason; they believe you will have the courage to let them go when the time comes. Remember this always.

What Would Josie Spencer Do?

Back to our imaginary family, the Spencers. On the next family call, Josie asks her parents if they have completed a living will and healthcare proxy form, something she is worried about with her dad's recent stroke. She is met with silence and some furtive looks between Mom and Dad. Mom confesses that all they have done is talk about it, but they never filled out the forms completely. Mom thinks they might have filled out one in the hospital when Dad was admitted for his stroke, but she does not know for sure. Josie is smart enough not to blame or find fault. Both John and Wendy pipe up about how important these forms are and declare they have completed these forms for themselves. Josie explains that not knowing what their end-of-life wishes are or what treatment they may or may not want to receive leaves the entire family in limbo and confusion. She tactfully asks, "Is this what you really want? The family guessing at a time like this?" She suggests they sit down together and look at the Conversation Project website, which will walk them through the decision-making process. She offers to do this with them if they feel like they would like her support. Sally and Bob agree to look at the website, take a few days to think about it, but agree to do the living wills by the end of the week. They will ask for her help if they need it. John and Wendy agree that choosing Josie makes sense since she will be near them in Raleigh, and states prefer an HCS who lives nearby. Bob and Sally will appoint each other as primary healthcare surrogate, and Josie agrees to be backup—or listed as secondary on the forms. Josie helps them review and compile a list of everyone they need to give copies to, including all doctors, the hospital, all the siblings, and anyone else of medical import. And of course, they set a date for their next meeting! John offers to do some research on what senior communities are available in the Raleigh area, and Wendy says she will scout for new doctors.

Pre-Need Guardianship

If your parent has a family history of dementia or their doctor feels that they are showing early signs of dementia that will progress, you should talk with your parent about what is called "pre-need designation of a guardian." He or she can choose who shall serve as their guardian in the event they become incapacitated. Talk with your parent and with an attorney to see if this is necessary, as appointing someone durable power of attorney may cover most contingencies. The best thing about this option is it avoids protracted litigation or actual guardianship by covering the possibility *ahead of the actual need*. Needless to say, the person chosen as potential guardian needs to be totally trustworthy and ethical. The law holds them to high standards and serious consequences should they betray this trust. In some states it is now a criminal issue, not just a civil issue, if funds are used for personal expenses that have nothing to do with the parent.

Is Guardianship Necessary?

If the family member with the diagnosis is past the point of participating and there is no power of attorney, it may be time to consider some form of guardianship or conservatorship. Most attorneys will tell you that guardianship is not recommended since it is a complicated, expensive, and very time-consuming process. Guardianship is viewed by most states as a last resort and will only be granted if it will safeguard the interests and affairs of a person who is so impaired that they can no longer make safe and sound decisions for themselves. Or perhaps their property/assets have become subject to fraud or undue influence by someone who no longer has their best interests at heart. Anyone who has gone through this process, however, will advise you to seek alternatives first.

I have watched many adult children stand by helplessly while their parents came under the influence of a shady person who proceeded to bilk them out of cars, cash, homes, and more. My friend's father, a widower who was retired military and financially comfortable, had "an eye for the ladies," as his son delicately put it. But he also had a serious drinking problem and alcohol-related dementia. It is not hard for someone unscrupulous to hook up with easy prey. Next thing George knew, his dad had bought a nice new Cadillac for his new girlfriend, and she had moved in with him. This is a common scenario today and much easier with dating sites often used by lonely older men and women and predators eager to take advantage. She left him after cleaning him out and took the Cadillac with her.

If you don't feel you have a choice about filing for guardianship, there are wonderful organizations that can help you. Google your state website for guardianship to be sure you know the rules in the state where you reside or where your parent lives. Also, check out the National Guardianship Association (guardianship.org), as well as seeking information from your state bar association. I would certainly advise you to consult experienced legal counsel first to determine your best course of action depending on the circumstances. It might be to become their guardian (make sure you understand the responsibilities completely before deciding!) or to carefully choose an independent guardian.

Additional Medical Information and Considerations

Here are some other important forms and issues to consider.

HIPAA Permission Forms

All the well-intentioned medical privacy laws have greatly hindered medical professionals from talking with family members. In case you aren't sure, HIPAA stands for Health Insurance Portability and Accountability Act, and it is a law that was passed in 1996 that restricts access to individuals' private medical information. I understand that limiting access to medical information may in some cases be the wishes of the parent, but often it is merely an oversight, where parents have forgotten to add their adult children's names. Medical professionals are still bound by law and will not speak with you about your parent's situation. Better to be a bit pushy with your parents and ask them to **make sure to include you on the list with all their important medical professionals!** Ask them to write a generic form you can use if needed, especially if you are not one of the healthcare surrogates, but you are a family member who wants to stay informed in an emergency.

List of Medications

Knowing the medications your parents are taking could possibly save their lives. In a medical emergency you might be able to tell the EMT (emergency medical technician) where your mom or dad keeps a list of their meds. In one community I worked in, they encouraged all members to keep the "vial of life" in their freezer in a clear plastic tube. All the EMTs knew to look in the freezer in the event of a medical emergency. Even a husband or wife can grab this simple plastic tube on their way to the hospital if they are driving the spouse themselves. You can order various vial of life products at vialoflife.com.

Mom or Dad may have all your contact information by the phone, or even plastered to their fridge, but if they are unconscious or not speaking or thinking clearly, this won't be of any use if the EMTs are trying to find out what medications they are on. I have known some seniors to tape a sign next to their phone or on the fridge that says, "LIST OF MEDS & CONTACTS IN THE FREEZER." At least if a doctor—or a neighbor—calls you, you may be able to help with critical information, even if you live hundreds of miles away.

Geriatric Social Worker or Aging Life Care Specialist

If your parents need a new primary care doctor for any reason, look for a practice that has a full-time senior advocate on staff. This person could become the one factor that keeps you sane and makes a significant contribution to your parent's well-being. They may be a licensed clinical social worker, they may be an RN or LPN who has become a certified geriatric-care manager, or they may be an aging life care specialist. What they all have in common is that they provide coordinated care for your loved one. Perhaps your mom or dad needs care when they get home from surgery or a list of qualified referrals for home healthcare? This person will function as the liaison communicator with you, the doctor, and your parents.

And if the doctor's office does not have a social worker or aging life care specialist on staff, you can find one on your own. Go to the ALCA (Aging Life Care Association) website (www.aginglifecare.org) and put in the appropriate zip code, review the specialist's credentials, and interview them. This website also explains what services you can expect from their members. Skills and experience vary, as does cost. This professional can hire and oversee home care and home healthcare, interact with the hospital, report back to you, and more.

USAging: Leaders in Aging Well at Home

The organization, USAging, is the national association representing and supporting the network of Area Agencies on Aging. As they say on the national website, www.usaging.org, they go by "many names, many partners," but have "one mission": to "improve the quality of life and health of older adults and people with disabilities, including supporting people with chronic illness, people living with dementia, family caregivers, and others who want to age well at home and in the community."

The original Area Agencies on Aging came out of the Older Americans Act, passed in 1965 as part of President Lyndon's Johnson's "Great Society." It now has over six hundred offices in fifty-six states with more than twenty thousand community providers who organize a vast array of "home and community-based services, including information and referral/assistance, case management, home-delivered and congregate meals, in-home services, caregiver supports, transportation, evidence-based health and wellness programs, long-term care ombudsman programs, and more." USAging "believes that every person should be able to age with optimal health, well-being, independence and dignity in their homes and communities."

For over fifty years, this organization was known as the Area Agencies on Aging, and some local organizations retain this name or call themselves "Elder Options," or some variation. The central USAging website can help you locate the office nearest you using your zip code.

You can also find your local office by using your zip code via the "Eldercare Locator" website, www.eldercare.gov, or you can speak with an information specialist by calling 800-677-1116.

Regardless of name, the association and its network are an invaluable free resource that is funded by both federal and state dollars and provides an amazing wealth of information for you and your family. Focused on providing unbiased information, they can supply lists of senior services and senior resources in your area, along with lists of free classes and training for caregivers. Start with them when looking for any type of senior living, healthcare, transportation, meals on wheels, senior centers, adult day care, Alzheimer's care, and more. They will even provide free help with financial planning and management and offer assistance with qualifying for any government programs or subsidies for seniors.

Medical Checklist Summary

My advice, dear reader, is to look through the list below and start prioritizing. Email it to your parents and ask them to respond, ideally via email. Make sure to share this information with siblings, and store both online and paper copies. Keep your paper copies handy, in case you need this information as you run out the door to the hospital.

1. Do your parents have advanced medical directives? Did they do it so many years ago that it needs updating?

2. Have they chosen a healthcare surrogate (HCS) as part of their advance directives? If so, who is it, and have they chosen an alternate or second person to fill this role if needed? Are they still willing and able to carry out these duties?

3. Who are their doctors? Compile names, addresses, emails (if possible), phone numbers, and the doctors' specialties. Do all the doctors have copies of advance directives?

4. HIPAA laws: Have your parents included you on the Health Insurance Portability and Accountability Act of 1996 (HIPAA) list with *all* their doctors and with their hospital of choice? If not, no one will talk to you unless you show up as the appointed HCS.

5. Is there a social worker or case manager in their primary care doctor's office who you can use as a resource, especially in an emergency? Is there an aging life care specialist nearby?

6. Do your parents keep a list of all their medications anywhere in their home? What meds do they take regularly? Do they have any severe allergies?

7. What pharmacies do they use? Do the pharmacies deliver?

8. What is their hospital of choice? It may not be the nearest one!

9. Do they have a home care company or home healthcare company they prefer?

Depending on your relationship with your parents, you can get some of this information over time or while you are visiting. With so many adult children living thousands of miles from their parents, you don't want to be in a panic during an emergency and try to scramble for these critical details.

Keep in mind that having all this information is no guarantee that you will avoid the pitfalls of helping your parents navigate major medical issues. If nothing else, you will feel some peace of mind knowing you did what you could to be prepared.

Chapter 3

Financial Information: What You Don't Know Will Hurt You

My friend's father, already widowed, is over ninety and has multiple real estate holdings all over Florida totaling in the millions of dollars. If my friend's life depended on it, she could not tell you where they are, and the sad thing is, neither can her dad. His dementia has relentlessly crept forward, and she kept meaning to ask him about his financial situation but was afraid he would "take it the wrong way." He didn't keep very good records, nor did anyone else. Believe it or not, he does not even have a will! She has no idea how to even begin piecing together the whole picture. It will take her years and lots of legal fees or private investigator fees to get the estate settled when he passes away. This is why millions and millions of dollars lie unclaimed in bank accounts all over the United States, and even real estate holdings are lost to future generations. This is far more common than you might think, and the money goes to either the state or Uncle Sam instead of the heirs or relatives of the owner.

As challenging as it is to talk with your parents about advance directives, sometimes bringing up financial issues is just as dicey. Different families have different rules, and maybe you're blessed with parents who want to be transparent about their finances. If so, you are in the minority. Given the prickly nature of this topic, go back and review some of the same principles you applied in Chapters 1 and 2 about having "the Conversation." Remember the "what if" scenarios?

- 📍 What if you and Mom were in an accident together?
- 📍 What if I was trying to help pay your bills because you couldn't? How would I know what bills you have, or where you bank?
- 📍 Mom, Dad, you already may have filled out some legal and financial documents. Are you willing to share these with me so I can feel more prepared for an emergency? Or tell me where I can find them?
- 📍 I'm worried about you getting scammed! What can we do to make sure this never happens?

I would reassure them you are not asking to read "the will," for example; you just want to know if there is one! Or a power of attorney? Or a trust? And where are the documents located? Are they filed with an attorney?

You might have a terrific relationship with your parents, but it is still hard to raise this topic. It is totally understandable that completing a will is scary. It brings up fear in adult children, and in many parents as well. Avoiding the subject of preparing a will may lull some people into a false sense of security. "If I don't make a will, maybe I'll never die!" But imagining the alternative should give everyone some courage. Do you really want to be totally in the dark about your parents' financial situation or their wishes for their treasured heirlooms, or how you might pay for their long-term care? Meet with your siblings and come up with a strategy that works for all of you. Involve them so this line of questioning does not come out of the blue or stir up sibling rivalry. This way, if your mom calls your sister and says, "Susie just sent me a weird email asking about our financial and legal documents," your sister can say, "Yes, Mom, I know. We talked about it together. We just want to make sure we are all prepared for the unexpected." Find your courage and trust that your parent(s) will accept your genuine concern.

The Importance of a Will

When my mother died, I moved my beloved stepfather, Bill, to my town. By then, I had worked for many years in senior living and thought I was fairly prepared for how his life might unfold as he grew older. I asked him if he had a will and he said yes. I did not ask to see it, and although I tried several times to talk with the attorney before Bill passed away, we never connected.

Eventually my concern was centered on Bill's health, which was declining. I assumed the will existed and naturally I did not want to be pushy. When he passed away, I contacted the attorney. "No," he said, "I never did Bill's will, only your mother's. He said he already had one."

I had never seen a copy of his will, nor did I ever find one. I am certain this was not intentional on my stepfather's part, but nonetheless, there was no will. His previous attorney had passed away and left no trail.

Luckily, I had done everything else right, and my name was on all his accounts since he had developed some cognitive impairment and I was paying his bills. I also had power of attorney before he died and had been acting on his behalf. I knew what his wishes were and carried them out, and my sister, stepsister, and I were always in full agreement. Have you discussed financial matters with your parents? Do you know if your parents even have a will?

What Is a Last Will and Testament?

A last will and testament is a legal document that communicates a person's final wishes pertaining to assets and dependents. Generally, it outlines what to do with property, investments, and possessions, indicating what to leave to whom—to other family members or to groups or charitable organizations. Importantly, it also advises on other things such as custody of dependents if needed, and management or distribution of accounts and financial interest such as a business. Writing a will gives a person some control over what happens with their assets after their death.

A person writes a will while still alive and leaves instructions about who will be their **executor or personal representative** to make sure the wishes stated in their will are carried out. This person can be a family member, a trusted advisor, or a friend whose main duty is to carry out the will's instructions to manage the affairs and wishes of the deceased person's estate. For a will to be valid, it must be signed by the "testator"—the person whose assets it covers—and he or she must be of sound mind and mentally capable. Wills usually require at least two unrelated witnesses, aged eighteen and over. Most people seek the advice of a law firm or an attorney in writing a will, but this is not required. The more assets, the more complicated a will can become, but even an online will may be better than nothing, provided one meets the legal requirements of the state a parent resides in, and the signee is competent to sign a will. *I strongly advise hiring an estate attorney, especially if there is property or lots of assets involved.* Expect to pay several hundred to thousands of dollars depending on the complexity of the will or trust.

When to Make a Will

What is a good age to see an attorney about making a will? Generally speaking, if someone is married, has children, and has even a small savings or investment account, they should make a will. And certainly, by the time someone is in their fifties or sixties, they need a will!

A gentleman I know died in a tragic motorcycle accident at age sixty-six; he was a very successful businessman, lots of property, grown kids, and a second wife. And despite his wealth and family, he had never executed a will. The result was a huge mess. The wife was stricken, the business tanked, the adult children were furious at the stepmom, and everyone started suing everyone else. You can be sure this is not what he wanted, but by inaction and procrastination, this is the legacy he left behind: anger, confusion, years of probate court, and a family torn apart.

So, if you have no idea if your parents have written a will, ask them. Do not wait. Make absolutely *no* assumptions as I did with my beloved stepfather. Plenty of people write a will long before turning sixty! Explain that you do not want to see the will, but you would like to:

- **♀** Know it exists;
- **♀** Get the name and contact information of the law firm or attorney, if they used one;
- **♀** Verify that *your* contact information is on file with the attorney;
- **♀** Find out if you're listed on file with the bank as someone who can open your parent's safety deposit box, if they have one, should your parent die. (If so, they should have given you a key. If not, welcome to a long legal hassle and possible probate before you can even open the safety deposit box.)

Making a will is not rocket science, but it gets close to rocket-science complexity if a person dies without one. Most parents want to leave money

---

Probate: What If There Is No Will?

If someone dies without a will (which is called "dying intestate"), the estate will be settled by a probate court, including the distribution of all assets. Probate is a legal procedure by which a court oversees the distribution of property left by someone who has died. The court appoints a custodian to take control of any assets, make sure any debts are paid first, and then distribute property to whomever they determine are the proper beneficiaries. This incurs legal fees and court and state costs, likely taking a chunk of what was left. In settling the estate, the state decides how to distribute the property and who receives payment first, without any consideration for a family's circumstances. Most courts follow a formula disbursing assets to a surviving spouse and children of the deceased. If no next of kin can be located, assets become the property of the state. There is a common misconception that if someone does not own a home, they do not need a will. People fail to consider the value of other things such as bank accounts, investment accounts, family heirlooms, art, cars, jewelry, and more. Everyone can benefit from a will.

to their children, grandchildren, or even an organization, but no matter how good their intentions, if they do not have a will, it just won't matter. Procrastination goes both ways. Do not assume you have all the time in the world to have this discussion.

Gift Lists

One of the purposes of creating a will is to specify who parents want to gift what assets to, as well as the disposal of specific items. Grandmother's diamond ring should go to Susie, while this ring should go to Ellen, etc. Encourage your parents to be detailed, as this is a kindness to children left behind. If you want to see grown adults turn into bratty kids, just ask them to decide who's getting what. I have seen otherwise lovely people become very ugly and have arguments with family members over the smallest things.

This kind of situation can be avoided with some forethought. The focus should be on mourning the loss of a parent, not the objects they left behind. Everyone will rest easier knowing that a list exists, the attorney has it, and there is no guessing about the wishes of the deceased.

I had one woman tell me her secret to getting her mother to cooperate. She had asked her mom to make a list, but the mother kept finding reasons to put it off. Finally, the daughter told her mother that she had heard a least-liked daughter-in-law telling someone in the family that she wanted and was going to get "Mom's diamond ring." That did it—Mom wrote the list!

The idea I like best is gifting things while you are around to enjoy the giving. Why wait? My beloved older sister had cancer and knew she was going to die soon. On our last visit together, she gathered all her sisters, her daughter, and her daughter-in-law, and gave us her jewelry. She enjoyed this gifting tremendously, and it was even more special because of the closeness around it. She asked me to take care of those who could not be there (dear friends, others) and because of her list, I knew who got what.

When Is a Trust Needed?

If your parents have total assets over $500,000 (home, bank accounts, investments, businesses), most attorneys will recommend they have a trust. A will becomes active only after one's death, but a trust becomes active the day you create it. Trusts tend to be more expensive than wills to create and maintain. A trustee will be named in the document to control the assets' distribution following the trustor's wishes and the trust document and its mandates. A trustee can be a spouse, an attorney, a friend, and just as with an executor, should be a person you trust implicitly. A trust is set up to protect assets from probate and to ensure that assets pass on to whoever the trust lists, usually surviving spouses first, children next (but not always), and grandchildren, etc.

However, a trust can be structured any way you choose and is simply a tool to protect the funds and property from the assessment of unnecessary legal costs. There are all kinds of trusts: irrevocable, revocable, living trust, and more, each with its own advantages depending on your individual situation and wishes. If your parents do have a trust, you can ask the same basic questions: who has a copy and where is it located, etc. Generally, you should feel assured that if they have taken the time to create a trust, then they are legally prepared for death and have taken the right steps to protect their assets and provide direction about these assets. If you are comfortable, ask your parents to explain the organization of the trust and what their wishes are generally. Unlike wills, trusts do not go through a probate process and are not usually a matter of public record. A trust, however, can only deal with property or assets that have been already transferred into the trust, so it is critical that assets are placed in a trust to protect them, or they will be subject to taxes and possible probate. Assets like any kind of checking, banking, savings accounts, investment accounts, property, homes, anything of value, can be owned by the trust.

Durable Power of Attorney

A power of attorney (POA) may be the single most important legal document your parents should have, secondary to a will. Hopefully your parent or parents have already executed a POA with their attorney. They may have asked you, a sibling, a good friend, or trusted advisor, but this is the person who can make big decisions for them if they are no longer able. This might be due to dementia, a sudden accident, or an incapacitating stroke or medical event. The "power" to act in this role ends when the appointee dies. This is not the same as the executor or personal representative in a will, a role that comes into play after death.

Your parent can assign POA for a single thing like selling just one item (for instance, a car), or they can assign a far greater authority to you (or whomever they have asked to be in this role). Should they ever develop dementia, this document will allow the POA agent to make a broad range of decisions. This is a very general statement, but having durable power of attorney you can:

- Sign a contract for your parent;
- Sell a car, home, or other property;
- Make financial transactions for your parent;
- Sign legal documents;
- Make investment decisions;
- Make health decisions if you have specifically been authorized with a medical power of attorney (see page 36). This is identical to being a healthcare proxy or surrogate.

If you are at least eighteen, you can be appointed POA. There is no test or required level of education, but you will be held responsible to always act in good faith in the role of POA for your parent. The law calls this your "fiduciary" responsibility, which means you are in a position of trust. Since you are managing the affairs of your parents, you have the responsibility to deal honestly and fairly with "the principal" (your parent or family member in this case) and make decisions that are both in their best interest and in the interests of their overall financial health.

You have the authority to use their money for their needs but not necessarily for yours. To avoid either conflict or even possible criminal allegations toward you, seek the advice of an attorney or a professional familiar with the law. If you misuse your POA, or make financial decisions in your best interest, not your parents', it is possible that you will be charged with a crime. Some states, including Florida, have passed laws making it a criminal act if it can be proven you acted improperly in the role of "caregiver or a person who stands in a position of trust and confidence" and stolen money (from your parent), used their money to purchase gifts for yourself or others, or attempted to influence them to change a will for your benefit.

Critical List of Financial Questions and Documents

While you don't necessarily need to have all this information now, this list represents critical documents and information you would need if your parents were to suddenly become incapacitated or pass away.

The answers to every question on this list will help you if you are suddenly faced with trying to help pay bills, pay taxes (possibly past due), locate assets, pay for long-term care, and in general, manage any of your parents' affairs if they can no longer do this for any reason. And if you are the personal representative, as I have been for two sets of parents, this information will be critical for you to settle an estate, pay outstanding debts, help your siblings attend a funeral, or even pay for a funeral. If Dad is the one who managed everything for Mom, you may be called upon to organize and manage her affairs. For older generations this is often the case, less so for younger couples. No matter if it is Mom or Dad or your favorite aunt, this information will come in handy.

If they are seriously uncomfortable giving you this information, they could answer all these questions and give the info to their attorney or leave it in their files . . . as long as you know where to find it!

1. Do they have accounts in more than one bank or more than one state? Ask for a list of account numbers and bank locations.

2. Who is their investment company/counselor or financial advisor? Is there more than one in multiple states?

3. Do they have a CPA? A different tax accountant? Where are the tax files/history? You may have to gather this for the IRS in the future.

4. Where are their retirement accounts (401(k)s, IRAs [individual retirement accounts], or Roth IRAs)? Are they part of a trust, their investment portfolio, or held elsewhere?

5. Do they have any CDs (certificates of deposit)? Often people will open CDs with whatever bank is offering the highest interest, not their usual bank, hence these accounts may be harder to find!

6. Did they serve in the military? Do they receive any benefits or is there a survivor benefit? Where do they keep their military history/ information? You may need these to file for benefits for a parent!

7. Do they receive any pensions, and do the pensions stop at their death? Does a spouse receive all or some portion of the pension?

8. Do they have a safety deposit box? What is the general list of contents, locations, keys? Are you listed as someone who can access the box?

9. Do they have any annuities? Do they end at death or continue for a spouse?

10. If they owned any kind of business, do they still hold an interest in this business, partnership, or LLC (limited liability corporation)?

11. Do they receive any continued income stream from this business?

12. In the event of their death, if they are still in business, is there a succession plan in place for their business?

13. What real estate do they own? In whose name is it, and is it owned jointly or corporately owned?

14. If your parents are divorced—remarried or not—what is their Social Security status after a partner's death? *They can switch to a higher Social Security amount from a deceased spouse if they were married at least ten years, or if they never remarried, and they are at least sixty-two years of age.*

15. Do they have copies of birth certificates, Social Security cards, drivers' licenses on file or can you get copies?

When my stepmom died several years after my dad, my sister and I spent weeks cleaning out their NYC apartment. We threw out old birth certificates from her side of the family that we saw no reason for keeping. We were wrong. While she did have a will and left the remainder of the estate to my sister and me, due to arcane laws of New York State, as stepchildren, never formerly adopted, the lawyer was forced to do a "kinship search" just in case *any* relatives of our stepmother wanted to lay claim to the estate. The birth certificates we threw out would have helped. The attorneys spent many thousands of dollars advertising throughout every state she ever lived in for anyone to come forward to lay claim to the estate. In addition, we had to hire a private investigator and research our stepmother's family for well over a year, even though she never had any children, had no siblings, and had a will! Please keep in mind that this was not for a large estate. Thousands of dollars had to be spent for attorneys out of a limited estate, just to settle anything, like it or not. For any families that have stepchildren or stepparents, remember that different state rules may apply. It never occurred to me to ask.

Your parents may have old birth certificates from past generations, as well as old family records and photos that are irreplaceable. If there is an ancestry buff in your family, make sure to ask if they want these kinds of records before throwing them out!

Let's Visit the Spencers

When we last checked in, Bob and Sally, the parents, agreed to complete their advance directives with help from their daughter Josie if needed.

Mission accomplished! Copies of completed living wills and healthcare surrogate forms have been distributed to everyone in the family plus all their doctors in New Jersey. John shares the information he has gathered since the last call about good doctors in the Raleigh area and information about the real estate market and two retirement communities he is looking into, which are mailing his parents full brochures. He has found a primary care doctor with a great reputation associated with the university medical hospital, who also has an aging life care specialist on staff and is accepting new patients. Bob and Sally want to check out the doctor first, as well as the retirement communities, and agree to report back.

Now the focus is to make a list of everything that needs to happen for this move. John is concerned about his parents' finances and financial information and asks them if they are willing to be transparent. He inquires if they have a will or have completed a trust. What about a power of attorney? Bob and Sally share that they have recently updated their trust and tell the family who their attorney is. Since Bob is the primary money manager and he has recently recovered from the stroke, he asks their son John if he will assume power of attorney. Bob plans on sharing information about accounts, investments, insurance policies, and household bills just in case something happens to him. Sally is grateful because she is already feeling overwhelmed. John says he has a list of questions and information he needs (taken from the list in this book on pages 48 and 49) that will be of immense help should Bob ever become incapacitated. The family sets another meeting in three weeks to see how things are progressing and to compare notes.

Smart Banking Practices

Encourage your parents to list each other's names on their bank accounts. Do not use the words Joe Smith *and* Jane Smith. It needs to be Joe Smith *or* Jane Smith. With the "or," either parent can access the account, even if the other is incapacitated or passes away. If the word "and" is used, an account could be frozen for months if the primary person dies or is incapacitated. The same is true if you are an adult child managing a parent's checking or savings account. If you are paying the bills, hopefully your parent will use "or" if they trust you to always act on their behalf. Ideally the bank staff should know you and you should know them. This scenario is rare these days, since the advent of online banking and the disappearance of small-town banks.

Banks also offer what they call *convenience accounts*. This is not a joint account, but it does mean that the parent can add a son or daughter to a bank account to write checks for them. You will still be held accountable in this fiduciary role, and this by no means allows you to write checks freely, but only when requested by the parent.

It is typically assumed that if your name is on the account, you would be the sole inheritor of the funds in the account in full upon the death of the second party. But that may not have been the intent of your parent at all. They may have assumed, if you have siblings or other family members, that any remaining funds in this convenience or joint account would be dispersed by the dictates of their will. To avoid any family squabbles (and money makes people weird), ask your parent. Is this joint account part of the "pot" or to be passed on only to you as joint holder of the account? Ask your parent to put something in writing or to clearly express to the bank and to their attorney exactly what they want. Better yet, have the distribution of *any* account listed individually in the will itself. Then there is no question as to your parents' intent or wishes.

Even if you have the sole designated power of attorney, you should find out what your parents' wishes are with these types of accounts. They may say something like: "Use this account for any unpaid bills I leave behind or for needed travel expenses having to do with family getting to my funeral etc., but then the rest can go into the estate." I have been the executor for two wills, and this is exactly what happened with any remaining funds. They were used as needed initially to pay immediate bills and eventually distributed to family members as the will indicated.

You can expect at least a fifteen-day delay between the death of your family member and utilizing the funds if you are not a joint signer of the account, says a banker friend of mine. And it will take ten days to two weeks to get a death certificate, minimum. Even with this, you will need to present the certificate to the bank and should expect delays. You will need to show them proof that you are the legal representative, not just show the previous power of attorney, since this document *ends at the death of your parent or family member*. Besides, no one will assume that the POA agent and the executor or personal representative is the same person.

I have also seen situations where a family member has to change the designated power of attorney due to the death of an adult child or in the case of mental illness or addiction to drugs where the parent feels their adult child is no longer capable. I did not know that you can file a new POA with the local court until my banker friend told me. Although this is rarely practiced, you can officially file the choice of POA through your local court system, and therefore revoke it more easily. No matter what, if your parent opts to change the designated power of attorney, you should file an official revocation with the court just to make sure there is no confusion. You should also make sure the attorney is in the know and alert other family members, if necessary.

Credit Cards, Passwords, and More

Of utmost importance is making sure there is a list of passwords to accounts that you can access when needed. Don't get carried away and ask for them now, unless it is an emergency. Your parents won't appreciate it. They will appreciate you asking to make sure a list exists. Half the couples I know don't even know each other's passwords! A sudden and unexpected death can wreak havoc with the best-laid plans. Having a will or trust won't help in this area if no one can access this information easily. All you need to know is **if** there is a list online, in writing, or in a digitally protected file. Many companies now offer online identity protection and password storage and protection. Encourage your parents to utilize these services or keep a password book hidden or locked up in a safe.

Do not forget how important it is to cancel credit cards when your parents pass away. Did you know scammers peruse the obits and target widows and widowers? Try to get a list of all the credit cards. You might want to see if Mom has cards in her own name or only in Dad's name. Why? Because if he dies first, and she has no credit, she will not have any credit history, and she will be unable to get any credit cards. As you can imagine, this is far more likely with older couples. I see plenty of lovely older women who concentrated on running a home and raising children and never worked outside the home. Usually, they are in their eighties and above. Just ask your elderly parents and see if this is an issue for them. I have also seen elders better with navigating online than I am, so you never know!

Many people use more than one bank. As mentioned, they may have CDs at whatever bank was offering the best rate. In fact, many couples don't even use the same bank as each other, especially if it is a second or third marriage. I have known wives who had accounts their husbands didn't know anything about, and plenty of husbands who had accounts their wives knew nothing about. Sometimes there are surprises that can be quite a shock. Hopefully someone does know, likely the attorney. My advice is for the personal representative to check in with an attorney to see if there are any unpleasant surprises before a will is read or distributed to all the family. Often these surprises can be resolved without too much anguish. It can be very difficult if your parents lived in many locations or live in two locations (winter somewhere and summer elsewhere) and have accounts in both places. This is likely for affluent couples, and it can be tricky for adult children trying to sort through where all the assets are.

Critical Insurance Documents

It is always a good idea to know what kinds of insurance policies your parents have. Often an employer, a pension package, or a top-notch retirement plan will have a life insurance policy automatically paid for. Many older couples have maintained life insurance policies for years that could pay an estate thousands of dollars. Some couples have what is called "accidental death" insurance as well. Hopefully they have all their insurance policies in one general location. Insurance documents are incredibly difficult to replace, if not impossible. Make sure that in a crisis, these critical documents are not tossed out accidently or put in an unmarked box you will never find.

I worked with a lovely woman, Emily, who took care of her mom for years after her dad passed away. Her mom had dementia, and she finally placed her in a memory-care assisted-living facility (ALF) and paid for this herself. A year after her mom died, she found a long-term-care insurance policy that would have paid for taking care of Mom, as some policies cover paying a family member! It also would have covered $150,000 of her memory care in assisted living.

Due to her father's sudden death and mom's dementia, Emily never knew this long-term care insurance policy even existed. Long-term care policies *do not pay after the fact*; they are not like life insurance policies! Ask your parents if they have a long-term care policy and ask for a copy. Review it every five years so everyone knows what it does and does not cover. Coverage and benefits could go up by hundreds of dollars a day over time if your parents purchased what is known as an "inflation rider," far more than the original policy will show! Please review Chapter 15, "Medicare, Medicaid, and Paying for Long-Term Care," where I provide more details on long-term care insurance.

Who Is Paying the Bills?

It is also a good idea to know general information about all household bills like rent, mortgage payments, utilities, and auto or property/homeowners' insurance.

With online banking, you should also find out if your parents have automatic bill pay through their banking accounts and if so, what bills are being paid this way. This will be critical should they become incapacitated, the bill payer dies, and no one knows the passwords, or some other scenario. This is also important so you can assist your parents should they need or wish to cancel any kind of automatic payments, for example, auto-pay insurance for a car or house that is being sold!

The husband of a couple I knew died suddenly and left his wife in a large, lovely home. While she certainly did not have dementia, she was accustomed to her late husband paying all the bills and managing the upkeep of the home. Her adult children did not realize the degree to which she depended on him until she confessed she had been ignoring the bills for months since he died. She was overwhelmed, grieving, and somewhat embarrassed, and did not want to burden her children by asking for help. She had a small car accident and discovered that her auto insurance had been cancelled, which is when she asked for help. In fact, it turned out her property insurance had been cancelled as well. Her car insurance was reinstated, but in Florida, it's not so easy to get homeowners' insurance these days. The company was only too happy to cancel and not renew the policy.

Do not assume if one parent goes first that the remaining parent can take over and manage if they are not used to doing this. You can always call the insurance companies and double-check that all is in order. If your parents pay annually, you could be paying for insurance they no longer need, and you may be eligible for a partial refund. If the premium is paid by automatic withdrawal, it would be helpful to cancel before the withdrawal. You may need to be with your parent(s) to make any changes to billing or cancellation unless you have their power of attorney.

The Crime of the Twenty-First Century: Scamming the Elderly

There is an epidemic of vast proportion going on in our country today. A recent Bloomberg survey found that criminals stole approximately $37 billion from the elderly through online scammers, telephone pitches, and family members. Recently, the US Centers for Disease Control and Prevention called it a "public health crisis." Most of the fraud is never reported, so this number is thought by experts to be the tip of the iceberg. And to make matters worse, according to AARP, 51 percent of the scammers were strangers, 34 percent were family and friends, and the rest were trusted financial advisors or attorneys. In 2020, AARP estimates that the average amount of money lost is up to $120,000 per individual!

Why are the elderly such tempting targets? With a lifetime of working and investing, older Americans hold a great deal of the wealth in this country and scammers know it. While it is easy to think no one could possibly fall for the "Nigerian letter" scam, apparently it happens all the time, or some close version of this. But if one-third of Americans over the age of seventy-one have mild cognitive dementia, according to Robert Roush of the Huffington Center on Aging at Baylor College of Medicine, then this, too, contributes to poor decision-making and creates an easy mark. The latest research shows that there are actual changes in the brains of the elderly that prevent them from perceiving truth from deception, making seniors more prone to being scammed.

Educating Yourself and Your Parents

So who can you trust, anyway? When you look at the stories and statistics, not too many people, it seems. Start by talking with your parents and making them aware of the most common scams on the market. If it has already happened, they may be too embarrassed to tell you, but again, be brave, and bring this topic up. Explain that millions of older Americans have been scammed financially; in fact, one in five over the age of sixty-five!

Ask your parents if they will allow you to monitor their mail or accounts for unusual activity, especially their credit cards and bank statements. There are now many apps on the market designed to help with this very issue. You can receive alerts for unusual activity in bank accounts, double bill paying, and more. These apps are also immensely helpful for any parent with early cognitive impairment who still wants financial autonomy but may need some oversight!

This advice also applies to an aging parent who may live alone or is concentrating on being a caregiver and who may not be paying attention to bills and financial statements. Some kind of oversight is a must if they have staff/caregivers coming in and out of their home. I hate to say it, but theft of financial information, account statements, and personal identification and belongings is rampant in the home care business. My mother lost a great deal of her jewelry this way. Remind your parents not to leave credit cards out, or checkbooks, or any kind of financial information where it can easily be seen or stolen. Lock up any valuables in a safe!

There are often free classes on preventing financial fraud offered by local police, senior centers, and even investment firms. Scammers keep upping their game and can even use apps that make it appear the local police are calling, or even the IRS or Social Security. Make sure your parents know that if anyone asks (by phone or online) for personal identification like Social Security numbers, account numbers, or money transfers, it is a scam.

Other steps you can take to avoid the scamming industry? Ask to meet your parents' banker, financial advisor, trustee, attorney, and broker if you have not already. Most of these professionals will be happy to meet you and

Avoiding Family Conflict

With 34 percent of scammers being family members, here are some tips to prevent this from happening to your family:

- Do not let the primary caregiver pay the bills if possible. Have another sibling or trusted person pay the bills.
- Require online access to copies of bills for more than one family member.
- Require permission from other family members for purchases over a certain agreed-upon amount.
- Require notifications/alerts from the bank when withdrawals or transfers over a certain amount are made.
- Consider seeking the advice of an "elder-law" attorney to write up a family contract or legal agreement that spells out individual family members' responsibilities, especially if a family caregiver is being paid.
- Have quarterly family meetings with fully transparent financial statements from the bank or investment portfolio, not just information provided by the person in charge of the money.
- Be vigilant and be suspicious, even of a family member. The facts show this is warranted!

talk with you, with your parents' permission, and ideally in their presence. They will be far less likely to be tempted to steal from your parents' accounts if they know you have a watchful eye on the statements. This is the single most powerful deterrent to this type of scam: an involved, responsible adult child. If you have power of attorney already, then you can explain you are trying to get to know your parents' trusted circle of advisors to be better prepared for whatever the future may bring.

Don't Procrastinate!

I realize that much of this may seem like overkill, and you may be wondering what your parents will say when you start asking for lists and copies of important documents or discussing the high incidence of seniors being scammed. But again, just remind yourself that a discussion now could prevent financial fraud. Completing documents and gathering critical information now will provide peace of mind for the future, no matter what life throws at all of you. Remind them you are trying to prepare to help them under any circumstances, including some kind of incapacitation. Many things contribute to a person's inability to carry on life as usual. It could be a sudden accident, an incapacitating stroke, dementia, or any number of things. *To be prepared means having this kind of information or knowing where to find it.*

The good news is that many couples do plan ahead and try to leave things well organized for their families. You might be one of the lucky ones with parents who are prepared. If so, be ever so grateful that they did "the heavy lifting" and made it easier for you. But please remember it is human nature to procrastinate, and life can deliver some nasty surprises that can lay waste to the best plans. No matter what, go ahead and ask your parents if they have this information written down and easy to find, so you can be prepared should they need help one day. As usual, prioritize based on your situation, and just get started. I promise this will give you some peace of mind.

Chapter 4

Do Your Parents Need Help Now?

When developing a plan, keep this question in mind: Do my parents need help now? It is sometimes difficult to know what your parents need, especially if you don't live near them or see them often. One way to approach this is to look at a measure used by many geriatricians and assisted-living facilities:

- Are they able to easily manage for themselves and do basic things like shop for groceries, cook for themselves, get to doctor appointments? These are often referred to as **IADLs** (instrumental activities of daily living) and can include managing finances and keeping track of their medications as well as the above.
- Another measure used is called **ADLs** (activities of daily living), which are often markers used to determine how much help a person needs. This list includes the ability to dress oneself, bathe and use the toilet independently, and feed oneself. How is their mobility? Are they walking and able to easily go up and down stairs?

If you are noticing changes in their appearance, their behavior, or housekeeping habits, you should also be concerned. Look for any underlying health conditions that could account for these changes, and please do not assume this is the beginning of Alzheimer's. Many things can mimic cognitive impairment. Suggest to them it is time to check in with their primary care physician to rule out a treatable condition.

If your parents need help in any of the areas mentioned, it is time to put a plan into place quickly. Any senior already falling into this category is far closer to a medical crisis than someone who is still fully independent. Please don't procrastinate hiring or arranging for help, even if it is only temporary!

There are simply so many reasons your loved one may need help either long or short term, but it can make all the difference in the world to helping them live safely in their home. Part Three will focus extensively on options and solutions when they need more help and care, but you can't "get the ball rolling" without accessing what help your parents need now.

Physical Limitations

If you notice that your loved one is walking less, their balance is off, or they are holding on to furniture and counters as they move from room to room, you should be worried. Perhaps they have already had mini-strokes, called TIAs (transient ischemic attacks), or are having trouble breathing due to heart or lung issues. Do they already have a diagnosis of COPD (chronic obstructive pulmonary disease) or CHF (congestive heart failure)? Have they recently fallen; do they have poor balance? Some of the red flags listed below apply in this category as well, not just for memory loss! Anything that is beginning to interfere with their ability to perform everyday functions (housekeeping, grocery shopping, preparing meals, bathing, etc.) should alert you that they need more help.

Memory Loss and Confusion: Causes and Preparation

There are very few things more frightening than coming to the realization that one of your parents is losing their memory. Usually this happens long

before any kind of formal diagnosis. Sometimes through your own obser-
vations or reports from your other parent or family members, you begin to
wonder if what you are seeing is serious or just signs of forgetfulness.

For many years, any senior who exhibited ongoing mental confusion
was thought to have Alzheimer's. According to the Alzheimer's Association
website (www.alz.org), Alzheimer's is a type of dementia that affects memory, thinking, and behavior.

Symptoms eventually grow severe enough to interfere with daily
tasks. Alzheimer's is the most common cause of dementia, a general
term for memory loss and other cognitive abilities serious enough to
interfere with daily life. Alzheimer's disease accounts for 60–80% of
dementia cases.

It is a progressive neurologic disorder that causes the brain to shrink
and brain cells to die, and eventually it affects a person's ability to function
independently. It is not considered a normal part of aging. Today, hopefully,
the general public is better informed. Without a full medical assessment,
the correct tests, and the passage of time, *you will be guessing*. I cannot stress
enough that it is never safe to make assumptions about what the cause of
confusion may be.

My dear friend Carol told me this story. Her father, who was ninety-
four at the time and still living independently, started exhibiting mental
confusion, poor memory, and the inability to recall normal everyday words.
She talked with her father, called the doctor, and insisted her dad show up
for an examination. After doing a CAT scan, they discovered he had a small
brain bleed, and the pressure of the pooling blood was pressing on his brain
and causing these symptoms. His condition was totally treatable and did not
have permanent effects since it was diagnosed early! If she had not insisted,
I'm not sure he would have gone to the doctor.

As an adult friend or family member, you cannot take the advice of the
person who is confused! I've known many seniors who simply avoid the doctor out of fear of a diagnosis of Alzheimer's.

Look for the Red Flags

Do any of these statements below sound familiar? If so, it is time to look deeper into what is going on. I have had many conversations with adult children who seem to overlook or make excuses for obvious signs of trouble. Sometimes adult children are the last to admit that their beloved parents may need help!

- "I don't know what's the matter with Mother lately. I called her last night to remind her I was coming over and then she acted surprised when I showed up today."
- "I've noticed Dad is losing weight, but he won't talk about it and keeps saying nothing is wrong. I wonder if he is eating enough?"
- "I wonder why Mom is socializing less these days. She used to go out with her friends all the time."
- "Don't worry about your father. He's fine. Just getting a bit confused, that's all. Nothing to worry about."
- "I keep finding pills on the floor or medications sitting around the house. I wonder if Mom is taking her meds correctly?"

If any of the above statements apply to you and your family, it is time to look at providing more help. If you see your parents struggling with paying their bills, losing interest in eating, experiencing declining personal hygiene, missing doctors' appointments or social engagements, and most importantly, losing track of medications . . . these are all red flags. It may not be Alzheimer's, but it *is* something!

Take these steps:

- Try to honestly observe what is going on; keep a log of the changes you notice.
- Talk with other family members or friends.
- See how long you think the symptoms have been occurring.
- Seek some medical expertise.
- And remember that any signs of confusion could be a treatable condition.

Read on to see many conditions that cause confusion in the elderly.

Proper Diagnosis

Many types of dementia mimic Alzheimer's symptoms, so it is critical to have a thorough diagnostic evaluation by a doctor trained in memory disorders. Don't assume your parents' primary care physician can accurately diagnose the true cause of your parents' confusion, but you may have to start there. They will likely refer you to a neurologist, but if not, ask for a referral! Other types of dementia include Lewy body dementia, vascular dementia (which my mother suffered from), progressive supranuclear palsy, corticobasal degeneration, multiple system atrophy, frontotemporal dementia, and sadly, the list goes on. Most of the diseases mentioned above have various treatments or medications that can treat symptoms or perhaps slow the progression of the disease.

Mild Cognitive Impairment (MCI)

Many doctors today will use the term "mild cognitive impairment" (MCI) to describe ongoing mild confusion that is generally beyond normal. The impairment can't be bad enough to meet the criteria for dementia, which would mean that the level of confusion is interfering with common activities of daily living. MCI is often thought to be an early sign of Alzheimer's disease or another type of dementia, but studies show that only 30 to 40 percent of people with a diagnosis of MCI will progress to dementia. *Some people never get worse and never develop full-blown dementia.*

If one of your parents receives this diagnosis, there are steps they can take now to help them cope with the possibility of increasing confusion. The doctor may find it is a hormone or vitamin deficiency or perhaps a sleeping disorder, all of which are treatable conditions. There are also classes called "cognitive training" that focus on planning daily tasks and setting up reminder systems and organizational calendars. Check with your local Alzheimer's chapter and local USAging center for local classes, which are often free.

Currently (2022) there are no FDA-approved medications for the treatment of MCI, as none have been shown to prevent progression to dementia. The controversial new Alzheimer's drug Aduhelm did get FDA (Federal Drug Administration) approval in 2021 and can be used in certain MCI patients, but it's a special case, and some medical professionals think Aduhelm should not have been approved due to poor effectiveness.

Cognitive Training

Cognitive skills are the core skills your brain uses to think, read, learn, remember, reason, and pay attention. For someone with early-stage MCI or early-stage Alzheimer's, they can benefit from cognitive training, which is a series of brain exercises that help with all of these skills. A person with memory loss can learn to cope better and compensate for some of their short-term memory loss when these skills are exercised through a series of regular mental activities. This is totally nonpharmacological, and classes can usually be found through senior centers, memory-disorder clinics, Alzheimer's Association support services, and Area Agencies on Aging websites.

What If You Know It Is Alzheimer's?

More than eleven million family members and other unpaid caregivers provided an estimated sixteen billion hours of care to people with Alzheimer's or other dementias in 2021, according to the PubMed.gov website. You may be one of these caregivers and know all too well the pain of losing a loved one to this terrible disease. Did you know that Alzheimer's disease was ranked as the seventh leading cause of death in 2021 in the United States, not far behind heart disease and cancer? It is the most common cause of dementia in the elderly, and according to the Alzheimer's Association in 2022, more than 6.5 million Americans have Alzheimer's type dementia. By 2060, the number of people aged sixty-five and older with Alzheimer's dementia is projected to reach 13.8 million!

At some point, doctors may tell you that the diagnosis is in fact Alzheimer's. Often it is a process of elimination as physicians rule out other possibilities. If there is a memory-disorder clinic near you or your parents, consider taking your loved one for full testing. While it can be grueling and is often three to more than four hours of consecutive tests, the results are as accurate as you could hope for. Search online for a clinic near you. They are commonly associated with a university, but top-notch hospitals will often have one as well.

Enter Their World

Try to approach the possibility of a parent having dementia constructively. Most Alzheimer's patients can still remember their past. It is their short-term memory that is primarily affected in the early stages of the disease. Some of the most frustrating moments in my professional career have been watching adult children behave badly with their confused parent. For example, Mom is repeating herself and the family member says with great exasperation, "Mom, you already told us the same thing three times!" While this kind of reaction is totally understandable, it is not helpful. I spent years working in an advanced dementia facility and learned ways of coping with repetition. A resident named Mr. Charles would often wait by the front door and tell me his dad was coming to take him fishing. Since he was well into his eighties, I knew Dad wasn't going to show up. But instead of trying to "make sense," I simply asked him to tell me about fishing with his dad, where they would go, what he would catch. He told me lovely stories about fishing in Ohio with his dad and brother.

This approach allows you to still communicate positively in a way that is enjoyable for both of you. Enter their world; it can make it much easier. Call your local Alzheimer's Association and get on their email newsletter list to learn about the many resources and support groups. If you are a caregiver, I would strongly encourage you to get involved with a support group. Family members have told me it has saved their sanity!

Common Causes for Confusion in Older Adults

The important thing to realize is that there are many potential reasons your loved one may appear confused or forgetful. Since many of these are treatable, it is important not to make assumptions but to seek medical advice. Don't assume the worst, and get a diagnosis before moving forward with decisions and plans.

UTIs or Urinary Tract Infections

Did you know that a urinary tract infection (UTI) often causes mental confusion in the elderly? I discovered this when my stepfather, Bill, was placed on the psych floor of a major medical hospital. He told me with genuine earnestness that he could change the television channels using the "Mr. Smurf" hat he was wearing! Another time he was sure the staff was going to blow up the memory-care facility he was living in at three in the morning.

The doctor explained that the elderly are extremely susceptible to mental confusion with almost any type of infection, but in particular with a urinary tract infection. Sometimes dementia can exist already but is not necessarily very apparent until the person comes down with an infection. Once the infection was cleared up, Bill improved.

If your parent has a sudden and unexplained change in behavior, such as increased confusion, agitation, or withdrawal, this could very well be a UTI or some other type of infection that is treatable! Women are far more likely to come down with a UTI than men. Even if your loved one does not say they have pain upon urination, they could still be suffering from a UTI.

When someone has dementia, they may not be able to articulate that they cannot urinate, and they may not even notice. Your loved one could also be running a mild fever, have some kind of lower abdominal pain, or if it is extreme back pain, the UTI may have spread into the kidneys. When in doubt, request a urine culture!

Most UTIs are treated with a regimen of antibiotics, depending on what the doctor orders. If you know your parent is allergic to any antibiotic, let the doctor know right away.

Anesthesia

Simply going through any kind of surgery will often result in a lingering fog due to the effects of anesthesia. It can take *eight to twelve weeks* for anesthesia to totally leave your system, and the mental confusion can last that long. Some people with underlying dementia do not recover from the effects of anesthesia, which is why any kind of surgery in the elderly should be treated cautiously. A few of the top hospitals in the country are now doing pre-screening of patients sixty-five and older prior to surgery to try to prevent exacerbation of any kind of underlying dementia.

If your loved one is due to have surgery, make sure to ask the hospital if they offer this kind of cognitive pre-screening and be sure to bring up your concern with their surgical doctor. The latest results have shown that with pre-screening, doctors can be on the lookout for those that test poorly. These patients are at much higher risk for prolonged cognitive impairment, surgical psychosis, and longer recovery times. On the upside, these patients won't be given a discharge plan that will send them home alone without companion care.

ICU Psychosis

Since we are discussing confusion in the elderly, I wish I had known about ICU psychosis or post-surgical psychosis before it happened to my stepfather. This is a condition that happens often to patients in intensive care settings and results in serious psychiatric symptoms. The patient can become very disoriented, agitated, paranoid, restless, and extremely excitable. They can hallucinate, hear voices, and become delusional. Knowing this situation was common would have been a huge relief for my family and me.

My stepfather, Bill, a World War II vet, was convinced that the Nazis were trying to kill him after undergoing a difficult ten-hour abdominal surgery. They had to restrain him since he was trying to get out of bed and wrestle with the nurses. It was difficult for all of us, but afterward, he remembered nothing. Some estimates are that one patient in every three who spends more than five days in an ICU will experience some form of psychotic reaction.

The cause of ICU psychosis is thought to involve a combination of environmental and medical issues such as sensory deprivation (no windows, away from friends and family), sleep disturbances or deprivation, room lights left on all the time, stress, constant disturbances by hospital staff, and lack of orientation to time and place.

Fortunately, this condition usually stops within twenty-four hours once the patient has had some sleep, is hydrated, and is surrounded by family members. If a person already has dementia of any kind, ICU psychosis is more likely to occur. Try to encourage hospital staff to allow your parent to sleep as much as possible, minimize shift change disturbances, keep lighting close to night-and-day cycles, and keep a calm, quiet environment. Talk to the doctor if they are recommending an antipsychotic medication (with potential serious side effects) and see if this is necessary.

Depression or Dementia?

Early Alzheimer's and depression share many symptoms, so it can be difficult for even doctors to distinguish between them. Plus, it is easy to see why people with Alzheimer's could be depressed! If you notice loss of interest in hobbies, social withdrawal, memory issues, sleeping too much, or impaired concentration, these are red flags for either diagnosis. If you notice any of these symptoms, talk with your parent and see if they are willing to open up. Needless to say, a proper diagnosis will help.

Plus, according to the National Alliance on Mental Illness (NAMI), one in three seniors do not receive treatment for mental health problems. About 20 percent of adults over age fifty-five have been found to have some type of mental health issue, so this is a fairly large percentage of the elderly population. They could be facing major health issues or lifestyle changes such as loss of a loved one, or a recent serious diagnosis. Either could trigger both depression and anxiety, especially if there is a previous personal history.

Did you know that anxiety disorders are the leading mental health problem for all women and the second most common for men, after substance abuse? While this is a common reaction to stress, it is not normal when it affects your activities of daily living, your social life, or your relationships with friends and family. If someone is living in a constant state of panic, fear, worry, apprehension, or dread that is excessive or disproportionate to the situation, they likely have an anxiety disorder. You don't want depression or anxiety to be diagnosed as dementia!

Ask yourself what is normal for your loved one. Start keeping a simple journal of symptoms and ask other people who interact with your loved one to do the same.

Dehydration

Is your mom or dad drinking six to eight glasses of water a day? I doubt it. A recent UCLA study says that 40 percent of seniors are chronically "under hydrated." In fact, many elders cut back on drinking water because they are afraid of falling at night due to frequent trips to the bathroom. But cutting back on drinking water leads to an increase in UTIs, dehydration, and mental confusion and is one of the primary reasons seniors are hospitalized. If a person loses more than 15 percent to 25 percent of the water in their body, this is invariably fatal. A 10 percent loss will result in physical and mental deterioration.

Symptoms of dehydration include confusion, headache, general discomfort, loss of appetite, dry skin, decreased urine volume, unexplained tiredness, irritability, and even tingling of the limbs. Even with only minor dehydration, heart palpitations can be a symptom.

If your parent is already exhibiting extreme symptoms, take them to the hospital immediately or call 911. Older people die every day from severe dehydration. Heed the warnings to go check on the elderly when summer heat waves hit. Without air-conditioning, they are very susceptible. Fans are better than nothing. Climate change, loss of power, and extreme heat will not be going away soon. Find out where the nearest cooling stations are and see if your city or county has a list of medical emergency transport for at-risk seniors. See if you can add your parents to the list now. In a climate emergency, they will be on a list of people to check and possibly help with evacuation.

The big problem for older people is that as we age, the body's thirst sensation diminishes so it no longer sends messages to the body and brain to drink more water or any kind of liquids. Try to get your parents into the habit of having a water glass nearby at all times. Many people like the athletic insulated mugs with a built-in straw. Much easier to drink from!

I have friends who simply hate water and just won't drink it. If this is true for your family member, make sure to provide healthy substitutes. Offer them sports drinks (beware added caffeine), fruit juice (beware sugar content), smoothies, Jell-O, popsicles, and any kind of fruit, especially watermelon.

Medication Mix-Ups

Medication mix-ups can be one of the first signs of cognitively impaired parents who are no longer managing their meds properly. This is also one of the top three reasons older people end up in the hospital—stopping their meds, not taking them as prescribed, taking too many meds. Not taking medications as prescribed can be both a sign of mental confusion or the reason for cognitive impairment! It is important to try and find out if the confusion you are seeing is the underlying reason they can no longer manage taking their meds. Or are the meds themselves contributing to mental confusion? If so, it could be that your loved one is not taking them as prescribed, or the combination of medications is causing symptoms. Talk with their doctor and the pharmacist to see if any adverse drug reactions could be occurring.

According to the National Center for Biotechnology Information (NCBI), approximately 30 percent of hospital admissions for older adults are drug related, with more than 11 percent attributed to medication non-adherence. Approximately 10 to 17 percent of admissions are related to adverse drug reactions.

Some of the reasons for medication mishaps are unbelievably basic! Elderly patients who have poor vision, can't open the bottle, or can't read English are going to have issues. Ask for bottles that are *not* childproofed, as they are difficult to open for anyone. Ask your parents if they can see the label on the script and *have them read it to you*. If not, ask the pharmacist to print in a larger font. Call your local USAging office for programs that help pay for medications and for pharmacies that deliver.

Over-the-Counter (OTC) Medications

There are many over-the-counter meds that are dangerous for the elderly but especially in combination with other prescription medicines. Often patients do not even think to tell their doctor what else they take regularly that might interfere with the absorption of a critical med or result in a lethal combination.

According to the American Geriatrics Society (AGS), a wide range of medications pose serious health risks to seniors. In 2019, the AGS updated a list of medications that are potentially inappropriate for seniors. The panel updating the list were experts in geriatrics and pharmacotherapy, and this report was based on the latest research. The list, called the "American Geriatrics Society Updated Beers Criteria for Potentially Inappropriate Medication Use in Older Adults," is considered critical for those in the field of geriatrics and it is updated every three years. The list groups medications as those ***best to avoid*** for most older people, medications to ***use with caution*** if someone has certain conditions or disease, and those that they deem ***high risk.***

You would be surprised at how many of these potentially dangerous drugs you will be familiar with, such as Aleve or naproxen. What about muscle relaxers like Flexeril, which can leave an older person feeling groggy and confused and can increase falls? If you take aspirin along with Plavix or Coumadin, you could be in big trouble. I doubt I need to educate you about the dangers of any opioid, including OxyContin and any form of hydrocodone such as Vicodin. Drugs that include codeine, tramadol, or hydrocodone are highly addictive with a long list of side effects. By the way, seniors dealing with insomnia often self-prescribe OTC meds with lots of negative side effects. It wouldn't hurt to ask your parents if they are taking any sleep aids.

Educate yourself about your parents' prescription medications, OTC meds, and even herbal or natural products they are taking. Talk with them and their doctor or other health providers.

Sleeping Potions

Many simple combinations of OTC drugs and prescription meds cause balance issues and severe drowsiness. What OTC drugs are they taking? Bring those to the pharmacist or doctor, too, if you can, or encourage your loved ones to include those at their annual doctor visit. You won't be surprised to hear that Benadryl is on the Beers cautionary medication list because so many seniors use it as a sleep aid, even though it is primarily an antihistamine used for allergy treatment. However, as a strong anticholinergic, it can cause a variety of dangerous symptoms, especially if taken with alcohol. Long-term use of this type of drug is also linked to dementia and dementia-related diseases like Alzheimer's, and the risk is greater if you are sixty-five years and older! The active ingredient in Benadryl is diphenhydramine, the primary ingredient of ZzzQuil and other sleep aids, but in fact it is associated with a reduction in sleep quality that can leave a person with residual drowsiness the next day.

Addiction to Prescription Drugs

It is currently estimated that in 2020, over 2.7 million older adults misused prescription drugs according to the SAMHSA, the Substance Abuse and Mental Health Services Administration. With older patients often given prescriptions for very strong pain meds, sleeping pills, or anti-anxiety drugs, it is no surprise. As a person gets older, the liver's ability to filter medicines out of the body decreases, leaving them more easily addicted or experiencing side effects from a lower dose than a younger adult. The SAMHSA website, samhsa.gov, has a lot of helpful information and referral information on both drug abuse in seniors and mental health in seniors.

Look for the Red Flags for Prescription Addiction

- The patient gets a prescription for the same medicine from two different doctors or uses multiple pharmacies for the same medication.
- They take the medicine at different times or more often than instructed on the label.
- You notice behavioral changes such as anger or withdrawal.
- They are afraid to go anywhere without taking the medication.
- They make excuses for why they need it or why they cannot stop taking it.
- They store "extra pills" in their purse or pocket or hide medication.
- They have any kind of history of alcohol or drug abuse in the past.

Keep this in mind when you doubt that your sweet little old mom could be addicted to anything—women are far more likely than men to become addicted. This can be attributed to the fact that more women take psychoactive medications (benzodiazepines) because of situations they experience such as divorce, widowhood, poor health status, depression, and/or anxiety.

If you think your parent or loved one is addicted, talk with the doctor who prescribed the medicine. Depending on the severity of their addiction, the doctor may even recommend a residential treatment program. You may be fortunate enough to live in a metropolitan area that has a specialized treatment program for an addicted elderly person.

Narcotics Anonymous is a free twelve-step program for anyone addicted to any type of drug. You can go online to find the nearest meeting. There is also Nar-Anon for any family member trying to cope with an addicted loved one. These types of programs offer a path to recovery for both the addict and family members, and they have saved thousands if not millions from death, despair, and insanity.

Knowledge Is Power

I know you are likely feeling overwhelmed at the amount of information in this chapter. Think of this as your reference guide. You aren't going to be tested, so there is no need to memorize all of this, thank goodness! But if you only remember a few things, like UTIs causing confusion, or making sure a parent does cognitive screening before surgery, you are better educated already, and you get an A+ from me! Reread this chapter as often as needed. Simply paying attention in our super busy world will make a huge difference to helping your parents, and yourself, especially as you move forward with plans.

Location, Location, Location?

The power of community to create health is far greater than any physician, clinic, or hospital.

Mark Hyman

Do you recall the first item on my list of the Five Pillars of Aging Successfully, from Chapter 1? The question I start with when consulting with my senior clients is: "Do you want to age in place or move, and if so, where?"

Deciding where to live during this phase of one's life is absolutely critical. It will usually determine:

- Whether or not your parents will age successfully,
- Whether or not they will be able to maintain their independence for the longest possible time,
- The level of healthcare they can access,
- Their overall quality of life.

When discussing future living situations, the goal is to generate a conversation that looks at all the options with an open mind. The framework goes back to Principle #1: **How can I help maximize and prolong my**

parents' independence as they age? When families sit down and take an honest look at the options with this framework, they will often come to some surprising conclusions.

Helping your parents think this through gives you a chance to apply Principle #2 as well: **the JITSP or "Just in Time" Senior Planning.** There is nothing wrong with a three- to five-year window of staying in one's home, with a plan B that involves moving into a senior retirement community or life plan community later . . . or closer to *you*! Plus, any plan can change if a medical or other crisis requires you to be flexible.

This section will delve into the various pluses and minuses of senior living options, including aging in place, moving closer to "the kids," moving in with "the kids," choosing a retirement community or life care community, and more.

Chapter 5

Where Should Your Parents Live?

The best way to approach the question "Where should my parents live?" is, first, to find out what your parents want and need now, before making any assumptions. Next, ask yourself what is realistic for you and for them. I am a big fan of making a list of pros and cons, and I suggest you start your own list and your parents start theirs. Begin with: "Where can my parents live where they will be able to receive the support they need, now and in the future?" Please add: "And we can all keep our sanity." See where these lists line up, and if you and your parents are on the same page. If you are lucky, you may all agree on "where." If not, go through the list of considerations I provide in this section and see how the options stack up.

You want your parents to be happy in the long run. Thinking strategically allows you and your parents to create a plan together that has a good chance of success. No one will be happy if plans are put in place that do not address what I call "the happiness factor." Where your parents live can be a critical factor for all of you in the happiness arena. Just living an hour away might be perfect, rather than five to six hours away. Ideally, your parents are not wholly dependent on you for their social life. Remaining where they are or moving nearby to an age-friendly city could be perfect, especially if they are still active and healthy. The story is different if they need care now or soon. Applying the JITSP model, the three- to five-year plan for your seventy-year-old healthy parents should consider their level of health, need for social engagement, and openness to relocating.

An important factor in creating a plan that will work long term is *you*. By "you" I mean your mental, physical, and emotional well-being. Remember those airline safety talks where the flight attendant tells you to "always put your oxygen mask on first before assisting others?" It's the same principle here. First, please take care of yourself. Risking your mental or physical health will be of no help to anyone, especially your parents. This is not the time for guilt trips, coercion, or agreement just to keep the family peace. It will backfire, I promise you. This plan needs to be one that addresses everyone's mental health!

To Move or Not to Move?
That Is the Question!

If a move is on the table as an option, always use the foundation of Principles #1 and #2, maximizing their independence and having a flexible plan. Start with asking these questions first about where they live now:

- Is their home senior friendly with modified bathrooms and few stairs? Is it well designed for safety, or can it be remodeled to make sure the home is safe? (See Chapter 6, "Aging-in-Place Considerations.")
- Is the neighborhood safe, with easy access to public transportation if needed?
- Do they have an existing support network nearby? Family or close friends who are available to help when needed in an emergency?
- How far away is the nearest family member? If a family member is also an HCS (healthcare surrogate), how far away are they?
- How close is the nearest hospital, and how is this hospital rated?

- Are there any excellent retirement communities nearby they would consider? (See Chapter 7, "Retirement Communities: Asking the Right Questions.")
- Is home care or home healthcare readily available? (See Chapter 10, "Next Steps: Options and Solutions for In-Home Help.")
- Are there well-rated assisted-living facilities in the area? (See Chapter 12, "Assisted-Living Facilities.")
- Are there well-rated skilled nursing facilities in the area? (See "Chapter 13, Choosing the Best Nursing Home or Skilled Nursing Facility.")
- Is there a top-notch senior center nearby?
- Are they connected to the community through a church or place of worship? Or otherwise socially engaged?
- Is their town rated "age friendly" by AARP?

If your parents' home is two or more stories, difficult to maintain, or in a high-crime area, how will this help them age successfully? Unless they can access help when needed, whether it is home care, an excellent doctor, or good hospital care, they are at risk of a minor medical crisis turning into something major.

If they are solidly entrenched, or already need care, then start interviewing home care and home healthcare companies *now* so you have a plan to address the inevitable crisis. I advise solo seniors to interview and decide on who they would call in an emergency for home care, even when they are totally healthy and independent. You can do the same! This way, the caregiver will know you and possibly meet your parent in advance of needing any care. This will give you some peace of mind if there is a medical crisis, as you will have a company or person lined up.

Don't Underestimate the Stress of Moving

If the answers are negative to more than 50 percent of the questions listed above, it is time for your parents to consider moving, and hopefully they will see the wisdom of this. If you both are looking ahead to their aging in place safely, then look **now** beyond a three- to five-year window if your parents are in their seventies. Why? *Because the time to make a move is now, not in ten years!* Did you know that relocating is on the list of the top ten stressors in life? Worse than a divorce! Translation: It does not become easier to move the older one gets. I have seen far too many seniors procrastinate about moving until it is so overwhelming they just can't do it. When you parents tell you they will move "in five years," depending on their age, you should question the logic. If a move is under serious discussion, I suggest moving in one's early to mid-seventies, and not later.

The ideal time to move is when a couple or an individual is young enough and healthy enough to make new friends and to enjoy what a community has to offer! My daughter-in-law's parents moved in their early seventies to be closer to her. They live about half an hour away, both are active, and both continue to work part-time jobs they love. They moved early enough to make new friends, join new clubs and organizations, help with grand-children, and be closer to their daughter. Everyone benefits! This is a plan well thought out.

Avoiding Family Conflict

If your parent or parents have been living independently up until now, but it is clear this is no longer working, there may be fierce family arguments about whether they should move, where they should move, who pays for their care if they are unable to do so themselves, etc. This type of situation is often aggravated if the parents don't want to move or two siblings both want a parent to move closer to them. The first thing to find out is what kind of help your parents really need, and who is best situated to provide that care?

Here are some basic guidelines that might help with this type of situation:

1. Get a professional in-home assessment that everyone can rely on as accurate. Hire an aging life care expert to help. A home healthcare agency will also do an assessment if you are hiring them.

2. Arrange a FaceTime/Zoom conference call with all family members. Consider asking the geriatric case manager/ aging life care expert to give their report as part of this meeting or call. Include your parents whenever possible.

3. Ask each family member to first email their ideas about what they feel to be the best outcome for the given situation and why. Look for agreement first and work toward consensus.

4. Is a family member able to move in with your parents? Build a tiny house on their property? (See Chapter 9, "Alternative and Creative Living Options.")

5. If considering a community, decide who will visit each facility and do the research to see what the state ratings are. Ask each family member to put their results in writing. Design a simple template so everyone is using the same form.

6. If your parents need assisted living now but may need skilled care later, look at *all* the facilities in your area and have a future plan as well. See if there is a nearby life care community (Chapter 12, "Assisted-Living Facilities") that does direct admissions into assisted living. This way, when your parent needs skilled care, they can possibly move up to this level of care without changing facilities.

7. Always work toward a long-term plan. You might have to come up with an emergency fix (such as temporarily moving in with Mom or Dad), but stay focused on a plan that helps your loved ones maintain their independence for the longest possible time!

Also, if you have decided that Mom and Dad must move, and they don't want to, try to come to a consensus as a family and show a unified front. This is a tough situation, and there needs to be agreement before proceeding. The worst outcome is when either the parents or the siblings choose the divide-and-conquer method, and the plan falls apart. Everyone has to be on board and be very clear they are choosing the best long-term plan. Decide as a group exactly how this is going to be communicated to your parent(s). Again, if possible, make sure all the decision makers are present when this conversation takes place. You can always add a trusted family advisor (minister, priest, rabbi, counselor) to this group (or a geriatric social worker) to take part in this difficult conversation.

What to Look for in a New Location

Start with the basics yet again. How is this potential new location going to help your parents age successfully and meet their needs *as they increase in age*? Did you know that the single most important determinant in aging well is the strength of your social network? If your parents have a very strong social network where they currently live, then keep this in mind. How will a move work for both you and your parent(s) in terms of family members who are close by and willing and available to provide support?

Start with this list of questions to help you evaluate a new location, but make sure to go back and look at the prior list above.

- Does the community offer things important to your parent(s) such as sports, culture, libraries, museums, lifelong learning?
- What about a nearby church, synagogue, or mosque if this is important to them?
- Is there *a cultural fit?* Are they used to urban, rural, or diverse neighborhoods?

♀ What about the availability of ethnic foods or specialty grocery stores? Let's not underestimate the importance of beloved foods!

♀ What living options are available? Are they affordable? (Costs vary tremendously from one city to the next.) Do they plan to buy a condo or a home, or rent an apartment?

♀ What retirement communities are nearby? Are they rental, entry-fee based, other?

♀ Can they live close to you and still be happy?

♀ Is there some city or town close to you (an hour or less) that meets the right criteria?

Ideally, whatever move is under consideration, it will be close to a family member who can help in an emergency AND meet the needs of parents looking for a great community to retire to and enjoy! All of these things add up to meeting your parents' needs as those needs increase over time.

Age-Friendly AARP Info

Did you know that, since 2012, AARP has developed a list of places that are "age friendly"? Cities that qualify to join this network are committed to offering walkable neighborhoods; safe, reliable transportation; access to quality healthcare; affordable and adaptive housing; respect and social inclusion; great public outdoor spaces; and more. For a full list of designated cities, visit aarp.org/livable-communities, and click on Age-Friendly Network. They believe that an age-friendly community is good for any and all ages!

How Important Is Cultural Fit?

I have a client who has a heart of gold. She decided to take care of her birth father in his old age, even though he had more or less abandoned her as a child. After many years, he'd contacted her and asked for help. She found her father and stepmother living in "unacceptable conditions," and she moved them from rural Ohio to Chicago to be closer to her. But she did not take into consideration their cultural preferences. The apartment she rented for them was in an urban setting. They did not like the noise, the ethnic diversity, the city pace. They kept asking: "Who are all these strange, different people?" They would not drive anymore for fear of having an accident, unaccustomed to city traffic and not knowing the area. It was a disaster. They were miserable and so was my friend. Please take into consideration what your loved ones are used to. If the adjustment is just too much, I doubt they will be happy. My friend now feels they would have been happier had she found a solution in their original community and set up help and visited them every three to four months.

Even with admirable intentions, this plan failed. Consider this a cautionary tale as you evaluate your options. The trade-off of moving parents closer to you may not be worth their misery in the wrong location!

Weigh the Risks and Benefits

Do not wait until your parents have made the move to discover that their supplemental Medicare policy is not offered in the state they just moved to! Almost all seniors have a policy that pays for what Medicare does not cover, called a "supplemental policy." Companies like Blue Cross Blue Shield and UnitedHealthcare through AARP have hundreds of different options. Costs vary, but they can be expensive. The fact is, these kinds of policies are not always transferable from one state to the next. Make sure to call and inquire specifically about the exact policy your parents have. One couple I know moved from New England to Florida and found out the hard way that his policy, paid for through the husband's retirement, was not offered in Florida. They had to buy a new policy out of pocket that cost them thousands annually.

If your parents' dream was to move to the country when they retired, and this location is an hour or two from the nearest hospital, please ask them to reconsider or at least have a Plan B. I met Betty and John Marshall shortly after his sudden heart attack. They loved their country home but admitted that living two hours from the hospital was not a plan that would work moving forward. The first hour after a heart attack is called "the golden hour" for a reason. If an individual can make it to the hospital in this magic hour, their chances for recovery are much higher, and permanent damage to the heart can often be avoided. The Marshalls sold their home and moved closer to a top-notch hospital.

The Spencers Move Forward

Remember our friends the Spencers? They are turning their attention to living options for Bob and Sally. They considered Colorado, where John and Sophia live, Southern California (where Wendy lives), and Raleigh, North Carolina, where Josie and Dan live, and evaluated the pros and cons of each option.

Bob and Sally decided against both California and Colorado due to weather and the very high cost of living. John and Wendy understand that choosing Raleigh makes the most sense when comparing all the facts. Raleigh checks a lot of the boxes: an excellent medical reputation, a top-rated hospital, plenty of cultural activities, reasonable real estate, and their supplemental health insurance policy is widely accepted by the doctors and hospitals in the area. They know that selling their home in New Jersey would generate enough capital to buy a new home or cover the costs of an upscale retirement community.

Bob asks Josie and Dan how they feel about being the default care-givers if he and Sally move closer to them. Josie expresses her willingness to help and so does Dan, and Josie shares she has done some research on the two retirement communities John mentioned in the family's last call. Based on her research of life care communities, she explains that Raleigh would provide an active lifestyle and higher levels of care for either Bob or Sally as their needs increase over time. This option takes some of the worry and pressure off Josie and Dan, since she knows a community like this would provide a long list of services, care, and social activities for her parents to enjoy. She asks her parents if they want to come to Raleigh to check out the city and tour the various options under consideration. Bob and Sally start planning for a visit in a month's time, ask to tour some homes as well as retirement communities, and the family sets another Zoom call for two weeks.

Your Parents Don't Want to Live with You

As you're planning your parents' next move, you may be assuming that they will want to move in with you. Maybe you're happy about that; maybe you are dreading it. Maybe you think you have no choice! Well, you do.

In fact, in all the time I've spent working in the senior living field, most parents have told me this secret: They never want to live with their kids. In fact, they were simply afraid to tell their kids this. Usually, there is no shortage of love, but there is also no desire to actually live together. Your parents love you and don't want to hurt your feelings, but believe me when I tell you that the majority of parents value their autonomy, and they don't want to be a burden. If they have been caregivers themselves, they understand what may lie in their future and yours!

For many older people who are used to a quieter lifestyle, it is just too big an adjustment for them to cope daily with young children, teenagers, dogs, noise, and vastly different schedules. Suddenly your mom can't keep her undercover smoking habit a secret anymore. Perhaps they only like to watch Fox News and your political opinions differ. Or Dad's habit of eating Cheerios at 2 AM is a problem.

Even for yourself, there are little things that contribute to your mental well-being and become hugely important under daily stress. What if you don't drink or you belong to AA, but Mom has a martini every night? Or your glass of wine keeps you sane, and you feel you can't drink in front of Dad, who is trying to stay sober?

By the time many parents are in their eighties, we shouldn't expect them to suddenly change their daily habits, or political opinions, or long-held beliefs. If you know they will be unable to accept your same-sex partner, for example, living together or perhaps even near you might not work.

"Negative sentiments about multigenerational living have spiked from 34 percent to 51 percent from 2019 to 2020," according to an AARP poll. This is another reminder that moving your parents in with you, or you living with them, may not be ideal. When families all lived in one geographical area and could share the tasks of looking after and caring for older family members, it was the norm. Current trends don't always allow for this.

The point of these scenarios is this: *Examine the assumption that your parents actually want to live with you or right next door.* Developing a plan that works for all of you takes communication and thoughtfulness. For some, an intergenerational family is the perfect answer to Mom's loneliness. It could be a blessing for Nana to help provide childcare, help with cooking, or pick kids up from school (or help homeschool). Grandpa may love gardening, fixing things, reading to the kids. Many people have wonderful memories of grandparents being part of their lives! Of course, they don't need to live with you to help with all these things or share in your life.

Each family is different, but I'd like to reassure you that "togetherness" or intergenerational living is not for every family. You will learn from upcoming chapters what other options exist for your parents and why those may be preferable to having them live with you. I have seen numerous couples move in with or closer to adult kids, only to be hugely disappointed when their "kids" did not have time to spend with them. Why? Working full time and managing their own families was overwhelming already.

If You Choose to Have Your Parents Live with You

Did you know that before Covid, 20 percent of all households in the United States were multigenerational? That adds up to about 51.5 million households! According to AARP, these numbers have now grown across all cultural spectrums. More families have merged households for financial survival, not necessarily "a desire to connect with each other or improve the quality of their lives," says AARP. Living together during Covid was not a choice for some families, it was a necessity. With the high death rates in nursing homes, families were frantic to get their loved ones out. I know friends who flew their parents out of high Covid areas like New York City and moved them in temporarily. The safety net of a "contained" family unit was paramount when we were all just trying to be safe and not catch Covid! Job loss also contributed to blended families: hard to pay rent, much less a mortgage, when you are out of work.

Covid or not, living together may be the most economical option for all. Pooling resources has always made sense, and sharing income and lowering expenses has tremendous advantages. When looking at the cost of renting even an average apartment, much less the average monthly fee for a full-service retirement community, living together may be the only option and could raise everyone's living standards!

If you do choose to blend families, experts suggest families make a *commitment of shared responsibility* that everyone signs and agrees to. My suggestion is that families who are contemplating a multigenerational home sit down and do their own version of "shared responsibility" for today's world. Families can put together an agreement that works for them. Likely you were brought up with a list of chores you and your siblings were responsible for. Having a clear understanding of who is helping with what can go a long way to keep the peace. Make sure to address shared financial responsibility as well. How are your parents helping (assuming they can) with the cost of groceries, household bills, transportation? It will be much easier if they are transparent about their finances, set monthly income, and agree to an amount every month to cover some of these costs, especially if home care is needed. All this changes if you have a parent who is bedridden, too ill to help, or is on very limited income. But the trade-off of having childcare that allows you to work or a parent who can help cook and run errands may be ideal for many reasons.

I like to remind "adult kids" that if parents are in their home, they get to set reasonable rules or guidelines. For example, I am an avid nonsmoker. My mother smoked three packs a day. When she came to visit, I requested she only smoke outside. Mostly she followed this rule and honored my request.

We made it work. Don't be afraid to set some limits, just like they did with you when you lived in their home.

When a Plan Works

Last year I spoke with Gail, a wonderful young woman trying to manage a full-time job, two kids, a dog, a partner, and a very sick dad. She was told she had a few weeks to move her father out of assisted living, all in the middle of the pandemic and long distance, since she lived three hours away. She was doing the best she could to take care of her dad and manage her family life. I told her she should give herself permission to be stressed out and to make mistakes. Anything she managed to do was better than nothing. Allow yourself to do what you can and remember something important: You will be of little help to anyone—to yourself, your own family, or your partner—if you burn out. Less stress for everyone in the long run will mean better family relationships.

Gail moved her father into her home because of Covid and hired home care to help for six months. When he recovered and the worst of the pandemic was over, she moved him back into an assisted-living facility nearby so he could have the care he needed. Her father accepted that living with her permanently was not an option and admitted he was happier with peers his own age and scheduled activities and trips. This decision followed Principle #1, by maximizing his independence for the longest possible time, plus Principle #2, by having a flexible JITSP plan that changes as needed and worked for them both in the long run. Gail can now see him far more frequently and oversee his care! As Gail told me, "I may not be able to have my dad live with me, but at least I know he is getting the care he needs, I can keep working, and meet my family obligations. It isn't perfect, but we can all accept this is the best option."

This is a solution that considers everyone's mental health, Dad's need for friends his own age, his daily care needs, and what will work financially in the long run for both Gail, who must keep on working, and Dad, who can pay for his care in assisted living.

No Unspoken Assumptions

Please remember you can be of help to your loved ones in many ways. Have the conversation before a crisis and talk it over with your parents. Which options work best for all of you? This is not the time for unspoken assumptions; clarity and honesty are needed. Talk it out, write it out, and be prepared to change your plan as required. Listen to your parents' wishes, but don't be afraid to point out unrealistic expectations. If their plan has big holes, you should gently point them out. If you are their safety net, *speak up and voice your concerns.* Just because your parents don't want to live with you, or you don't want them to live with you, does not mean you can't forge a solution that will work for all of you. And remember, you are already building flexibility, resilience, and the tools you need by reading this book!

Chapter 6

Aging-in-Place Considerations

Over 90 percent of seniors say they want to age in place, a figure that has only gone up in the last five years. So, what is aging in place? It means staying in one's own home and not ever having to move to senior living. But I like the broader definition given by the CDC (Centers for Disease Control and Prevention), which defines aging in place as "the ability to live in one's own home safely, independently, and comfortably, regardless of age, income, or ability level." I am guessing that a high percentage of my readers have parents who wish to age in place. This could mean staying in the house they are in, but it can also mean moving to another home or a new location, and aging in place there.

This may be the most important chapter in this book, especially if your parents don't want to move and are determined to stay in their home. I am not a fan of this plan because I have seen so many lonely older people become prisoners of their own homes, isolated and at risk for scams. Aging in place will only work well *if the following basic safety measures are applied, and your parents have a support network.* We can all agree that aging in place successfully is more than grab bars and good lighting. This chapter looks at the numerous steps you can take to improve both the safety of their physical home and their personal safety with home security and medical alert systems.

Getting the Conversation Started

Aging in place successfully is not impossible, but lots of people assume it will "just happen," without much planning. It won't. I suggest you begin this process with another version of "the Conversation." Something like: "Mom, Dad, you have said you want to stay in your home for the foreseeable future. Can we talk about some things that need to be done to make your home safer? Let's make a plan so you can age safely and successfully in your home. I know you want to stay independent for as long as possible, and I want that, too. Can we make a list of priorities to start with?"

Let them make the list first, and then, after you've read this chapter, you can add things they may not have thought of. My experience is that older people often become so accustomed to their settings they can't see them with fresh eyes. Don't forget you can always ask their doctor to have an occupational therapist come in for an assessment of their house/apartment specifically looking at safety factors.

Fall Assessment and Prevention

You may be surprised to learn that falls are the second leading cause of death worldwide, according to the World Health Organization. Adults over the age of sixty suffer the greatest number of falls, and 37.7 million falls are severe enough that they require medical attention each year. Keep in mind that a bad fall can immediately affect someone's ability to maintain their independence! A broken hip or pelvis means surgery, and maybe never recovering one's mobility, leading to the need to move into assisted care.

Given the statistics above, and the fact that one-third of people over the age of sixty-five fall at least once a year, it is worth looking at ways to prevent falling. Do a quick assessment on your own to see if your parents (or you!) are at risk for a fall. Here are categories usually considered to determine risk:

- History of more than one fall within the last six months (with or without injury);
- Impaired vision (can't see without glasses or contacts, glaucoma, macular degeneration;
- Foot problems that cause pain, balance issues, or any kind of neuropathy;
- Frequent toileting or incontinence issues;
- Taking any type of opiates, sedatives, psychotropics, anti-hypertensives, diuretics, laxatives. (See Chapter 4, "Do Your Parents Need Help Now?," for more in-depth information about risky medications for seniors.)
- Existing mobility issues: unsteady gait, balance issues, use of cane, walker, wheelchair;
- Any degree of cognitive impairment;
- Generally frail or limited physical strength/endurance.

All occupational and physical therapists are trained to assess fall risks. If you think your parents are at risk based on the list above, ask their primary care physician for a professional evaluation. Don't wait for a fall, and if they have already fallen several times, statistics show they will likely fall again. If they have limited physical activity, their risk jumps to "high." If they have impaired vision, bad feet, bad knees, and make frequent trips to the bathroom, they are far more likely to fall. Keep in mind that advice from a trained physical therapist about clutter or needed modifications will likely be better accepted and acted upon than if they hear it from you.

A history of falls might mean a need to change some medications, learning how to use a walker, strength or balance training, new glasses, and more. Even taking up yoga (chair yoga!), Tai Chi (particularly recommended to improve balance and very low-key), SilverSneakers (free exercise classes designed for seniors and often taught at the YMCA or senior center), or any kind of exercise program will go a long way to help them with balance and flexibility.

Household Environmental Factors and Safety Concerns

Most falls occur in or around seniors' homes, and more falls happen during the day than at night. Environmental factors such as poor lighting, clutter, areas of disrepair, loose carpets, and slick floors contribute to falls. So take a survey and see what changes could make the home safer.

Here is a helpful checklist that includes both commonsense items and things you may not have considered:

1. **Flooring:** Remove area rugs, throw rugs, plush thick rugs. Try to use only low-pile carpeting. Carpet stairs for safety. Use nonslip or slip-resistant flooring. Use cork flooring or vinyl planking rather than tile—they're not as likely to break something if a fall occurs.

2. **Accessibility:** Remove all clutter and fall hazards such as magazines, boxes, decorative items, and tchotchkes. Make sure hallways and stairs are clear, especially the path to the bathroom. Move furniture or downsize items to create easy passage around the house.

3. **Appliances:** Are the washer and dryer on risers to make them easier to load and unload? Is the stove well designed with easy-to-use controls for arthritic hands? Would a split dishwasher (top and bottom drawer) with a small top-load capacity be a great idea? Does the microwave need to be moved to a lower shelf?

4. **Slip-proofing:** Are there nonskid rubber suction bath mats in the bottom of the shower and outside of the shower and tub? There is now a nonslip spray you can apply and permanent stick-on nonslip strips to use anywhere in the tub or shower, or on stairs.

5. **Closets and cabinets:** Are frequently used items within easy reach or up on high shelves? Lower the shelves in any closet to make items more accessible.

6. **Stairs:** Is there a secure, sturdy handrail? This is an absolute must! Any loose carpeting that needs to be fixed? If steps are tile or wood,

consider some kind of nonslip adhesive strips. What about a handrail for exterior steps? Add a ramp: Instead of steps, would a simple ramp (interior or exterior) solve a stair issue?

7. **Doors:** Does the bathroom door swing in or out? Much better if it swings **out**. If your parent has a serious fall, the outward-swinging door will allow someone (or emergency personnel) to get into the bathroom.

8. **Lighting:** Is lighting bright and functional, and are light switches flat-panel lever style? Are night-lights installed in hallways, bedrooms, bathrooms, the kitchen, and at exterior exits or stairs? Switch to LED lights for a brighter, stronger light and change manual night-lights to sensors that go on automatically.

9. **Entrance, exit walkways:** Is access to the outside well lit? *Can an emergency vehicle easily see the address or house numbers?* Check for loose bricks, broken pavers, and slippery moss or mold on pathway or stairs. Is it time to power-wash the walkway?

None of these items are very expensive and many can be done by anyone who is handy with tools. Half of these are a matter of observation and action, like reorganizing a kitchen or closet so it is easier to reach things. On your next visit, see what small projects you could do together. If you see your mom using a shaky step stool, go buy one that has a handrail and nonskid legs. Consider moving the kitty litter box to a safer location and the dog bed away from the stairs. This is the time to add that handrail to any set of stairs, interior or exterior.

And while you are at it, please check to see if your loved one has a top-rated fire extinguisher in any area where there is gas heat or a hot water heater, etc. Also check for smoke detectors and carbon monoxide detectors. All of these items add to the overall safety of the home and will save lives.

Bathroom Safety Measures or Remodels

Another scary statistic? More than 235,000 Americans fall in bathrooms every year and wind up in the emergency room. It is often called the most lethal room in a house, and it is an unforgiving place to fall with all its hard surfaces and corners!

But there are many simple, inexpensive things you can do to improve the safety of any bathroom without a major remodel. Start with the basics:

- **Add grab bars next to a toilet, in the shower, or anywhere needed!** Good grab bars cost roughly $75–$150. They are designed to support the full weight of any adult and there can be more than one in a bathroom. Typically, you should install one to hold on to as you **enter and exit the shower,** and one on the back wall of the shower or next to a built-in bench. Adding one near the toilet is also a must. They even make attractive grab bars that also hold toilet paper but can be used to aid in getting up and down from a toilet seat and do not even look like a grab bar!

- **Buy a raised toilet seat that adds inches to a toilet height.** The most common height of a toilet in older homes is only 14.5 inches. The ADA (Americans with Disabilities) handicapped toilet height is 17–19 inches tall as measured from the top of toilet seat to the floor. Rather than buying a whole new toilet, you can buy something called a "toilet raiser." There are numerous options, ranging from a plastic seat riser that is attached directly to the toilet to an apparatus that is placed over the existing toilet with secure handrails and an elevated seat. They are as inexpensive as $25 to over $100 and available online at Walmart, Wayfair, or any large retail or medical durable-equipment location. You might think that raising a toilet seat a few inches is no big deal, but to a frail older person with mobility issues, "reaching" the toilet seat at a height of seventeen inches is a lot easier than lowering your body down to fourteen inches. And getting back up is a struggle for someone sick, frail, or weak. This simple addition can make a bathroom experience tolerable!

- **Buy a shower chair or shower bench to allow for a senior to sit while showering.** You can purchase an inexpensive shower bench direct from Walmart for around $40–$50 or a shower chair with handrails for around $50–$100. Some are built for larger persons/ frames, but all should comply with basic safety measures like non-skid pads or padded seats. Most have adjustable heights and adjustable seats. I have noticed that the local Goodwill often has very inexpensive secondhand shower benches/chairs, all of which can be easily sanitized. And they almost always have walkers as well! Look for a "repurpose" recycling center that sometimes practically gives these away for free.

♥ **Add a handheld shower nozzle that fits over the faucet or shower-head and can be more easily used while sitting.**

If you decide to remove a tub to add a shower, this can range from $200 to $2,000, depending on options. If you want a custom tile shower, the cost jumps quite a bit—usually around $1,000 to $3,500 depending on complexity, size, and the type of tile and fixtures you choose. Add another $500 to $1,000 for tear out, new plumbing pipes, fixtures, and custom carpentry. Total costs are usually closer to $4,000–$5,000 and can exceed $20,000 if you are remodeling an entire bathroom. But this is still less costly than moving!

CAPS Certification

Consider hiring a CAPS-certified builder to do this kind of project. The Certified Aging-in-Place Specialist (CAPS) designation is a joint program of the NAHB (National Association of Home Builders) and AARP, which can be attained after completion of a three-day program of required courses. You can find CAPS-certified builders at nahb.org/education-and-events/education /designations/Certified-Aging-in-Place-Specialist-CAPS. Look for someone with great references and solid experience, and get more than one quote.

More Expensive Options

When is it appropriate to spend a lot more money to remodel or add some of these more specialized items? When it seriously contributes to your loved one's happiness and helps them maintain their independence! If your mom loves taking long baths but can't manage getting in and out of a tub, then look at walk-in options. If she or Dad have restless leg syndrome affecting their sleep or a bad back, and all the lovely jets in the new tub help, buy the new tub. If a move is in their near future, maybe not. Look at the overall cost; if it is affordable for you or your parents, do it.

Walk-In Tubs

How many times do we have to see Pat Boone on TV, getting in and out of his walk-in tub? Despite the repetition of these commercials, a walk-in tub is a godsend to someone who loves baths but can't climb in and out of one. The cost varies, but they usually run around $1,500 to about $5,000. If you get a fancy one with water jets and more, it could be as high as $10,000 and Medicare will not contribute, so it is all out of pocket. Make sure to have it professionally installed and check the warranty. *Consumer Reports* researches the best walk-in tubs yearly, so check before buying. Expect out-of-pocket expenses, but in some cases Medicare might help (read on).

Stair Lifts

Many homes are multilevel, and with so many elders opting to age in place, getting up and down stairs is a real problem. Many say it keeps them young, and going up and down numerous times a day is their best exercise! But if they don't want to move to a new one-story house, and they suddenly cannot go up and down stairs, then a lift may be the answer. Stair lifts are available either powered by battery or electricity. Unless your parents have a whole-house generator, batteries offer more peace of mind. With climate change, severe weather, and more hurricanes and rolling blackouts, batteries may be the way to go—if the power goes out, so does an electric ride. Stair lifts run around $2,500 to about $5,000 installed. Again, expect to pay out of pocket.

In-Home Elevators

Recently, I met with a couple who had installed a simple elevator to be able to get to their second-floor master bedroom and bath. It was small, attractive, and accommodated one person. I have seen more and more ads for elevators, so this is clearly a solution for some people to age in place. They can take up as little as nine square feet of space and range from an average of $19,000 to as high as $40,000 installed. They can lift about 500–750 pounds, but some can lift a great deal more. They can be hydraulic (more expensive) or pneumatic, which are easier and less expensive to install. Always an out-of-pocket expense, but a lot less than moving!

Cost Considerations

By now you may be thinking that all this remodeling or adaptive equipment is just too expensive or too much work. Let's not pretend that cost is not a factor for millions of seniors, but aging in place in one's home will always be less expensive than senior living. Even spending $5,000 to $25,000 on modifying a home for safety reasons is a drop in the bucket compared to the annual cost of assisted living or skilled nursing care: $60,000 to $80,000. Skilled care could go even higher. Home care or home healthcare starts at $25 an hour with a three-hour-per-day minimum. (See Chapter 11, "The Confusing World of Home Care.") This immediately provides some perspective on cost! Even an investment of a few thousand dollars could help someone stay independent longer in their own home! And if this keeps a parent in their home another three to five years, it will be worth every penny.

When you think of it like this, any money you or your parents spend now could be saving you tens of thousands of dollars over time. And keep reading to discover that some of these improvements can be paid for through a variety of means, or at least be tax deductible!

Medicare Benefits for Home Modifications

According to payingforseniorcare.org (a great resource), Medicare pays for some adaptive equipment. If your parents are in the category of "frail," they may be in need of more than just modification and require durable medical equipment like walkers, wheelchairs, and oxygen. But even a shower chair is considered "durable" and would be paid for if medically necessary.

Medicare *may* pay for assistive-technology devices that are part of the modification process provided they are required for medical reasons and pre-scribed by a doctor. You can also receive assistance from Medicare in helping to determine what home modifications are needed and **medically required.**

Medicare Part B will pay for an occupational therapist to evaluate a home and determine what changes are required. In fact, recent updates to Medicare lifted the caps on occupational therapy. Finally, in some rare instances, Medicare will pay for bathroom modifications and walk-in tubs. However, to be clear, the vast majority of home modifications for the elderly are not paid for by Medicare. If Medicare does pay, it will be for the hard-ware associated with the modification, not for the actual construction or labor costs. Keep your receipts just in case, as reimbursement will take time.

If paying for either modifications or equipment is a financial burden, make sure to check with your local USAging office. They are a wealth of information and will save you lots of time with lists of resources and refer-rals. If your parents receive any kind of disability check or are on Medicaid, they will likely qualify for help with home modifications.

What Is Tax Deductible?

Almost all home modifications or improvements made to accommodate age-related disabilities can be tax deductible in some way. The cost of pur-chasing any special equipment like handrails, grab bars, and walk-in tubs, as well as the service costs for the installation of this equipment, are tax deductible as a medical expense if they are "medically necessary." Ask your parents' primary care physician for a Certificate of Medical Necessity as proof positive if the IRS asks. Make sure to remind your folks to keep their receipts for both materials and installation. Always check with your CPA or accountant to see what the current tax law allows.

The Spencers Remodel

Remember the imaginary Spencers? Let's rewind and remind ourselves that, before moving to Raleigh, Sally and Bob Spencer decided to prioritize modifications to their bathroom in their current home to make it safer. Bob found a CAPS-certified builder, and she helped the Spencers design a senior-friendly bathroom with a walk-in shower, grab bars, better lighting, all within their budget. They decided not to replace the bathroom sinks or cabinets since they knew they would be moving, and they could save the money. They did an easy retrofit for the shower, which is premolded, has a low threshold, and is much less expensive than real tile. Their son, John, reminded them that since Dad had a heart attack, maybe some of the modifications could be paid for through Medicare or Dad's veterans' benefits. Bob kept a file of all the receipts so they could claim a tax deduction for the medically necessary modifications. They checked with the doctor and the VA and found out that the grab bars and the raised toilet seats would be covered.

On John's next visit home, he added extra lighting to the exterior stairs, some handrails, and nonslip strips on the stairs. Wendy visited from California and helped Sally reorganize closets and the kitchen and begin the downsizing process. All of these improvements added value to the home for resale, so Bob and Sally felt it was a good investment, and they kept the costs lower knowing they were moving. It gave them over a year using their new bathroom, even with moving to Raleigh sooner. And for Bob especially, it was a tremendous help. Moving forward, they decided to make sure to find a home using the *universal design* concept. (Universal design is the process of creating products that are accessible to people with a wide range of abilities or disabilities that can be easily used regardless of an individual's body size, height, or mobility.) Josie agreed to check with the retirement communities to see how they measured up. Did they have grab bars, walk-in showers, high toilet seats, easy-open door handles, spaces that are wheelchair accessible, and more? They set the date for their next meeting and agreed to compare notes.

AgeTech

We can't address safety issues for your parents aging in place (or even in their new stand-alone home) without looking at available technology. Suffice to say that an entire chapter could be devoted to this topic, but here are a few pointers to think about. The term "AgeTech" is now being used to describe the field of applied technology and geriatrics, including home security systems, medication management and alert systems, and health monitoring in general. The array of products is truly both amazing and overwhelming, especially some that I mention in Chapter 10, "Next Steps," such as robot companions. Since all of these systems are constantly being improved, it is best to do your research on *Consumer Reports'* top recommendations. Many large healthcare organizations and medical corporations are spending millions of dollars developing technology to allow seniors to age in place. Both telemedicine and technology will go a long way toward allowing seniors to stay in their homes successfully and safely. With this in mind, it is a good idea to take an honest look at how such technology can be utilized by your parents. My only word of caution: Choose technology that they *can and will use*, otherwise it is useless. They may be open to learning new skills when you explain the connection between staying in their own home and learning to use the new laptop, new app, new home security system, and new medical alert system!

Home Security Systems

Some home security systems require professional installation, and some do not. In all cases, it will be important to choose a system designed to address the unique needs of your parents. What product you choose will also depend on cost, reliable customer service and response time, and senior-friendly technology. Are your parents worried about home invasion and thefts or medical emergencies? A good system could solve both these fears. Plus, if they are in the "go-go" years and traveling, they can monitor things from afar, or if they have mobility issues, they can turn lights on and off from a wheelchair, lock or unlock doors, control temperature, and more.

Most of the best home security systems for the elderly are designed to be exceptionally easy to use. Calling for help may be as simple as pushing a button. And for arming and disarming the system, control panels with larger letters and brighter screens can be helpful, so keep this in mind.

Home security systems without automatic monitoring can keep costs lower for seniors, but this may limit some of the protections you can expect. For seniors who are always at home and capable of caring for themselves, however, monitored systems may not be necessary.

Medical Alert Systems

For a senior who lives alone, I would recommend an alert system. It saved my stepdad's life, so I am a true believer. What is the best way to evaluate medical alert systems? Almost everyone understands that medical alerts are devices that allow users to contact emergency services in the event of a fall or other emergency. **PERS** or Personal Emergency Response Systems are especially useful for anyone who is at risk of falling, suffering a heart attack or stroke, or who may have some kind of serious mobility issues. But there is great variation among features and services, not to mention customer service. I would strongly advise choosing a company that has *24/7 monitoring that results in a two-way conversation* with a knowledgeable dispatcher who can decide either to notify caregivers or call 911. Seconds count in this type of situation, and having someone to talk to who has medical training can make a huge difference. (There are websites that will give you average response times for each company!)

Start with this question: Do your parents already have a home security system that has the option of adding medical alerts to it? If they don't have a security system, think about looking into one that can offer both security features and medical alerts. Most systems work off a cellular option now (not a fixed landline) and allow someone to call for help while they are out and about as well as in the home. If you are using some kind of shared app, you will be alerted, too, if a parent "presses the button" or calls for help.

Are they already using Amazon Alexa or Amazon Echo or a similar product? These products are being fine-tuned to help seniors age in place. They can do much of what a home security system can do and also function as a medical alert system. There are apps that can connect your cell phone or your Alexa to your parents so you can visually monitor or respond immediately to a call for help.

If your parent is frail and rarely leaves the house, then a standard home base unit is sufficient, but this has its limitations. Most base units have a range, typically about six hundred feet, for the emergency button to be effective. If the home is large or has several floors, look for additions to the system to increase the range. Any base unit must be connected to an electrical outlet, but some come with battery backup to guard against power outages. Don't even consider one without backup. Look for a minimum of *twenty-four hours of battery life and a backup battery with twenty-four more hours available.*

I am a big fan of a pendant or wearable emergency "button," but only if your loved one will actually wear it. I have seen some that look like necklaces or bracelets, and some that clip on a belt or a key chain. Again, what will they willingly use? Wearable devices are often designed to be totally waterproof and can be worn in the shower or tub where most accidents happen. Check *Consumer Reports* to see which products are completely waterproof. Visit the Resources tab on my website for a list of questions to ask when shopping for a medical alert device: starbradbury.com/resources/.

Aging in Place . . . Is It Ideal?

When I did admissions and assessments for assisted living, I often visited seniors in their homes to see if they qualified for acceptance into assisted living. I met so many lonely, unhappy seniors who had become isolated and withdrawn, some of whom had lost their ability to carry on conversations and socialize. If they had cognitive impairment of any kind, living alone had made it worse. This is when I realized that aging in place is not always the best option, *even if this is what a senior starts out wanting*. If they are isolated, maybe not driving anymore, and have no family nearby, then living alone is simply not the best option.

Even though they may have been afraid of change, I saw many older seniors come back to life after moving into a community with services and care, new friends, meals provided, recreational options, and safe places to walk or exercise. Please keep this in mind as you watch your parents age. Understand that choosing to age in place may not help them maintain their independence and could make their chances of aging safely much less successful. Your parents may be imagining some awful "nursing home," so it is imperative you both see how lovely some of these communities can be. I have often suggested a trial period of three months (no less) with the option of returning home if a parent insists. Usually, three months allows enough time to adjust, make friends, and appreciate all the help.

Make That List!

I started the chapter by advising you and your parents to make a list of priorities based on immediate safety concerns for aging in place. Even though a bathroom remodel is one of the most expensive options, this should be at the top of the list. Technology might come a little later unless a medical alert system is clearly needed now. Do an honest assessment and guide your parents if needed. Offer to help in any way you can: by doing the work, helping pay for the work, and/or vetting/hiring/managing the company doing the work. Do the research on what benefits they may qualify for through the VA, Medicare, or Medicaid. If they already need help in their home, add this to your conversation! Hiring someone to come in two or three times a week to help will also keep them independent longer. There are lots of ways to contribute and make a big difference to your parents aging in place in a home they love. You have the tools, you have the list, you know what you're doing!

Chapter 7

Retirement Communities: Asking the Right Questions

There is a reason this is one of the longest chapters in the book. There is a very steep learning curve when it comes to educating yourself about the many varied types of retirement communities.

First of all, what are retirement communities? Generally speaking, a retirement community is a residential community or housing complex designed for older adults who are typically able to care for themselves and are mostly retired. These communities offer many services and amenities such as meals, housekeeping, maintenance, transportation, classes, and more.

Some of these services are included in a monthly fee and some are fee for service. Some communities are age restricted, like the ever-popular Del Webb locations in many states that advertise "Active Adult Living for 55+" or the newer (2018) Jimmy Buffett Florida community called Latitude Margaritaville. Often, a resident of one of these communities is buying a home, just like in any planned community. Nevertheless, these communities can still be called retirement communities. They promise lots of fun, but usually no healthcare of any kind as part of the services on-site or included in any contract. Residents typically have access to a clubhouse, pools, dining options, and activities of all kinds. This chapter will spend more time looking at what I refer to as full-service retirement communities that are more than just "adult active," but if your parents are parrot heads (Jimmy Buffett fans), they may just love Margaritaville!

Full-service communities are often for older seniors, sixty-five and up, mostly retired, who are still active and independent but want a maintenance-free lifestyle and/or access to healthcare nearby or on-site. (Life care communities that offer continuing care, if ever needed, are so complex, they get a chapter to themselves coming up next!) But make absolutely no assumptions about what the term "retirement community" means. Every place is unique in what it does or does not include in a monthly fee, the services provided, if there is any kind of fee to join, a move-in fee, a wait-list fee, and more. And every place is unique in that it just might have a religious affiliation, a political inclination, or a reputation that could be appealing or not.

Getting Started

Let's begin by looking at what you need to know to help yourself or your parents. Take your time, educate yourself, make a list with your parents about what they want in a community, and see how this decision fits into your JITSP three- to five-year plan.

While it is somewhat daunting, choosing the right retirement community is of huge importance. Moving is traumatic, and you want to help your parents to make the right choice. Moving out of a community because your parents are unhappy is even worse, and I have seen this happen. This is likely going to be the last place your parents ever live. Think about that for a moment. They may be leaving a house they lived in for thirty or forty years. The factors that will make this a success are complex. Discovering what is crucial to their happiness will take time and effort on everyone's part. I am 100 percent certain that the lists in this chapter will suggest questions you would never even think to ask.

If your parents tell you they are considering moving to a retirement community, you should be grateful they are open-minded about moving! I say this because for years I heard people tell me their plan was to be "carried out feet first" from their house. Then they would laugh as if this was really funny. I like to reiterate that this approach is *not a plan*; it is really a default, and the results are never amusing, especially for the spouse left behind.

Benefits of a Full-Service Retirement Community

I am a fan of community living because the research is so positive! People live longer, age better, and maintain their independence at a much higher rate than aging alone in their home. Keep in mind I am not discussing nursing homes, just independent retirement communities. The keys to aging well are more or less the same no matter what research or website you look at:

- Physical exercise
- Healthy diet
- Mental/cognitive stimulation
- Social support/connectedness/meaning
- Resiliency/flexibility

It is far easier to access most of what is listed above when you reside in a senior full-service community. Even the most basic retirement community will offer a gym, various exercise classes, dining options, lectures and seminars of some kind, and numerous social opportunities. Plus, all maintenance needs will likely be covered, either with a cost or included in the contract. No worries about climbing a ladder to change a light bulb!

As one ages and it becomes more and more difficult to stay connected to the outside world, living in a community keeps these connections going. If you can no longer drive, transportation is often provided. If you need help, you can call security, and in some communities, a middle-of-the-night call results in both security and a nurse arriving at your door.

Food, an ever-important topic, adds to one's health and overall happiness. Since poor nutrition and hydration rank as the top reasons seniors end up in the hospital, access to regular meals, already prepared, that don't require your widowed father, for example, to cook or grocery shop, may add years to his life. And now, almost any retirement community you visit these days has healthy menu options with no salt or no sugar added for heart or diabetic concerns. Many offer vegetarian and even vegan options as well. Expect full kitchens in all independent-living apartment floor plans, and some kind of flexible dining option that allows residents to choose when they wish to eat in community dining rooms, with some number of meals included in a monthly fee. And if you have a parent who is close to no longer driving, most retirement communities offer group transportation to grocery stores, medical appointments, events, and more.

All these things add up to an improved quality of life, less stress, and longer lives. Their circle of friends usually expands, and it is easier to face illness, the loss of a spouse, and life's tragedies when residing in a community. People reach out to help each other in a community, not just staff.

Part of exploring communities will be meeting the current residents, without any marketing staff, and having lunch or dinner, seeing their apartment or home (ideally), and asking any questions. Don't just view models; ask to see a real apartment. Usually this is possible with planning. Expect a free overnight to be offered to your parents as they evaluate any community! The good news is that there are so many great options out there. Some of the questions I've highlighted in this chapter won't apply, but most will. And see "Questions to Ask When Touring Any Senior Community or Facility" at starbradbury.com/resources for a fuller list of questions to consider.

A wide range of options exist, from down-home to very upscale, some targeting artists, retired military, outdoor enthusiasts, urban or country settings, LGBTQ specific, and even nudists! Some are urban apartment towers, while others are houses in the mountains, on the golf course, or by the ocean. Some offer a vast array of services, and costs can vary tremendously. You name it, it's out there. There are communities that focus on ethnic commonality such as a high percentage of residents who are Chinese or Indian, and some with religious affiliations as well, although this will never be in print in a brochure, just evident from a tour and asking the right questions provided in this chapter!

Some communities provide only independent living, while others provide additional levels of care as well. Some are rental, some are entry-fee based (almost always some kind of life care), and some are just like any real estate transaction, sometimes referred to as "equity based." There are rental communities that offer access to assisted living or memory care on-site should your parents ever need it, but many do not. *You will almost never find skilled nursing on-site unless it is a true life care community.*

But Buyer Beware!

As with any service, buyer beware. I have talked to many seniors who have moved into a community only to find out they did *not* provide the services they thought they were going to receive. Taking the time to educate yourself and your parents is critical. Make sure you really understand the fine print that details cost, services, and termination provisions by the community or facility, and termination by the family or parent. If you have access to an attorney, you should consider having them read through the contract, or hire an expert who has worked in the industry and can make recommendations based on your wants and needs.

And please keep two important things in mind:

1. Some full-service retirement communities may require a basic physical assessment of a "prospective resident" to determine if they can live safely in independent living before formally accepting them. It's a good idea to ask! If your parents actually need assisted living, they may not be accepted into independent living.
2. A community may also ask for some kind of financial statement or declaration that confirms your parents' ability to pay ongoing monthly fees that will increase over time.

Is Community Living for Everyone?

You may ask whether, in my twenty-four years working in senior living, have I ever met someone not suited for community living. Yes, I have. If your parent is a total introvert, prefers their own company, doesn't like other human beings, and/or finds socializing painful, community living may not be for them. If they have severe mental illness, serious addiction issues, or anger issues, it's likely a bad idea to move them into a social setting. All communities have a clause that will allow them to break a lease or contract if a person "is a danger to themselves or others," or some verbiage close to this. When it gets bad enough, they will ask your loved one to leave, if they are living in independent living. Are they making life miserable for their neighbors? Are they leaving the stove on or flooding their apartment due to cognitive issues? It is rare, but it happens. If they are already in assisted or memory care, the criteria are far broader, but I have still seen residents asked to leave if they were aggressive or violent with staff or other residents. No community will risk the liability of severe property damage (think fire), or injury to the resident themselves, other patients, or staff.

Have a Conversation

Holidays are often a good time, when families are together, to schedule a tour as long as you plan a month or more ahead. If there are excellent options in their area, suggest touring these. If you are asking them to consider moving closer to you or another sibling, don't spring this on your parents as a surprise. Let them know you would like them to consider moving closer to you and ask them if they are willing to visit some possibilities in your area. You could offer to send a list of communities and ask them which ones they might like to see. Most senior community websites now have excellent virtual tours, including "seeing" various apartments or homes. A good marketing department expects things to get very busy during the holidays and will only be closed Thanksgiving Day or Christmas Day. Do not drop in or you will be disappointed. Most marketing offices do not handle surprise tours, as a thorough tour takes hours. One community manager recently told me she was planning tours six weeks out!

Not Your Grandparents' Nursing Home

If you are the one suggesting moving, your parents may have no idea what these new communities are like today. They may hear "retirement community" and think "nursing home." The older they are, the more likely this is what they are thinking! Usually if you visit some of the lovely upscale options, they will realize just how many great choices they have.

Make a List

If they are open-minded about moving, ask them to make a list of what is important to them in a community. Maybe it's an indoor pool for year-round swimming, or beautiful safe walking trails, or a lifelong learning program? Maybe it is a bridge club or higher levels of healthcare? This list will grow and help guide all of you as you see the options available. Eliminate touring any community that does not offer something critical that could be a deal breaker. Narrow the list to the basics and expand from there. Are they looking for a fifty-five-and-up active lifestyle, a retirement community focused on lifelong learning, one near a top hospital?

I recommend that husbands/wives/partners create their own lists and then compare and merge them. Let both parties have their say. This works better if one person is more dominating than the other. Both of their wishes need to be considered. Maybe a Bible study class or investment group is important to Mom. Maybe Dad wants to play golf nearby. A good list will take time. If they are considering a major relocation to another state, then this will help you choose by city or state. Be specific when you do your search, and include things like "near the ocean," if this is relevant. I strongly advise choosing a community that has healthcare options on-site, or quality care nearby. Remember it is not a question of "if" your parents will one day need help, it is "when." Why move to a community only to have to move again in a few years if help is needed, and it is not available?

How to Find a Retirement Community

Begin by doing an online search. You will be overwhelmed with ads from all kinds of organizations. I am sorry to tell you that you will need to sift through the ads and the lists. Most websites are corporate sponsored and have a reason for placing a community on their list. Sift and then sift again. Look for general lists that have no direct reason to try and sell you. Here are some ideas:

- I liked the website realestatewitch.com/best-retirement-communities -florida because the criteria were solid and based on lots of data showing how they chose the best retirement cities and top retirement communities in Florida for their list.
- Look for larger not-for-profit senior organizations that also compile lists, like seniorhousingnet.com/care-types, that you can search by state and level of care, but be sure to do your own research.
- Another good list can be found every year on the Retirement Living website at retirementliving.com/best-places-to-retire. They present great criteria that include "age friendly cities" with excellent healthcare and cultural amenities.
- *Where to Retire* magazine (wheretoretire.com) offers an annual list of the best places to retire. And you can check out back issues for even more cities to consider.
- Some states have websites focused on affordable, sustainable senior living, like housing4seniors.com, the website for the not-for-profit group SHAG. SHAG stands for Sustainable Housing for Ageless Generations, and is based in Washington state. I promise you, if you search for "retirement communities" in any state, you will eventually find the one you are looking for!

Expected Costs

The website seniorliving.org has a complete list, state by state, of average, minimum, and maximum monthly costs in independent living communities.

According to investopedia.com, the average national monthly fee is about $2,500–$3,000. The most expensive states are Connecticut and Massachusetts, coming in at an average monthly cost of $4,000–$5,000, and the Northeast in general is one of the most expensive areas. Fees can go as high as $6,000–$8,000 a month in states like New York, Florida, and California. The lowest fees were close to $1,000 a month, and I can tell you those are few and far between, and they may not be communities you would ever choose. Remember, these fees are *not* for life care communities, which have entry fees and tend to have higher monthly fees as well. You can see that fees can vary tremendously depending on services included and location. The lower fees may include very few services or allow you to opt in or out of things like meals, housekeeping, etc. All communities will provide you with a list of services included in the fee, plus those that are available on-site but cost extra.

There can also be some kind of one-time "processing" or "move-in fee" in some communities, so don't be surprised. Some communities have a move-in coordinator—usually at no cost, but ask. This person can be extremely helpful in making a move go smoothly. Sometimes communities provide two or more hours of free maintenance help to hang art and move furniture. But even paying for this help is worth it if you can't be present to assist your parents.

What's Included in Most Monthly Fees?

Although services vary considerably from community to community, I feel comfortable providing a list of what you can expect to be included in most full-service retirement communities. If they are simply "adult active," don't expect any of these.

- All utilities (except personal telephone)
- Alert system within the living unit

- Standard cable TV lineup (premium channels extra)
- Basic high-speed internet
- Basic housekeeping twice a month
- Basic maintenance of the living unit, including maintenance or replacement of refrigerator, stove, dishwasher, washer, and dryer
- Basic maintenance of common areas and grounds
- Scheduled transportation to shopping, performances, special events
- Access to common areas such as libraries, game rooms, movies, pools, for no fee
- Activities and fitness classes at no charge
- Twenty-four-hour security
- Dining plan of some kind: often X number of meals per month or even per day. Sometimes a dining allowance is given monthly, and the resident can "spend" it as they choose on breakfast, lunch, or dinner or only dinners, for example. If they spend beyond this amount, the difference will be billed.
- One designated parking spot. (There is often a charge for a second car unless the unit is a house with a two-car garage.) Check to see if covered parking is available. Often it is not. How far will your parents have to walk to get to their car? Think snow or rain factors.

What Services Will Have a Fee?

Again, this varies a great deal from community to community, and most fees make sense and are expected. The grander the community, the more amenities you can expect. It is rare to find a dentist's office on-site, but not impossible. The life care community I worked in had everything listed below, all for additional fees. But things like beauty and barber shops are standard and should be expected.

- Beauty and barber shop
- Home healthcare services
- Physician/nurse's office

- ♥ Dental clinic
- ♥ Podiatrist
- ♥ Audiologist
- ♥ Physical, occupational, or speech therapy
- ♥ Massage therapy
- ♥ Veterinary clinic
- ♥ Guest accommodations

What Is a Wait List and Why Is This Critical?

Many excellent retirement communities have a wait list, and for some it could be years. It is not uncommon for some couples to have wait-list deposits at three different communities in different states. Knowing it could take years to get into a community means planning ahead and having more than one option, especially if your parents are open to moving to more than one location near one of their children, or for any reason. This is what I call having a flexible plan! What does this mean for your parents? The last thing you want is for them to fall in love with a community, be ready to move in, and find out that the apartment or home they want won't be available for years.

Please believe me when I tell you this. At the top life care community I worked in for over eighteen years, it often took years of waiting before the average two-bedroom, two-bath unit became available. I told families, and still do, that being placed on a wait list *does not mean you are moving into this community.* From your perspective, it is just an option (perhaps one of many), but it gives you the possibility of moving. If you are not on the wait list in some communities, you will not get the home you want, and you may not even have the opportunity to make the move at all.

While there is usually a fee, it is almost always fully refundable for any reason, and that fee may allow you to be on the list for two different residences. If you are in a hurry, ask if they will accept two wait lists for four different apartments, for example, as this increases your chances of being offered something!

Here are some basic questions to ask any full-service retirement community:

- Do you have a wait list? How large and long is it?
- Is there a cost or fee (typically $1,500 to $3,000) and is it refundable?
- What is the average length of time it takes to get a one-bedroom or two-bedroom apartment, etc.? (Use a floor plan you are interested in!)
- What if a unit becomes available that I am wait-listed for and I am not ready? Do I lose my spot on the wait list?
- What is considered *standard* in all units as far as appliances, counters, cabinets, and flooring? How often do you replace these items?

(For a full list of questions, see "Wait List Questions" in "Questions to Ask When Touring Any Senior Community or Facility" at starbradbury.com/resources.)

Sometimes the "penthouse" top-floor units have an upcharge. Some communities will charge more if a unit already has spectacular upgrades or the best view. Many communities will have an "allowance" a new resident can use for upgrades before they move in. I have seen communities that have an on-site decorator who helps new residents choose new counters or cabinets or flooring. Every community is different. It may be "as is," especially if a unit has recently been remodeled. Do your parents want morning light? A view of the sunset or lake? You may or may not pay more, but you can ask the marketing office what units face what direction! I can assure you that this was not unusual where I worked.

Touring a Community

Before making an appointment for a tour, check out the website and ask them to mail or email you a full brochure with pricing and contract information. Give them a list of what you and your parent(s) would like to see on your tour. Narrow your options to no more than two or three floor plans such as a one-bedroom and bath with a den, or two bedrooms, etc. All the floor plans will be online so you can "shop" ahead of time. Keep in mind: some popular floor plans will not be available any time soon.

Ask if you can stay for a meal or join some residents for lunch without the marketing person. If they say no, be suspicious, as any good community is happy to accommodate that request or should even offer it without you having to ask. The importance of good food cannot be underestimated, both nutritionally and emotionally, so you definitely want to try the menu. The culture of a community will show in the dining room. Are people happy, talking, enjoying their meal?

Do Your Homework First!

Do your homework first or you could be wasting your time. Don't wait to read the brochure in front of the marketing person the day of the tour. If, for example, a full tour is two or three hours and involves lots of walking, and you know Dad can't handle this, you can instruct the marketing person to limit the tour. What will be the most important part of the community for him? Maybe skip the outdoor pool in favor of seeing the woodworking shop. You get the idea. If the gym or fitness center is amazing, and your parents love to work out, make sure this gets included. A decision like this will usually take more than one visit, so no sense in overwhelming your folks on their first visit. But first impressions are everything, so don't skip what is most important to you or your parents.

In addition, visiting a community *before* the actual need or desire to move gives both you and your parents the chance to formulate several options for their future, with absolutely no pressure. Waiting for a medical crisis to get motivated is not a good idea and inevitably limits your options, especially if a pre-admittance physical is required.

It may take more than a visit or two to really get a feel for a community before making a final decision.

Basic Checklist Prior to Tour:
- Was staff warm and friendly when you called?
- Did the marketing office follow through with getting you the information you requested, either by email or mailing you a brochure?
- Did the staff answer your basic questions about services and cost?

- Did the marketing person ask you pertinent questions about your parents or rush you through the process?
- Did the marketing person advise you on the length of the tour?
- Did they ask you what type/size of apartment you want to see?

When to Tour by Yourself First

Word of advice: *Consider visiting the community first by yourself.* Do the full tour and see everything on your own. Sit down and review the contract options and get a complete and thorough understanding before you bring your parents. Why is this so critical? If you don't like it, they probably won't either. If it is unaffordable, better to learn this sooner, not after a day of touring.

Touring the community first allows you to educate yourself with no distractions. When you return with your parents, you can focus on them and their reactions, and be prepared to jump in if needed to point things out or explain things. If your parent has any level of mental confusion or physical limitations, then absolutely, visit first on your own. If your parents are totally independent, then only go along if they ask you to. Before they make a final decision, however, I would encourage you to respectfully ask them if you can tour as well. You will see things they may not; you will ask questions they may not.

Plan for an Overnight

Most communities have a "guest house" or guest suites and offer visitors a one- to two-night stay at a very low cost (or free) that includes all meals. This is not unusual at any upscale retirement community. It gives potential residents a chance to experience what it would be like to live there and test it out. I would strongly encourage your parents to do an overnight stay of a day or two to really get a feel for a community before making a final decision.

While all of the questions above are basic, your initial experience is a precursor to what the community will be like. If staff is unfriendly and unhelpful, or they don't seem to want to take the time to listen, you might decide to take that community off your list.

What to Look for on the Tour

I've included a full list of questions to ask when touring any senior community (or facility) at starbradbury.com/resources for easy download and use. For now, here are some overall thoughts and a sampling of those questions.

Grounds

Before going directly into the marketing office to start your tour, make sure to simply drive around first and take a good look. Take lots of photos or videos and record your impressions, especially if you are trying to tour multiple communities in a day or two. Here is a partial list of what to look for when doing your initial drive through:

- Buildings and grounds must be clean and landscaping well maintained. Same for lobby and all common areas.
- If there is a security gatehouse, was the staff professional and courteous? Did they give you a map and clear directions for parking? Is it staffed 24/7?
- Are there tennis courts? Bocce ball? Pickleball? Walking trails? Gardens?

Transportation

You will find a great deal of variation in the transportation department. Do they offer bus transportation for large groups to a big event or for weekly grocery shopping? You might also check out the condition of the buses and the cars. Well maintained and comfortable?

- Is transportation of any kind provided? Is it free?
- If the community is large, how many buses do they have?

- Do they have cars/drivers for individual private transportation, and what are the fees?
- What is the policy to reserve a "ride"? (Note: One- or three-day advance reservation?)

Dining

Next to medical, I'd have to say that dining is listed as one of the most important aspects of any community experience. For many seniors, it may be the highlight of their day. Often, if meals are part of a monthly contract, people make their own breakfasts and use dining rooms for lunches and dinners. The larger the community, the greater the options. Things to look for:

- Is the dining room attractive and inviting? How often is the menu changed?
- Is it buffet style? Or cafeteria style only?
- Are there multiple dining rooms, including upscale and casual options? Do they all serve the same menu? What are the hours of operation?
- Is there a full bar? More than one?
- Can they accommodate special diets (diabetic, gluten free, low salt, vegetarian)?
- Is there a dress code?

Some more formal communities may require a coat and tie at dinner or in a specific on-site dining room. This is an indication of community culture and may or may not be a plus for your parents.

Amenities

This is another area that will vary tremendously. You will be absolutely amazed at the variety of amenities offered at some communities. Find out what hobbies or interests your parent(s) have or had. I met residents who resumed playing musical instruments they had not played since high school because the community had an "open" musical group, as well as residents who became accomplished artists and had never painted in their life.

- Do they offer a wide variety of classes? Lectures and seminars? (See educational questions.) Ask to see an activity schedule and/or fitness class schedule.
- Are there many interest groups like book clubs, investment clubs, movie clubs, genealogy, bridge, chess?
- Is there an auditorium or performance hall? Movie theater? How many people will it accommodate?
- Is there a woodworking shop? Artist studio? Pottery kiln? Library? (Other parental interest?)

Fitness Center

I have seen fitness centers that consist of one exercise bike in a small room to gyms that could rival any top-notch national club. I have seen pools that would fit about five people and Olympic-size lap pools, inside and outside, to give you a choice. Any fitness center is an excellent indicator of the culture of the community. Are residents into staying fit, active, and healthy, or is no one in the gym?

- Is the fitness center sparkling clean and up to date with good-quality equipment?
- Is it staffed at all times and what are the hours of operation? Is it open to residents at all hours or are weekend hours limited?
- What are the qualifications of the fitness staff? Do they have degrees in any of the exercise sciences? Do they help a resident develop a fitness plan? (Note: Can they safely oversee someone with balance, heart, or mobility issues?)
- Is there an indoor or outdoor pool? (Note: Is the pool easy to get into and out of? Is there a ramp?)
- Lifeguard on duty?
- Do they offer Pilates, aerobics, water aerobics, yoga, chair yoga, Tai Chi, balance classes, etc.? How often? (Ask for class schedule.)

Education

Lifelong learning has become so popular in the last ten years that almost all retirement communities have started classes. If they happen to be near a university, they usually have an added advantage. For some, this is their main focus, and they are called UBRCs, or university-based retirement communities (see page 141). Great questions to ask:

- Are you affiliated with any national lifelong learning organizations such as the Osher Lifelong Learning Institutes? Are they nearby, or are classes on the retirement campus?
- Do you have any affiliations with a college or university? Do residents have access to the university libraries?
- Do residents need to enroll, or can they audit classes on campus? Do you provide assistance with enrollment? Transportation?
- How many residents participate in these educational classes? (Note: You can tell from enrollment how vibrant these programs are.)

Medical Alert Systems and Medical Services

If you are looking for a community that includes any higher level of care, this section is critical. If you are looking at an "adult over fifty-five" type of community, almost none of these questions will apply. If they are "independent living only," they may not even have alert systems in any living unit. However, even *proximity* to higher levels of care or a hospital will be important to this age group, so keep this in mind.

- Does each living unit have an alert system? Does it call security or a nurse or both? Does it work only on-site? What happens if my parent calls 911?
- Do they have an affiliation with a local hospital, home health agency, or physicians' group? Do they have offices on-site? Any physical therapy on-site?

- Is a nurse available 24/7 or is there a nurse's office residents can go to during the day? What are the hours of operation? What about weekend emergencies?
- Do they provide transportation to medical appointments?

Levels of Care

Most independent retirement communities do not offer higher levels of care unless they are a life care or continuing-care retirement community (CCRC) but because some do, I have included the list below. Ask them:

- Do you offer any assisted living, memory care, or skilled nursing care on-site?
- What is the cost? Is there any discount offered for residents of the community?
- Are your healthcare facilities open to the public?
- Are residents given *preference for placement in assisted or memory care*?
- Is any care included as part of the residential contract? (Note: Even some rental communities include a limited number of free days in assisted living, usually based on twelve months of continued residency.)
- Do you have an *evacuation plan for an emergency or natural disaster*? May I see it? Have you ever had to evacuate?

Corporate or Financial Issues

I consider the following questions to be tier-two types of inquiries. No need to ask unless you are getting serious. These might be addressed on your third or fourth visit. They may be asked only by you, if your parents lean toward the older or frailer side. Many adult children did the "nitty-gritty" of vetting communities I worked in. Often, we would have conference calls involving other siblings, attorneys, CPAs. Why all the scrutiny? Because there have been, over the years, many shady retirement communities that have gone bankrupt and left residents stranded or worse, if large entry fees were involved. Some states have far stricter rules and oversight governing life care communities than others. No matter what type of community you are considering, part of this will be a financial investigation. Ask:

- Are you not-for-profit or for-profit? Are you affiliated with any other senior communities?
- Who owns the community now and for how long? Has it changed hands in the last five years? (This may indicate financial instability.)
- Who operates the community? (Often these are different contracts and companies.) Ask for full disclosure of any corporate entity involved with the ownership, operation, and management of the community!)
- Is there an administrator or director on-site or on call on the weekends? How long have they been there? (You're looking for stability.)
- Do you have quarterly or annual financial reports you can share with me? (Note: How financially stable are they?) History of monthly fee increases?

Ideally, in my opinion, the same company should own and operate a community. If they don't, there can be problems. The company that owns the community is looking for profit margins and not necessarily the well-being of the residents. They may be reluctant to replace carpeting or increase the food budget. Of course, these issues can still happen if they are one and the same. Look to see if either the ownership and/or the management company keeps changing, as that is never a good sign. Companies in this business squeeze profits, then sell off the location, and it starts all over again. Ask a lot of questions and ask to see financial disclosures. Also, check with any oversight organizations for the state or ombudsman complaints. General retirement communities are much harder to track than life care, licensed assisted living, or skilled nursing facilities, all of which have lots of oversight.

Political Affiliations

You may be able to easily determine if a community leans right or left after an initial visit, but often it may be difficult to tell. Marketing staff may be reluctant to say, but generally they know. You can also look up voting demographics, and this might help. Living in such a polarized political environment has made this an important question. The Villages in Leesburg, Florida, for example, voted 78 percent Republican in the last election. It is a popular election stop for many Republican politicians. This would be either great news or misery making, depending on your parents. These are tricky questions that marketing people hate. Ask them anyway. If a community is 90 percent one party or another, it may prove fatal to being happy living there. Here are some questions to ask:

- Does your community have any formal or informal political affiliations with any political parties?
- Is there a Republican club or Democratic club? How many members in general?
- Is there an active League of Woman Voters?
- Are there any guidelines about political signage within the community during elections?

Religious or Group Affiliations

Historically, retirement communities grew out of religious organizations addressing the needs of their aging members. The general population was heavily slanted toward whichever group founded the community, although this has changed in the last ten years. Some very well-known communities still have religious ties. Kendal senior living communities were founded by the Quakers and still promote the Quaker spirit of community and collaboration and respect for the individual that is associated with the "religious society of friends." National organization Westminster Retirement Communities was founded by the Presbyterians, so the tradition continues. Here are some questions to ask:

- Does your community have any formal relationships with any religious groups or military organizations or any other group organizations?
- Was it founded by any religious organization?

- Do you have a chapel, church, synagogue, or meditation center on-site? Nearby?
- Do you offer free transportation on Saturday or Sunday for religious services?
- What is the religious makeup of the resident population?

Demographics and More Questions

If your parents are in their late sixties, they will not want to move to a community where the average age is mid-eighties. If the majority of residents are single, couples may not be happy. If they have to pass a health assessment prior to being accepted, find out the requirements. If you have to sign a lease, what are the termination policies? Here are some general questions to ask:

- Are you offering any kind of discounts or move-in specials now? When do they end? What about in six months?
- What is the average age of your residents?
- How many women? Or men? (Note: Mostly couples or single elderly women?)
- Do you plan to expand anytime soon?
- Where will you be building? (Note the noise factor and proximity to living unit.)
- Do my parents have to sign a lease? What if they break it? What if my mom passes away or has to move out?
- Is there any move-in or community fee? (Expect one.) When does it need to be paid, and is it refundable?

Complete Question Lists

Please remember that these lists have been reduced and the full list of questions is available for review and download at starbradbury.com/resources. Pick and choose the questions that are important for you and your family. You are now informed and knowledgeable about what to ask and why!

Please do not ask all these questions on your first tour; many can wait until the third or fourth tour. If you have siblings touring, split these questions up to make it easier. Schedule a Zoom meeting just like the Spencers, and compare notes and plan for action steps!

The Spencer Family Goes on a Tour

Bob and Sally drive to Raleigh for a five-day trip as planned. They are trying to decide if they want to buy a home or live in a retirement community. Following the guidelines in this book, Josie and Dan, who live in Raleigh, vetted about six communities and helped Bob and Sally narrow tours down to three. They already ruled out several as either too expensive or too religious, and one was primarily retired military, not a good fit for them. They plan for one tour a day, knowing each will take from one to three hours, depending on how much they see and if they stay for a meal. Dad's energy is limited since the stroke and even Mom tires easily, so this makes sense. Before the tours, they review the list of questions, and they make their own list to ask the day of the tour. Bob says he is leaning toward a community that could provide more care if he needs it. They are only looking at full-service retirement communities with plenty of provided services and maintenance. All three have some degree of healthcare nearby or available on-site, and one life care community (Maple Village, a fictional name) has assisted, memory, and skilled care built into the contract. Dan agrees to take plenty of videos, photos, and notes, so Josie can concentrate on her parents' needs and questions. They gather all the data: services and amenities, costs, fees, wait-list information, availability of apartments, and more. Time to narrow things down to first and second choices. They inch closer to a decision but don't want to rush. The move is planned to take place in about a year, so they have time. John agrees to do a little more investigating of the communities' financial info, as well as any issues or complaints he may uncover. Mom says she will need help with packing. They schedule a Zoom call to share the results with John and Sophia and Wendy.

Making a Final Decision

Now that you are educated, I hope you and your parents will feel more confident as you "go shopping." Having years of experience in the senior living business, I have shared with you the tools to develop an insider's knowledge about every community you visit. Make a list before shopping but save the in-depth questions for your second and third tours. Never make this decision based on one tour, no matter how convinced you are or what the marketing person tells you. Always ask the marketing office if you can visit and chat with several residents who have lived in the community for a minimum of one year. These kinds of conversations will help you make your final decision, along with a one- to two-day overnight visit by your parents. And remember, get on wait lists early . . . and for more than one community! Doing all this work ahead of time will help ensure success!

Chapter 8

Life Care Communities: Are They Worth the High Cost?

Even though life care communities (LCCs) have been around since the early 1900s, many people have no idea what a continuing-care community really is. And to make it more confusing, full-service retirement communities will "borrow" the term "continuing care," even though they are not a true licensed life care community. Life care communities come in all shapes and sizes, but the most important fact to remember is this: Residents typically start out in independent living, but when higher levels of care are needed, the community provides assisted living *and* skilled nursing care on-site. Only a life care community or CCRC (continuing-care retirement community) offers the safety net of both assisted living and skilled nursing care (and usually memory care) on-site, in the same location.

Residents have the true flexibility of receiving *whatever level of care they need within this framework, for as long as they need it,* without moving to a new location. Most LCCs guarantee residents access to higher levels of care through a contractual agreement, and some also offer this care at various discounted rates well below the normal market rate for assisted or skilled nursing care. But understand: The word "access" varies tremendously as well as the cost of care. As you will see, contract options are complex and can be confusing.

Because most LCCs charge a hefty entry fee up front, when someone first moves into independent living, this option tends to appeal to more affluent families who can afford this. Typically, though, a couple will sell their home to pay the entry fee, making this option more affordable for many. Most LCCs are not real estate based, so don't assume an entry fee means your parent owns the house; usually they don't. However, you may come across some LCCs that are "equity based," which means your parents do have some kind of equity in their residence that they can eventually sell. Can you begin to see why these communities have a reputation for being confusing? Keep reading, I promise it will get better.

How Do LCCs Differ from Full-Service Communities?

As I mentioned, full-service retirement communities will often use the term "continuing care," yet they are not a true LCC. They may indeed have assisted care and even dementia-specific "memory care" on-site, but they are not *licensed as a life care community through the state they operate in*. Most states require a special license to operate as a continuing-care or life care community. Ask the facility how they are licensed and pay attention to their answer. If they say, "Yes, we have assisted living, but not skilled nursing," they are *not* a true continuing-care community. Are all residents of independent living *guaranteed* a room in assisted or skilled care when they need it, and is this promise in writing in a contract? Does the community have to adhere to any state regulations that often govern life care communities? Will residents have to continue to pay rent or a monthly fee for their apartment/home in independent living while *also paying the full cost for care in assisted living or another level of care*? I advise reviewing the "Wait List Questions" in my "Questions to Ask When Touring Any Senior Community or Facility" at starbradbury.com/resources.

Another factor has to do with skilled nursing care. I have never seen a non–life care retirement community that has skilled nursing care on-site. It just never happens. Many states require that a corporation complete what is called a "certificate of need" to even get permission to build a skilled nursing facility. Each state is slightly different, but the ACHA (Agency for Healthcare Administration) website for Florida states:

> The Certificate of Need program is a regulatory process that requires certain health care providers to obtain state approval before offering certain new or expanded services. The CON program currently regulates hospices, freestanding inpatient hospice facilities, skilled nursing facilities and intermediate care facilities for the developmentally disabled.

A "CON" is very expensive and time consuming, and does not guarantee the state will give a company permission to build. The state always evaluates what skilled beds already exist in the community and wants to make sure these beds are utilized before granting permission to build more, even if the available beds are in awful nursing homes! And even if they do get a green light, in today's world, building costs, staffing costs, and regulatory mandates make it an even more expensive option. No regular retirement community is going to go to the great expense of adding skilled care unless their mission and purpose guide them and they want to be a true life care community. Remember I mentioned that many life care communities started out with affiliations to religious organizations? For many, the mission may be serving the needs of an aging senior population, possibly of the same faith, by offering a high-quality lifestyle, plus the continuing care they will need as they age. No present-day LCC limits residency due to faith, but it never hurts to ask what the general makeup of any community is as far as religious affiliation goes.

What Are the Advantages of Life Care?

Again, having worked in one of the top LCCs in the country, I have seen firsthand the many advantages, and it has made me a fan of this general approach to aging successfully. An LCC typically provides:

- ⚲ *Easy access* to long-term care, plus assisted living, memory care, and skilled nursing care on-site;
- ⚲ The *flexibility of accessing care* without a spouse or children having to provide that care;
- ⚲ A possible *cost reduction for long-term care* that is smart for the financial long term and is often part of the contract;
- ⚲ *Access to healthcare ancillary services* like full rehabilitation such as physical therapy, occupational therapy, speech therapy, podiatrists, and more;
- ⚲ *The ability for couples to stay near each other* in the same community and not be forced to be separated during a stressful situation such as after surgery or a heart attack, or even prolonged long-term care;
- ⚲ *An active lifestyle with intellectual stimulation and a variety of social and recreational activities on-site that help keep residents engaged in life.*

Residents can go to a hospital for surgery or the care only a hospital can provide, but afterward, they can return to their LCC to receive all the care they need until, ideally, they can return to their home in independent living. But if they can no longer live independently, they can transition permanently into assisted living or skilled nursing care and still live in the same community as their partner or friends.

How This Can Work

Let's say Mom is diagnosed with dementia, Dad is fine, and they are living in a life care community. Dad could stay in his apartment, and when he can't manage Mom anymore, she can transfer to memory care on the same premises. They could still eat dinner together every night and see each other often, but this way, Dad can sleep through the night and not worry about Mom wandering away in the middle of the night and getting lost. They can walk to see each other, no driving needed, and neither will ever become a 24/7 caregiver. Can you see the appeal? This example has a built-in assumption, by the way, that they have lived here for several years, and made the move before Mom's dementia diagnosis. Remember I mentioned a required physical assessment? Already having dementia would mean they might not be able to move into independent living together in a life care community.

If you ask older people what they worry about most as they age, it is often the question of "Who will take care of me if I can no longer care for myself?" Couples worry about burdening their spouses. Parents worry tremendously about burdening their children, or perhaps they don't have children they can count on. Sadly, I have met with countless families who have adult children with addiction issues, illness themselves, financial woes, or who live too far away to help. Add the millions of "solo seniors," with no spouse and no children, and the worry is just as bad. No matter how you look at it, *knowing how you will receive the care you may need, who will provide that care and where, as well as how you will pay for it, goes a long way toward providing peace of mind for both adult children and their parents.* Tens of thousands of seniors are willing to pay a large entry fee to live in an LCC for this very reason.

A small percentage of LCCs are rental only, with no entry fee. These types of communities say they have continuing care, which is true, but be aware that they usually do not offer either guaranteed access to long-term care or lower costs for care. Always ask what levels of care are on-site, what access is guaranteed by the contract, if the days of care are limited in any way, and what the cost of care should be if you ever need it. Expect anything from two weeks of care at no extra cost to ninety days over one's lifetime. If the days are limited, find out what the fees for long-term care revert to once those contract days are used up.

LCC Basics

There are over two thousand life care communities in the United States, with close to a million residents, with lots of options to choose from, ranging from simple to lavish.

- ◉ The average entry fee today is about $350,000, but fees can be as high as $1 million. Sometimes these fees include built-in refund options, so be sure to ask. The larger the floor plan, the higher the entry and monthly fee.

- ◉ Average monthly fees range from $2,500 to $4,500 but can go as high as $8,000–$10,000 a month for large homes and two people. Monthly fees cover lots of services and amenities, such as all utilities, all maintenance, housekeeping, and some meals.

- ◉ Many LCCs offer more, such as 24/7 emergency response, a fully equipped gym, and a huge variety of social and cultural activities. Remember, the vast majority of residents sell their home to cover all or some of the entry-fee costs.

What (and Who) Does an Entry Fee Pay For?

Entry fees almost always apply to those moving into independent living—though recently I have heard of larger life care corporations charging *much* lower entry fees for direct admission into assisted living or skilled nursing care. The advantage of paying an entry fee is almost always a lifelong discount for the cost of care plus a guarantee of admission from assisted into skilled care (something that will become more of an issue as access to long-term care becomes competitive).

It bears repeating that most entry-fee communities do not typically include ownership of any property, a fact that often comes as a great shock if this concept is new to you! It was common for people to say, "You want HOW MUCH for a house I don't own?" Think about it this way: the entry fee is covering *unlimited access to long-term care at discounted rates for your lifetime*.

Another surprise? Expect what is called a "first-person" entry fee, and a "second-person" entry fee. The good news? The second-person fee is tremendously less than the fees I have quoted above. The average second-person fee nationally is between $25,000–$35,000. A second person could be any two people who choose to live together, as in a mother and daughter, a brother and sister, a same-sex couple, or two friends, as well as a husband and wife.

Gone are the days when same-sex couples were discriminated against. It took a few legal suits, but no one should ever experience this type of discrimination, and if they do, go talk to a good lawyer. When looking at total cost, don't forget to add in both fees for any two people.

Same goes for the monthly fee. There is always a "second-person" monthly fee, always much lower than the $3,500, for example. Expect this to be in the $1,200–$1,600 range nationally. Services will be identical for both residents. Make sure to keep reading to educate yourself about required physical assessments and financial reviews, if your parents are moving into independent living *together*.

Oversight

No matter where you live, find out if life care communities are regulated or have to operate under state law and then read the statute! Continuing care communities are regulated at the state level, and some states have little to no regulation. The state agency that oversees a licensed life care community can be the state regulatory insurance office, financial services, aging or elder services, or another agency entirely. Stricter states with a high number of life care communities, such as Florida and North Carolina, require a number of documents to be submitted annually to the state, including a disclosure statement, actuarial studies, audited financial statements, and much more. They also have strict cash reserve requirements and escrow requirements related to entry fees for start-up communities. This oversight is to protect the potential resident from financial fraud and abuse.

State regulation of continuing care retirement communities, which tends to focus mostly on financial regulation, should not be confused with health-care-related regulations. For instance, the on-site healthcare facility will be strictly regulated by the appropriate licensing body within the state. Remember, a life care community will have both assisted living and skilled nursing care on-site and must comply with any state and federal laws governing these facilities. Any facility that wishes to receive Medicare and/or Medicaid reimbursements must be certified in accordance with federal guidelines.

An LCC vs. Long-Term Care Insurance

A life care contract is, in essence, like a long-term care insurance contract. Instead of paying for long-term care insurance over twenty to thirty years, you pay a one-time lump sum (entry fee!) that typically promises access to higher levels of care when needed *at a lower cost*.

Since the average long-term care policy for an older couple could easily be $5,000 to $6,000 a year, this easily can add up to well over $100,000 over time. If it is a traditional policy, this money is totally lost if never used, and it does absolutely nothing in the way of guaranteeing quality care. And to be clear, a typical policy today will have a limited maximum payout, meaning it will cover some costs for a period of three to five years. Many long-term care insurance companies increase their fees multiple times over the life of a policy so you can expect significant increases over time. I have seen many couples forced to either drop their policy when it became too expensive or decrease the benefits to make it affordable, just about the time they really need it! Please read Chapter 15, "Medicare, Medicaid, and Paying for Long-Term Care" to find out more about different kinds of long-term care insurance options such as hybrid policies that might work for your family.

Please understand that no long-term care policy will ever pay for an entry fee to a life care community, and neither will Medicare or any government program. Entry fees are for those individuals moving into independent living who may need future long-term care and want financial protection for the future cost of this care. A typical long-term care insurance policy also addresses future cost and will help pay for home care, assisted living, memory care, and skilled nursing care *wherever you live*, even in a life care community. Ask any life care community you or your parents are considering if they have a contract that will complement your long-term care insurance contract, if you have one. It could mean a much lower entry fee!

If you are considering a life care community in a state with very little oversight, it will be even more important to look closely at their financial information and patient care surveys. See Chapters 12 and 13 for more detail about oversight in general.

Refund Options

Some communities offer refund options if you move out or when someone passes away, as a way of recouping your entry fee. As I have said, most LCCs are not real estate transactions, so there is usually no selling a unit. Some communities offer the options of a 50 percent or 90 percent refund by asking for considerably higher entry fees up front, and some *automatically build this into the initial entry fee*. Some adult children who can afford it offer to pay the higher entry fee for refunds to ensure a large portion of the entry fee reverts to the estate when their parents pass away. Many life care communities restrict refund options to those *eighty and under*. If refunds are important to you, be sure to ask the community if there are any *age restrictions on their refund plans*.

For those LCCs that say they are equity based, this often means the "owners" of the home can sell the home at market value or their heirs can sell the home. Often there is some kind of restriction such as a percentage of the profit above *the cost initially paid* returned to the community. This helps the community manage costs and stay financially stable. Again, read the fine print. It is rarely just a normal real estate transaction. States often have rules about how long an LCC can take to pay back a refund that is due. It can be up to six months in some states. It will always be in the contract somewhere. They may not have to pay back anything until "a like unit sells that is equal to the amount of the refund," and they may first have to reimburse anyone already waiting for a refund!

For either a single person or a couple, there are advantages you might not think of to choose a refund contract, even if you are not interested in leaving money to anyone. What if one of you dies first and the remaining spouse wants to leave the community and move closer to a son or daughter?

Then you should consider a plan with a refund option. Refund options pay not only when someone passes away but typically pay if the person (or persons) breaks the contract and leaves the community entirely. This gives you the freedom to take a good portion of the initial entry fee with you should you decide to leave the community.

Expect Increases in Monthly Fees

All communities will increase the fees they charge. Usually there is an annual increase in both entry fees (paid in full only once before moving in) and ongoing monthly fees. In Florida, the average increase has been between 3–5 percent annually. All communities should be able to give you a history of all fee increases for at least the past five years (or longer), which you will need to predict future costs. If one year stands out as being a particularly high increase, ask why. Was there an emergency, a new roof for the entire community, a flood or fire? You can always request a meeting with the CFO to pose very direct financial questions and ask to see annual financial statements. You and your parents have the right to educate yourselves about the financial stability of a community when you are considering making such a significant investment. Any resistance to your questions should be a red flag.

Does the Community Have Specific Affiliations?

As mentioned, historically, LCCs were developed by religious organizations to meet the needs of their congregation as they aged. You have likely heard of a community being "sponsored" by Methodist, Presbyterian, Quaker, Lutheran, or Jewish groups. Many of these groups have large national not-for-profit corporations that have developed multiple locations all over the country. I have visited several communities where the religious influence is strong enough that they did not serve alcohol in the community restaurants, but that was some years ago. It is a good idea to always ask if a community is affiliated with a particular faith or religious denomination. Questions like "What percentage of your residents are Lutheran?" are appropriate. Do they celebrate Hanukkah and Christmas? How? Other religious holidays in some way? Understanding the culture of a community before moving your parents will be key to choosing the right one. Some communities cater to retired military, LGBTQ, or pilots!

The same question goes for political affiliations. Obviously if your parents are very conservative, living in a predominantly liberal, progressive community may not be a good fit.

University-Based Retirement Communities or UBRCs

About twenty years ago, universities began to develop retirement communities on or near their campuses, referred to as UBRCs. Most UBRCs are also life care communities, but not all, so again, always ask. They tend to attract lifelong learners who may have an academic background or a high level of education. They usually have access to university libraries, classes on campus, cultural events, and large performing arts centers. Another advantage? Excellent healthcare, especially if the university has a teaching hospital or large medical center associated with it. At some UBRCs, classes are held on-site and taught by both professors and qualified interested residents. Classes typically covered are politics, history, science, languages, philosophy, art, music, and much more. Classes are typically offered for a minimal cost or low annual dues and are usually not for credit.

Some communities are affiliated with the Osher Foundation, started in 1977 and named for its funder, philanthropist Bernard Osher. There are now over 125 Osher Lifelong Learning Institutes operating on various college campuses and oriented to seniors interested in high-quality lifelong learning programs. Check out the national "Lifelong Learning Institute Directory" at osherfoundation.org/olli_list.html.

Perhaps the best-known lifelong learning program is the Elderhostel Institute that morphed into the Road Scholar Lifelong Learning Institute Network. There are hundreds of classes to choose from and most are open to local area residents (not just community members).

Buyer beware: Some UBRCs may or may not offer true continuing care. Some are strictly for independent living and have no long-term care on-site, or if they do, it is not part of their contract. Always ask a full range of questions.

Types of Life Care Contracts

Do not rely on the LCC's brochure description of their contracts. It will take time to come to a complete understanding of the possible contracts you could enter into. At the highly respected life care community I worked at, we had four main contracts with over ten options to consider! Contracts vary from one LCC to another, and communities can offer hybrids of the three contracts discussed below. The contract a family chooses, or will even be offered, will be based on age, health, and finances. If someone has an excellent long-term care insurance plan or long-term care annuity, this should influence their choice of contract. I highly recommend you seek the advice of a professional who is knowledgeable about life care contracts before signing one. They are notoriously complex and confusing to most people. *Once you choose a contract and move in, most communities do not allow you to change or switch contracts!*

LCCs basically offer three types of contracts: Type A, Type B, and Type C, also referred to as extensive, modified, and fee for service. These terms are for general use within the industry, but expect variations.

"TYPE A" CONTRACT

A "Type A" contract is considered within the senior living industry to be the "Cadillac" option. Ninety percent of all life care residents will choose this option if they qualify healthwise and financially. It is the preferred contract because it offers the most financial protection in regard to the cost of long-term care when needed in the future. A true Type A contract is assumed to mean that there is no change in the monthly fee someone is paying for their independent-living apartment when they have to transition to assisted or skilled care permanently. It is a *lifetime guarantee of access to care when needed, at the lowest possible cost.*

Here is an example: Let's say your Aunt Alice is living in Seaside Village, a true life care community. She is paying $3,000 a month for her one-bedroom apartment in independent living. Unfortunately, Aunt Alice has a stroke and even after weeks of rehab (offered on-site), she has to move permanently to a higher level of care and give up her apartment in independent living. With a Type A contract, Aunt Alice is only charged $3,000 a month even though she is in assisted living full time now. Having paid an entry fee of $350,000 for a Type A contract on a one-bedroom-and-den apartment, she is now guaranteed this lower cost over her lifetime. If you called Seaside Village and asked what they charge someone not on a contract, it would likely be $5,000–$6,000 a month for the same room and level of care in assisted living. For skilled care in a private room, it would be as high as $10,000–$11,000 a month. But your Aunt Alice is only paying $3,000 for the exact same level of care and services, and it does not matter if she is in assisted living or skilled nursing or memory care. That is why these types of contracts are so attractive. They allow a person to secure high-quality care, in top-rated facilities, with a steeply discounted rate once you pay the one-time entry fee associated with the apartment chosen. Since the industry broadly defines Type A contracts, you need to double-check what this term means at each LCC.

There are also modified Type A contracts within the industry. They are typically similar to a traditional life care contract but have a few exceptions to the rule of absolutely no change in the monthly fee. With a modified Type A, any scenario that includes a resident in a higher level of care automatically triggers a change in what they are charged on a monthly basis. Even with a modified Type A, *it will still be at the lowest cost of any contract the LCC offers*. It would not be unusual for someone to be receiving assisted or skilled nursing care within the community and be paying approximately half of the public rate they would normally be charged if they were not on a contract of any kind.

"TYPE B" CONTRACT

A "Type B" contract will always have lower entry fees than a Type A contract. While this might sound attractive at first, I like to remind readers that this also means the cost of long-term care will be higher when needed. Using the analogy of a long-term care insurance plan, a Type B contract covers less of the cost of long-term care. How? By limiting the time period you can be in assisted or skilled care at a discounted rate. The contract may say you can be in assisted or skilled care for *only thirty days within a year at a lower cost*. After the thirty days, the rate they charge will go up to the public/market rate. Often this is twice the amount you were paying! Another example of a Type B contract would be a flat discounted rate applied to any care you receive. For example, in one community I worked at, we offered 20 percent less than "the then current market rates." Translation? If a community is charging $5,000 a month for assisted living now, but in five years' time, when you need the care, the cost increases to $5,500, the LCC will give you a 20 percent discount and charge you $4,400 a month. Again, when reviewing contracts, be cautious about those with a limited time period with a reversion to high market rates—or some type of discounted long-term care applied for only a short period of time. If the discount is high enough, this type of contract works well if you already have a long-term care insurance plan that will pay for a high percentage of your care.

"TYPE C" CONTRACT

A "Type C" contract is a fee-for-service arrangement. Care is provided, but the cost will be *the open market rate; no discounts are offered*. These contracts have significantly lower entry fees because you are not prepaying for any long-term care. If the community charges someone from "the public" who is directly admitted to skilled care $300 a day, then your parent, who already lives there, will be charged $300 a day with this type of contract. However, any contract should *guarantee access* to long-term care when needed, no matter what the amount billed to the resident.

Recently I have researched several very nice life care communities but discovered that they only offered ninety lifetime days in their health center, and after that, the cost for care was at the market rate, despite high entry fees. The market rate was $455 day for a private room in skilled care, not out of the ordinary for a high-end life care community and this is 2022 pricing! This is why it is so important to find out what is covered, for how long, and what your loved one will be charged!

Why Would You Choose a Type B or C Contract?

There are good reasons to choose a Type B or Type C contract, although these may not be immediately obvious. If your parents have a great long-term care insurance plan, or could afford to self-insure, then they would not need to pay the higher entry fee cost for a Type A contract. Sometimes these savings are in the hundreds of thousands of dollars. Here is an example from an actual fee schedule. Let's say a two-bedroom, 1,300-square-foot apartment entry fee for a Type A contract (for one person) is $444,000. For a Type B contract, the same apartment is $362,400. For a Type C contract, the same unit is $331,400. Keep this in mind: *The higher the entry fee, the lower the cost of long-term care when your parent(s) need it. The lower the entry fee, the higher the cost of future long-term care.*

I have seen very wealthy clients choose a Type C (lowest entry fees) because they could leave their money invested in the market and benefit potentially from these earnings. They were not worried about paying the cost of their future long-term care, but they still wanted to live in the community, even though they could afford any lifestyle they wanted.

The other less obvious reason? If your parent does not qualify for a life care contract, they may have no choice but to consider a Type B option. Even with this option, long-term care will cost less, so don't dismiss this as unacceptable. Many states have rules governing life care contracts that could dictate who is offered what, especially since most states do not let you "mix and match" contracts. Any two people residing together are often ***required*** to be on the same contact and are charged the same fees. There is no allowance made if, say, Dad is healthy but Mom has dementia. In this scenario, neither will be offered a Type A or true life care contract. Both would have to choose a Type B or C option.

It really comes down to your comfort level related to risk and how best to insure against the high cost of long-term care. If you or your parents are more comfortable with risk, you can always opt for the lower fee contract options at any age. But keep in mind that the fastest-growing demographic are those living over one hundred! So even an eighty-year-old could be looking at paying for long-term care for twenty years! Do the math.

As always, ask to see the full contract before choosing which one is best for you or your parents' circumstances, age, health, and finances, and find an independent expert to consult with.

Required Health Assessments for Admission

All life care communities require potential residents to take a basic health assessment prior to being accepted into the community. The purpose of these assessments is twofold: to determine the individual's ability to live safely in independent living, and to predict their need for future long-term care. If someone already has a serious diagnosis that is neurological or neuromuscular and predictably debilitating, they may not be offered the traditional Type A life care contract, but they may qualify for a modified alternative. If someone already has advanced symptoms that impede their ability to live safely in independent living, they will likely not be admitted at all on any version of a life care contract.

These assessments are not full medical examinations, but they are very thorough. The forms must be completed by the person's primary care physician and include complete lab work and full medical history. The doctor has to verify and sign that the information is current and accurate. In addition, an in-person health interview is required and usually includes testing basic activities of daily living such as walking, sitting, reaching, and balancing. It will also include a "mini-mental" review to screen for dementia. There are many typical senior health conditions that will not prevent you from being accepted, so never make assumptions. Even having cancer may not disqualify someone. Ask the community before taking the health assessment. These assessments are usually done two to three months prior to moving in, and not before.

Just getting on the wait list years in advance of the actual move does not mean you can take the health assessment then or that you are guaranteed admission! Why is this important? Because a major health event can prevent you from being accepted on the contract you may want or from being accepted at all. I often warned families that procrastination or waiting for a crisis will ruin even this type of plan! Keep in mind no LCC can accept 100 percent of future residents who will likely need skilled care, or they would need four hundred skilled nursing rooms, for example. The health assessment is a tool used to predict the likelihood of needing care so that the community can meet that need and continue to remain financially stable.

What If One Parent Is Already Ill or Has Dementia?

Keep in mind that it could be possible for a couple to move into an LCC, with one person on a life care contract of some kind living in independent living, and the spouse *needing care already moving directly into assisted, skilled, or memory care.* The rule mentioned above does not apply (the same contract for a couple) because only the person moving into independent living is taking the health assessment and is on a life care contract of some kind. The person already receiving care would pay market public rate for care and would *not pay any entry fee.* Should the well spouse eventually need care, they would get a discount based on the contract they chose.

Required Financial Assessment
for Admission

All LCCs require a financial review of all applicants. The intent is to prevent a community from accepting someone who might run out of money as they age. Ideally, the applicant and the LCC's marketing office work together to mutually determine the financial feasibility of your choice of plan. Remember, entry fees vary tremendously. Are you considering a one-bedroom apartment unit with a $250,000 entry fee or a large home with an entry fee of $1,000,000? Are you sixty or eighty? Will your funds need to last you fifteen years or thirty? The larger the floor plan, the higher the entry fee, just like when you are buying a home.

You will typically be asked to list your full assets, current and projected income, debts, and anticipated changes in income like survivorship rights with pensions, etc. *The LCC needs to see that your assets will comfortably last your anticipated life span.* Their projections are typically based on actuarial tables and life expectancy software estimates and should also take into consideration any increases in monthly fees over time, as well as increases in your own personal expenses. A good financially solid LCC cannot afford to have too many residents going broke! A general rule of thumb to apply without doing a full financial disclosure form was this: Your assets should be two and a half to three times the entry fee you expect to pay. This allows for a comfortable margin of error and some assurance that you will likely qualify financially.

Most not-for-profit LCCs have, as part of their contract, a benevolent fund that is available for residents who outlive their assets. This fund is designed to pay the monthly fee for someone who runs out of money if they qualify. Before a community would "pick up the tab," so to speak, they would look to see if a person intentionally impoverished themselves or gave all their money away. But the existence of benevolent funds in most not-for-profit life care communities offers tremendous peace of mind for families who wonder what will happen if parents run out of money. Ask a community if this is part of their contract, and then read this to make sure you understand how it works!

Waiting Lists

Just getting on a community's wait list does not mean you are "accepted." All it means is that you have an interest in moving to the community one day. You can request a preliminary financial assessment to make sure you are getting on the wait list for a unit you will be approved for, but expect to complete another one if more than a year has passed.

Consider more than one wait list deposit if your parents are very serious about getting into a high-demand community. Expect a wait of years for some midrange popular floor plans (1,200–1,600 square feet), so ask the marketing office which floor plans are in the highest demand, with the longest wait. If you want to move sooner, place more than one wait-list deposit for another two apartments, if the community allows.

If your parents' plans or time frame changes, or they decide on a smaller apartment, it is up to them (or you) to communicate with the marketing office.

If a community calls, and your parents say "I'm not ready yet" (a phrase I heard often), they may forfeit their chance to move in. Do not assume that your parents will be called again soon. I dealt with many disappointed couples who regretted procrastinating, only to discover an unexpected medical crisis kept them from getting in on the contract they wanted and needed.

The Spencers Consider an LCC

On the last family Zoom call, Bob mentioned his interest in a community that offered levels of care. Josie brings up the possibility of a nearby life care retirement community she read about near Raleigh, called Maple Village. They have a great reputation and many excellent services, amenities, and classes since they are near multiple universities. She checks out the community online and does some research. Josie explains to her mom and dad about moving into independent living to begin with, but also having access to higher levels of care should they need it in the future. Since Bob's stroke, the family recognizes he is now more at risk for needing long-term care. Bob and Sally express interest since Bob was worried about being a burden to Dan and Josie if either parent needed more care in the future. The family discusses if this option is better than just buying a house. They go back to the framework and Principle #1: What option will maximize Bob and Sally's independence and allow for flexibility as their needs increase over time? How does this fit into Principle #2 JITSP for a three- to five-year window? They like the idea of moving into a more manageable apartment, rather than a house, with all the maintenance taken care of. And they like the idea of not worrying about where they would get care if needed. They decide to get an appraisal of their New Jersey home to see what will be affordable if they are paying an entry fee of some kind. This option is becoming more appealing, but they are still not sure.

Josie calls Maple Village first. She makes a list of questions to ask prior to touring and decides she should tour with Dan before her parents come. They see several apartments that should work financially, and she talks openly with the marketing rep, Nicole, about her dad's prior stroke. She learns that he won't qualify for a life care contract due to his stroke, but he will qualify for several other contracts. She asks for copies of the contracts, and she and Dan review them.

Josie learns that there is a requirement that both Dad and Mom are on the *same contract*, so even though Mom has no major health issues, Dad's health prevents her from coming in on a life care contract. Nicole asks if they have a long-term care insurance plan, and Josie says she doesn't know but she will find out. Josie calls her parents that night to tell them about Maple Village and how nice it was. She asks about the long-term care insurance and finds out that Dad took out a policy when he worked for the university. He hasn't looked at it in years, but he will find out what it covers. Both Bob and Sally agree they want to find out more about Maple Village.

Nicole sends a full brochure to Bob and Sally, and they set up a virtual tour so they can see all the common areas, the dining rooms, the fitness center, and more. It includes two to three apartments as well. Bob and Sally pay a refundable $1,500 fee to get on a wait list for two apartments: a one-bedroom and den 1,200-square-foot apartment, and a larger two-bedroom 1,600-square-foot unit as well. They are still not sure of their plans, but they want to broaden their options. They plan for a visit to Raleigh soon to tour Maple Village as well as to see one other retirement community and a few houses. Josie knows Dad will tire easily after his stroke and Mom can handle about three hours max, and she already knows the full tour will take at least two hours, and longer if they stay for a meal. She schedules the tour for two days after their arrival, with the other tours on the following days. They are still on target for a possible move in about six to nine months.

List of Critical Questions to Ask an LCC

Sort through this list and prioritize into Tier 1 and Tier II questions, depending on your level of interest and the timing of a possible move.

I would start with Tier I questions:

- Are you for-profit or not-for-profit? Part of a larger corporation or one of a kind? Any affiliations of any kind?
- Are you a rental community, a purchase (equity based), or entry-fee based?
- What levels of care do you offer: independent, assisted, and skilled care? Are they all offered on-site?
- Is access to these levels of care part of a contract or guaranteed? Limited number of days? Is the cost reduced or at the market rate?
- How many different types of contracts do you offer? Are any true Type A or life care contracts?
- Do you offer refund options? Any age restrictions on any of your contracts?
- How long is your wait list and what is the cost? Is the deposit refundable?
- What services are included in the normal monthly fee? What services cost extra? May I see a complete list?

Below are Tier II questions:

- What are the accommodations for assisted or skilled care? Private rooms or semiprivate? May I tour this area? (The answer should always be "yes" for a tour.)
- Do you offer secure care for people with dementia in a memory-care wing? (Important for people who wander and are confused.)

- Who is the medical director in skilled nursing care? Who is your licensed healthcare administrator? May I meet them? (You should meet both at some point and ask how long they have been in the job. Think credentials and stable leadership.)
- What are the staffing ratios in the different levels of care? (Do they meet state requirements or go beyond, hopefully?)
- How do you screen your employees? Do you do background checks, drug testing, credit checks? (Think safety of your vulnerable parents; abuse and theft are big problems.)
- Do you have an affiliation with a specific hospital in the area or can your residents choose any personal doctor or any hospital? (What hospital is nearby for emergencies, optimally no farther than thirty minutes max, and are they top rated?)

Plan Ahead to Keep Your Options Open

All in all, choosing a life care community is one of the best options for meeting your parents' needs as they age, if the family has the resources. Do some research years before a possible move and find out what life care communities are located near you or your parents.

Life care communities offer either a single person or a couple all the benefits of both Principle #1 and Principle #2: a way to stay independent for as long as possible by living in a community that offers many of the services and support they may need, over a long period of time, as their health needs change, without having to relocate or provide twenty-four-hour care for each other, or depend on you—their children! And many LCC contracts actually offer a solid approach to paying for long-term care that can protect assets in the long run. It is hard not to be a fan. My only complaint about life care communities is the cost puts them out of reach for many people. The next chapter provides alternatives you may never have considered that are financially feasible for many families.

Chapter 9

Alternative and Creative Living Options

Let's face it, not everyone can afford a retirement or life care community. Plus, plenty of people told me all the reasons they would not choose this option even if they could afford it: "not enough diversity in age, demographics, ethnicity, gender, and more," was common. True; many retirement communities are homogeneous in nature. And, as we have discussed, many parents do not want to live with their adult children. So, what are the options if your parents don't like the idea of a retirement community, don't want to live with you or move, or in fact do need some help financially to stay in their home?

Remember the go-go, slow-go, no-go years phases in Chapter 1? The ideas I propose in this chapter are more suited for the first two categories, not the no-go years when your parents are likely to need more care, either in-home or in assisted living. This category by the way is not age specific. I have seen plenty of eighty-year-olds who are spry, still driving, and in the go-go category, and plenty of sixty-five-year-olds who are in assisted living already.

Often, when consulting with families, I listen to seniors who are worried about living alone for many reasons. It could be a safety issue, a money issue, a health issue, or a companionship issue. This chapter will offer solutions you have not thought of that can work for you, your parents, and your pocketbook . . . and perhaps your mental health (and theirs).

Live-In Companion or Roommate

With millions of Americans living alone (many of them women) and at risk financially for losing their home to foreclosure, the idea of a paying roommate could be the answer. This concept, called "home sharing," may be a godsend for many aging seniors and their families. The typical situation involves an elderly woman, often widowed or divorced, who has an apartment or home with an extra room. The reasons for inviting someone to live with them could be financial, companionship, safety, or assistance with shopping or upkeep of their home. There are now agencies that provide background checks and other screenings, including checking to see if the potential roommate is a nonsmoker, if they have pets, and general compatibility.

The roommate, often as not, is another older woman, but it could be a younger man or women. Usually when a match is made, an agreement is signed by both parties covering chores or overnight visitors, and usually a reduced rent. Google "home sharing" and see what agencies exist in your area. Vet the agency doing the matchmaking to make sure they are very thorough in their screening process and talk with families who have already used their services. You should also do your own reference checking!

If you have a parent who lives alone, does not want or refuses to move, and/or needs basic help you cannot provide, then seriously entertain a roommate as a viable option. If your parent resists, it may be time to have a real heart-to-heart reality-check kind of meeting.

It may sound something like: "Mom, I want to help you get what you want. You say you want to live alone, and you do not want to move. But I cannot move here, and we can both agree that you need help. I am asking you to please consider a compromise. I am contacting a senior roommate company to look into finding a roommate for you that can help with some things and contribute to household expenses."

With more and more seniors experiencing retirement insecurity and losing ground financially, I think this alternative may become more viable. Some companies have finders' fees, some are free, some only help woman over fifty years old. Check out silvernest.com, a company that has found much success in safely matching up roommates for elders. They are active in Florida, California, Colorado, Arizona, Oregon, and more, and are part-nered with well-known national organizations. They believe in offering seniors a new way of obtaining financial resilience, income, and sometimes assistance. Other websites include seniorhomeshares.com, a free national service that helps with roommate matching. Let me remind you to do your vetting and make sure whoever you call is everything they say they are. With rents going up every year, finding the right roommate for a lonely elder could solve financial problems by bringing in an extra $500 to $1,500 a month (just an example) and offer someone a nice place to live in an area they otherwise couldn't afford.

I have a friend in her sixties who lost her job, had to sell her lovely home, and could no longer afford to rent the home she was in. I put her in touch with an older woman, quite disabled, who was trying to maintain her inde-pendence in her home. She wanted a roommate who could assist her getting up in the morning and helping her to bed at night. Other people helped with meals, etc. For these services, her rent was greatly reduced. My friend has her own room, own bathroom, shared kitchen and living room space, and access to the garage for storage or a car. This situation was a tremendous help to both of them and worked well for years.

Some seniors might consider younger housemates, who can help with chores such as gardening, cooking, taking out and retrieving trash and recy-cling cans, doing some heavy cleaning, and perhaps even helping to walk dogs if the senior's back is out, for instance. Many younger people these days cannot otherwise afford to live in desirable neighborhoods near their jobs or schools. College or grad students may be helpful (though they will graduate eventually), but in some towns, housing is very difficult to find for nursing students or nursing assistants. What better housemate than that?! You may be able to use a neighborhood site such as Nextdoor.com to find reputable people in the community looking for a living space. Of course, you will need to thoroughly vet them.

Airbnb: A Solution for Senior Financial Woes?

I know of two older women who began an Airbnb business. One was in her late sixties, had an extra room, and liked the idea of both company and making extra money. Typically, she brought in $500 to $800 extra a month. The other was in her eighties and had just lost a large chunk of her monthly income when her ex-husband died. In the divorce, she was supposed to receive income for life, but due to a loophole, the income stopped at his death. This was a very frightening situation for her. We brainstormed together and came up with a plan she liked. She did not like the idea of a permanent roommate or constant guests, and she did not yet need any help. She spruced up the spare bedroom and found out she could provide housing for traveling nurses for a very nice fee. She was a retired nurse herself, so this worked out perfectly. She could also control the length of time a nurse stayed and accept one-month contracts, for example. At eighty, she was willing to try something new that gave her the financial stability she needed and allowed her to continue to stay independent in her home!

There are at least four or five websites that specialize in housing for traveling nurses such as furnishedfinder.com and travelnursehousing.com.

Cohousing Options

According to AARP and the Cohousing Association of the United States, cohousing may be the answer to the twenty-first century's social, economic, and environmental challenges. Why? Because cohousing "offers an ideal balance of privacy and community." These intentional communities provide the social connection seniors need, sustainable design, and shared resources.

Private homes of varying sizes are typically clustered around shared public spaces, shared facilities, a common clubhouse, and are self-governed. For an older person with no family, this could be ideal.

The website cohousing.org has a list of all existing and forming cohousing communities state by state.

There are approximately 113 established cohousing neighborhoods in the US, with many more coming. They more closely resemble a traditional village or close-knit neighborhood of earlier generations. They average about twenty to forty homes per community and often have a central courtyard or car-free walkways and play areas for children. Some seniors love the inter-generational nature of most of these communities, although the cohousing development in my town is made up mostly of retirees, but it's very child friendly, with playgrounds on-site. Meals are shared several times a week in the "common house," and responsibilities for running and maintaining the community are often shared. You may find a common garden area, various shared tools, and a common laundry room, for example. It's easy to understand the appeal for seniors who may not have family nearby or any family at all.

NORCs or Naturally Occurring Retirement Communities

Naturally Occurring Retirement Communities (NORCs) are self-help communities that started springing up in 1992 with the founding of "Community Without Walls," in Princeton, New Jersey. They are not formal communities but occur naturally in neighborhoods in both small cities and urban areas, thanks to a significant number of seniors having aged in place there or moved in. They offer a very popular alternative to moving into a senior living community, as the aim of a NORC is to keep seniors in their own home and allow them to age in place safely, by helping them access the care and services they need. And note, there is typically only a membership fee of some kind that does not come anywhere close to the entry fees of a life care community.

Often started by grassroots elder activists, NORCs link seniors with other seniors and leverage the numbers so they can collectively provide the typical services seniors need. If seniors need help with minor repairs, a ride to the doctor, groceries, meal drop-off, the NORC can often coordinate these services and usually for a reduced price. Volunteers are a huge part of the success of these groups. Some "villages," as they like to be called, include coordinating healthcare as well. Expect the larger NORCs to have a central office that will coordinate home care, access to a twenty-four-hour-a-day emergency hotline, transportation, and more.

Typically, they form alliances with home health agencies and other healthcare providers and vendors. Dues are associated with these communities and can vary from $25 a year to $750 a year for a couple depending on the level of services offered. There is now a national organization called the Village Movement (helpfulvillage.com/the-village-movement) that has helped establish over three hundred of these "village" communities. Sometimes a NORC is not a physically connected location but loosely organized around a church, synagogue, or fraternal organizations. Even the federal government has funded about forty NORCs, as the elder population is increasing so rapidly all over the United States.

NORCs are geographically defined either by the boundaries of a neighborhood or they can be an entire apartment building. While NORCs were first identified in urban settings, they can be found in communities large and small, and many varied settings including a more rural type of NORC comprised of one- and two-family homes over a large geographical area.

NORC programs are generally supported by a combination of public and private funding, which could be a combination of government agencies, corporations, and not-for-profit organizations. These core partners connect to many other stakeholders in a community—typically local businesses; civic, religious, and cultural institutions; public and private funders; and local police and other public safety agencies. By harnessing these resources for a common interest, NORC programs help to transform a community into a great place to grow older.

There are some very famous NORCs like Boston's Beacon Hill Village. Founded in 1999, it is recognized as one of the nation's oldest and most successful NORCs. I highly encourage you to visit their website, beaconhillvillage.org, to get an idea of just how these communities can work. You will see that Beacon Hill Village serves an older population (must be fifty and up) that happens to live in surrounding neighborhoods, who wish to age in place. It reminds me of a top-notch life care community without a high entry fee or having to move! However, for highly organized NORCs like Beacon Hill, with a complete list of services, you should expect annual fees of about $ 675 for one person and around $1,000 for a couple. They do offer lower fees to those who qualify based on income ranges. But when you compare these fees to the monthly fees of any retirement community, you will see that this is still a bargain!

These communities have group fitness classes, lectures, educational opportunities, social groups, travel groups, and group transportation to art and cultural events and more. Most importantly, they "provide access to household help, health and wellness services, home maintenance, technical support, and transportation. One phone call offers easy referrals to screened service providers." Notice the critical words "screened service providers." Seniors are often easy prey, and screening out shady businesses is important. The world is full of scammers, and this added protection is an important safety factor for seniors.

Affordable or Subsidized Senior Housing

There is such a high demand for affordable housing that typically there are long wait lists to get an apartment, even for seniors. I am choosing to include this information in the hopes that this situation will improve with so much focus on the need, especially post-Covid. With millions of families (and elders) facing eviction, this is now a pandemic of its own. Affordable housing is defined as housing where the cost to the tenant is less than 30 percent of their income. For a senior on a fixed income at poverty level, this is a very low rent. Public housing authorities can set a rent as low as fifty dollars a month in some cases. The government measures income classification by looking at the "Area Median Income" or AMI and considers extremely low income as below 30 percent of the AMI. There are lots of categories to consider but a few to research are:

- Low-Income Housing Tax Credit or LIHTC apartments
- Project-Based Section 8 apartments
- Section 202 Senior and Section 811 disabled apartments
- USDA Rural Development Section 515 apartments
- Public housing apartment communities

Check out the website affordablehousingonline.com to find out how these various programs work. Your local public housing authority and HUD (Housing and Urban Development) offices will also be helpful, and so will many local social service agencies (like your local USAging office) if you are trying to find affordable housing for your parents. If either of your parents were ever in the military, don't forget to look at the benefits offered to veterans, especially in the affordable housing arena. Check the list of helpful websites at starbradbury.com/resources for more.

USAging

To find out more about senior housing in general, aging in place, cohousing, senior affordable housing, or NORCs in any area you are considering for relocation, check with your local USAging office (usaging.org or call 1-800-677-1116). As I've mentioned, they are a wealth of information on *any senior issue* you can think of, and there is no cost associated with their information or referral services.

You may be especially interested in their Housing and Services Resource Center, their National Aging and Disability and Transportation Center, their Livable Communities information, and their Caregiver Support classes. This is a mere fraction of the information on their website. They are particularly useful if your parents are on a limited income and can often point you in the right direction for help with costs of all kinds, including home modifications and community-based services.

Tiny House Option

I have friends who are considering building a "tiny house" on their property for Mom or Dad (or both). They could have their own space, be yards away, not miles away, and still have a measure of independence. This is today's version of a mother-in-law suite but with a tad more space since it is an actual separate residence but nearby. This option is far more economical in the long run than most retirement communities, much less assisted living. Don't forget that Mom or Dad might be willing to pay for construction costs if they can afford it. The average cost of a tiny house in 2021 was about $45,000, with most people paying between $30,000 and $60,000, according to homeadvisor.com. There are plenty of do-it-yourself kits to choose from if you are handy.

The size of a house in this category is about 100–600 square feet. Much larger than 1,000 square feet, and it becomes a "small house." However, when compared to the average size of a small apartment in assisted living (about 400–600 sq. ft.), a tiny house could offer about the same size, for a fraction of the cost, if you are able to provide any assistance your parent might need. Compare approximately $5,000–6,000 a month for assisted living with the expenses of a tiny house. Make sure to crunch the numbers and look at utilities, maintenance, food, and more. Factor in some home care a few times a week, and you will still come out ahead, costwise.

It is an enhancement to your property in the long run and may eventually be a source of rental income in the future. See if your neighborhood is zoned for this option. More and more cities are adding this option to their building codes, and not just for seniors but to address the problem with affordable housing in general!

Keep an Open Mind and Don't Make Assumptions

Before you eliminate any of the alternatives listed in this chapter, I'd like you to think about this in reference to Principle #1 (independence) and Principle #2 (JITSP). One of these options could extend your parents' independence for years before hitting the no-go years. Getting a roommate could mean your mom or dad gets some companionship, and some help with household chores or the financial help they need. Maybe it prevents a move to assisted living for two or three years.

This is exactly what my friend did for her mom. She converted the upstairs of her mother's house to an apartment with its own entrance. She then rented it for a modest amount to Elaine, a woman in her thirties who agreed to look in on "Mom," be available in the middle of the night for an emergency, and help with grocery shopping. Mom aged in place for another four years before she finally had to move to assisted living! Mission accomplished. She not only gave her mom what she wanted (staying in her home for as long as possible) but she generated income for her mom, and she saved approximately $240,000 by keeping mom out of assisted living for four years, and that is modest with factoring only $60,000 a year in assisted-living costs.

Maybe talking about building a tiny house lets Mom know she can move closer to you in three or five years. She has the peace of mind of knowing you want her closer, she can sell her current home when she is ready, help pay for her new tiny house, and have money left over. Keep in mind that many seniors welcome and are prepared to downsize. This could be the missing piece of your JITSP three-year plan for Principle #2. You don't know what she will say if you don't ask! Your parent(s) could be so grateful for the option of maintaining some autonomy in their own space and still be nearby. Initially, they could be helping you, with roles reversed as their needs increase.

Who knows, perhaps you are lucky enough to discover that your parents live in a well-established NORC and all they have to do is sign up! You may be totally surprised at what is available in their town or yours *once you know what to look for.*

When Your Parents Need More Help and Care

There are only four kinds of people in the world . . . Those who have been caregivers, those who currently are caregivers, those who will be caregivers, and those who will need caregivers.

Rosalyn Carter

In Parts One and Two, we've learned a lot about the importance of talking with your parents about crucial medical and financial issues and sharing this information. Principle #1 provides a framework for developing a plan that focuses on maximizing their independence, and Principal #2 focuses on a three- to five-year JITSP window. Previous chapters took an in-depth look at all the options open to your parents as they decide if they are going to age in place and stay in their home, relocate closer to you, or move to a retirement community of some kind. But what happens when your parents need more help and care?

No amount of planning and preparation will eliminate the likelihood of your parents needing help. Even with an emphasis on maximizing their independence, if they live long enough, they will most likely need help.

Sometimes it is simply a slow progression or physical decline, such as increasing memory loss, and sometimes it is sudden, such as a stroke. With people living well into their nineties, age and frailty is reason enough to need more help! Any preparation or homework you do now will save you time and energy in the future.

This section educates you on options and solutions for more care and support for your parents. You will learn the difference between home care and home life care, what assisted living is and their requirements for admission, and how to vet a skilled nursing facility and look up their ratings. The final two chapters will help you with long-distance caregiving and options to consider paying for long-term care.

Chapter 10

Next Steps: Options and Solutions for In-Home Help

The truth is, if either cognitive impairment or physical decline affects your parents' ability to safely live independently, yet aging in place is the only available solution at this point, it is time to figure out how you are going to get your parents more help. Stay focused on finding the best possible option for maintaining quality of life for your loved one and keeping some balance in your own life. Go back to developing a plan centered on helping them maintain their independence and safety for the longest possible time. Your goal will likely be helping them live safely in their home with additional help, whatever their needs, and working on your backup plan. It could be something as simple as a medication reminder system and home care two times a week. It may mean twenty-four-hour supervision! I suggest also reviewing Chapter 6, "Aging-in-Place Considerations," as a refresher on basic safety considerations and information on security and medical alert systems.

This chapter will give you lots of creative suggestions you may not even know exist and serve as an overview of your options. Look to the following chapters to give you in-depth information and tips on how to find the right home care, assisted living, or skilled facility, should your situation for in-home care change.

How Do You Know If Your Parents Need Help in Their Home?

Is the mail piling up and the house looking disorganized? If one parent is the caregiver to the other, is the caregiving parent becoming overwhelmed and exhausted? Perhaps a surgery is planned, they live alone, and you know they will need some temporary help as they recuperate. There could be so many reasons someone needs help *either long-term or short*, but it can make all the difference in the world to help someone age well and *maintain their independence*. The important thing is to educate yourself on the options!

Begin by making a thorough list of the kind of help they need. They may need help with:

- Shopping
- Meal preparation
- Housekeeping, house maintenance
- Laundry
- Transportation
- Dressing
- Bathing and personal hygiene
- Managing money, bill paying
- Communication, using computers, or any technology

Everything listed above falls into the category of ADLs or activities of daily living (dressing, bathing, toileting), or IADLs, instrumental activities of daily living (shopping, money management). You should be familiar with these terms as they are often used by both doctors and facilities as a way of evaluating a person and their level of need.

Are you looking for a temporary solution or long-term commitment from a company, or a private person, or a family member? By the time you finish this chapter, you will know if your parent(s) require home care or home healthcare. If you have noticed them struggling, it is time to consider getting additional help in your parents' home. Also, keep reading to find out more about hiring an aging life care professional who can help you.

The Difference Between Home Care and Home Healthcare Companies

While the terms "home care" and "home healthcare" sound similar, they are not. Home care companies offer *nonmedical help* with ADLs, while home healthcare agencies provide medical assistance, nursing services, and therapies like physical or occupational therapy.

Since the services provided by *home healthcare* are always thought of as necessary for a safe recovery from some major health event (a fall, surgery, stroke, heart attack, injury, etc.), it almost always follows a hospitalization, is always ordered by a doctor, and is usually short term during a recovery phase. This is the major difference between home care and home healthcare and is why Medicare and your Medicare Supplemental plan *will help pay for these services if they are ordered by a doctor as part of a rehabilitation plan*. If you are hiring home healthcare privately, for a longer period of time, you will likely pay privately.

There is no need to hire a home healthcare company if these kinds of services are not needed by your loved one. You will save your parents a great deal of money if a home care company can meet their needs. Cost estimates and comparisons for home care vs. home healthcare can be found in Chapter 11, "The Confusing World of Home Care." Hiring *a nonmedical home care company* that can assist with making meals, shopping, and transportation can keep your loved one independent for much longer. Having someone who can give simple medication reminders is a godsend. Even with all the downloadable apps that help you and your parent track medications, there is no replacement for someone standing in front of Dad, pills in hand, and watching him swallow!

I hired such a company for my stepfather, and it allowed him to age in place for at least another year before I had to move him into an assisted-living facility. A personal care assistant came to his apartment, made him lunch, did light housekeeping, and took him grocery shopping and to doctors' appointments. We carefully chose someone who would be compatible with him and enjoy his constant conversation.

These companies are mostly national franchises, individually owned, and will vary tremendously from area to area. Some of these companies include Visiting Angels, Home Instead, Comfort Keepers, and many more. Sometimes finding a *locally owned*, independent, well-run home care company is ideal. Ask friends, doctors, or hospital discharge planners for recommendations. Make sure your information is current. One company may be excellent for years, then sold, and things change.

Private Premium Live-In Care

If you have a parent who needs twenty-four-hour live-in care, you can now hire someone through a company that does all the vetting and screening before recommending that person to you and your family. Typically, he or she would move into a spare furnished bedroom in your parents' home. They assist as needed from morning until bedtime, but they are "on-call" overnight for any help needed, such as assisting someone to use the bathroom or some kind of emergency. They have regularly scheduled time off such as one weekend a month, or a three-day weekend, or one week every six months. They also have some downtime or scheduled unpaid leave time so they can leave the home. Often a payroll service is utilized that includes payroll taxes, workers' compensation, and HR (human resource) services. Expect to pay for the helper's groceries while in the home. This person would provide assistance with a long list of services such as medication aid, help with personal hygiene and care, meal preparation, shopping, transportation, household errands, pet and plant care, communication and technology assistance, and reporting and monitoring.

Caregivers can make almost three to four times more as a live-in than they can as a certified nursing assistant (CNA) in a senior facility. Many are foreign-born minorities with experience in senior care who prefer live-in work at a higher pay. The monthly average for a live-in companion is about $9,000–$10,000 caring for a single person and about $10,000–$13,000 a month if taking care of a couple. The cost is similar to what you would expect from a skilled nursing home, and somewhat less than assisted living, depending on the level of care the person needs. However, *the cost is about half of the twenty-four-hour home care costs* as charged by the hour, estimated to be well over $240,000 a year. This is because the live-in is off the clock during the eight hours they sleep at night. Most households that hire a live-in caregiver directly are exempt from paying the live-in overtime and for paying them for the eight hours of the sleep time, under certain conditions. Always check the rules in your state. The only company I know of at this time to provide this service is called Grandma Joan, and their website is grandmajoan.com.

They are extremely helpful, have excellent reviews, and will do a free consultation to discuss options with you and your family.

If this is an option you are considering, check to see if your parents have a long-term policy that will help pay for this type of care; otherwise, it will be an out-of-pocket expense and out of reach for many families.

Adult Day-Care Centers

Adult day care is the most economical approach to provide supervision and personal care for an elderly loved one on a daily basis. This might be ideal for an adult child who is still working but in the same town, or a burned-out spouse or partner. Their loved one can get the supervision they need during the day but be home at night. This option is much less expensive than others. Daily fees range tremendously from state to state, but expect an average of about fifty dollars a day. Look at the website seniorcare.com for a state-by-state list. Adult day care (ADC) provides frail seniors and persons with Alzheimer's with supervision and care in a structured setting during daytime hours, and most offer several schedule options, such as five days a week or just one or two. They don't usually operate on weekends.

There are two primary types of adult day-care programs.

- Adult social day care offers basic health services, meals, and activities.
- Adult day *healthcare* (ADHC) provides intensive health services for individuals who might otherwise need to reside in a skilled nursing community.

Some centers offer both types of care, and there are some centers that specialize in Alzheimer's or dementia care, referred to as Alzheimer's day care. Many centers provide transportation to and from the center at no cost or on a per-ride basis.

No matter where an adult day-care center is located in the United States, it is required to have a state license and will have to comply with specific state regulations. If they get any type of public funding, and most do, they will have even more regulations to abide by, but the cost could be subsidized, so ask if they have any free options for income-qualified individuals.

Since this is a group setting, unlike a home health–type setting, the state mandates the staff-to-patient ratios and minimum staffing requirements. Look for one care worker for every six clients. Ideally it would be 1:4, especially if it is an Alzheimer's day-care center, but it could be as high as 1:10. Obviously, the lower the ratio, the better the care.

Here's a quick checklist if you are considering this option:

- Make a list of the care centers in the area you are considering and call them all first.
- Find out if they specialize in dementia care, and if this is not what you need, eliminate them.
- Ask about providing transportation, hours of operation, and the type of participant that usually attends. Most day care centers will

not accept someone who has advanced dementia, is a wander risk, or has advanced mobility issues.

- Ask about the activities they provide and staffing ratios, etc.
- Once you have narrowed the list (if you are lucky enough to have several choices), plan a personal visit *without your parent*. You can concentrate on absorbing all you need to without worrying about Mom or Dad.
- Then go again, with your parent and any other family member, before making a final decision. They will likely have a trial period before making any kind of contractual arrangement. If a person is too disruptive, they may decline to accept them. It has to be a good fit for both.
- Ask if they require a deposit or have some kind of base fee.
- Do they provide a place to rest or nap during the day?
- Some assisted-living communities do provide adult day care but not many, so call and ask.

Who Pays for Adult Day Care?

The question of whether or not Medicare will pay for adult day care is very common and there is much confusion about this. Why? **Because Medicare never pays for any form of adult day care, but certain Medicare/Medicaid combination programs do!** To be clear, a person with **only** Medicare insurance coverage will not receive adult day care as a benefit. If your family member receives **Medicaid**, it will cover adult day care or adult day healthcare. All states are trying their best to keep Medicaid costs down, and one way to do this is to keep people out of skilled nursing homes, which are very expensive. Paying for someone on Medicaid to go to adult day care of any kind will be far less expensive than 24/7 skilled-facility care! Check the rules for your state, or ask any licensed day care what types of payment they accept.

Low-Cost Home and Community-Based Services Through Medicaid

If your parents are on Medicaid (NOT Medicare), they will qualify for free assistance in their home, and each state is a little different. **Medicaid** is an insurance program for low-income persons, and sometimes it will pay for nonmedical home care, home healthcare, and other in-home support to *help individuals remain living in their homes.* However, Medicaid rules are state specific, and therefore eligibility and benefits vary tremendously in every state. Please, **never ever make assumptions about whether your loved one does or does not qualify for Medicaid.** Do not sell a house, spend down your parent's assets, or make any major decisions before talking to a knowledgeable Medicaid counselor, even if you have to pay for it. I promise you it could save you heartache and thousands of dollars. The website medicaid.gov is very informative. Find out what services are offered in your parents' state through Medicaid's home and community-based services (HCBS). These programs help individuals remain living in their homes and communities by providing the necessary support services. In 2022, these funds increased drastically as the issue of aging in place reached national attention. Chapter 13, "Choosing the Best Nursing Home or Skilled Nursing Facility," will provide more information on what Medicare or Medicaid will or won't pay for, and so will Chapter 15, "Medicare, Medicaid, and Paying for Long-Term Care."

Senior Center Options

I am a huge fan of senior centers and have mentioned them in several chapters. If you feel your parents are coping fairly well in their home but are becoming isolated and lonely and just need more social interaction, a senior center may be the perfect solution. Many communities, even small ones, have senior centers where seniors can go and enjoy a variety of activities for little or no cost. Often sponsored by local government or not-for-profit organizations, they offer seniors exercise classes, yoga, arts and crafts activities, education classes, lectures on interesting topics, card games, and yes, even bingo! Usually, they serve one or more meals a day for free or very low cost. They are a fun place for seniors to gather and enjoy each other's company, and the main focus is social interaction with their peers. Many offer classes on health and wellness, and some are even sponsored by local hospitals or home health agencies. There is a staff, but they are not there to babysit or provide care. It's generally assumed that the seniors who come to these senior centers are living independently. Some cities even provide transportation to and from the senior center or provide subsidized Uber rides for qualifying seniors. See what is available near your parents. I have known of very small towns that provide a senior center, so check with the local chamber of commerce in any little town or call the local USAging office and they can tell you.

Think of combining some home care along with a senior center schedule that provides support for your loved one, such as combining a personal care assistant one or two times a week with two days a week at the senior center.

AgeTech Assistance

Just about every day, there are more and better technological aids for all aspects of senior living. Let's look at a few of them.

Robots

A few years ago, no one could have foreseen the degree to which AI (artificial intelligence) and robots of various shapes and sizes would exist to help anyone with a disability or the elderly to age in place. The new generation of "assistive robots" are specifically designed to help anyone live more independently. They can now do everyday tasks like help with laundry, deliver meals to a specific room, or carry things too heavy for someone with limited mobility, or a person who had a stroke and is paralyzed on one side. Watch the videos for products like the Labrador "Caddie" or Labrador "Retriever." As their website states: "Labrador robots are designed to serve as an extra pair of hands, to help move large loads, as well as keep smaller items within reach." You can load the Caddie with a full set of dishes, food, and everything you need to set a dining room table and direct it to the dining room. This relieves the person with limited strength or mobility from trying to carry heavy dishes or food back and forth. These robots will not be available until the second half of 2023, but they are already taking reservations for them. It looks like there will be a first payment of about $1,500, with monthly installments of about $100–$150 for thirty-six months. Total estimated price tag is about $6,500. The company is betting that seniors and their families will pay the price when compared to paying for home care.

ElliQ (elliq.com) is the brainchild of Intuition Robotics, a start-up pioneering social-companion technology company. ElliQ is designed to use machine learning to acquire a person's preferences, behavior, and personality. The robot's mission is to be an "active aging companion," keeping older adults engaged by helping them access and connect to today's technologies, including video chats, online games, social media, and other ways to stay in touch.

ElliQ recommends TED Talks, music, or audiobooks, and suggests physical activities like going for a walk. It's also a personal assistant and reminds users about appointments or taking medications on time. As of now, there is a $250 or so "enrollment fee," with a twelve-month commitment of about forty dollars a month. After one year, you can either cancel or continue with monthly subscription fees. It is emotive, even likable, and designed as a companion.

I am certain these types of devices will become more useful and add an entire new list of options for those who can afford robotic devices to help them maintain their independence or deal with loneliness. There are even AI robot "pets" that are great for people with dementia who want something to hold and snuggle that don't require care.

Medication Reminder Apps and Systems

Did you know that there are 181,000,000 Americans taking prescriptions drugs and a full 50 percent are not taking them correctly? Of this number, 34 percent are over sixty-five, totaling 61,540,000. In fact, on average, adults between the ages of sixty-five and sixty-nine take nearly fourteen prescriptions per year. Those aged eighty to eighty-four take an average of eighteen prescriptions per year! Yikes! No wonder they have issues.

Are your parents on a complex medication schedule? Do you know how many meds they take a day? If they have no cognitive decline, then a simple app could help them (and possibly you) keep track of their medications. It is worth asking how this is going, especially if you have noticed any kind of cognitive decline. Do they seem knowledgeable and sure of their regimen? There are now numerous medication tracking reminder apps on the market, in addition to pill dispensing options. First, ask yourself if your parent will use an app to help them with med reminders and tracking.

The best system with top reviews is called Medisafe (medisafe.com). It has over 3.7 million downloads and is a Google Play Editors' Choice winner, meaning people download it, keep it, and use it. It uses GPS to track the user, so if your loved one is out and about, it will alert them to take their med once they get home.

If your parents don't use apps or would benefit from a dispensing system that organizes, reminds, and notifies, check out seniorsafetyreviews.com for the latest reviews and information.

There are lots of studies about the importance of "medication compliance" and an equal number of studies about how pill dispensing/reminder services don't work. Take a good look at all your options before purchasing anything. If you think your parents may do best with an old-fashioned plastic pill organizer from your local drugstore, then just buy it and see how it works.

One other consideration, if the options above are overkill, is asking your parents' pharmacist if they will organize your parents' meds into blister packs, which groups pills by dose, by day, by week. This is a free service (usually) that allows people to track any medication easily.

Financial Support and Monitoring

There are now multiple choices for families to help parents with tracking and paying bills. Many apps send alerts to an assigned person, often a family member, about bills paid twice, or not paid at all, or large transfers or withdrawals, etc. One app, called Carefull (getcarefull.com) is getting positive reviews. They offer a thirty-day free trial and text alerts for unusual transfers or activity, late payments, excessive donations, identity theft, and more.

When it comes to finances, many parents want their autonomy and are hesitant to admit they need help. I only discovered my own stepfather was having trouble paying his bills when I looked at his checkbook. SilverBills is especially effective because it is not an app, it is concierge bill management. If your parent does not want *your* help, but needs help, this is the perfect solution. Every individual SilverBills (silverbills.com) customer is assigned a US-based professional account manager who they form a relationship with and is a dedicated point of contact. Business is conducted the way most seniors are familiar with: through the phone, mail, email, and text, whatever their preference. They do not even need to own a computer to work with SilverBills, which may be critical for non-tech-savvy parents or grandparents. As a family member, your parent has to grant authorization for you to access this account. Given the amount of financial abuse and exploitation perpetrated by family or on those who have no family, having a full-service company that can relieve an elderly person from managing their bills is a godsend. The cost ranges from $10 to about $100 a month depending on how much service they provide.

Home Food Delivery Options

There are now excellent food delivery options that did not exist only a few years ago. They can solve a big issue for a loved one who needs some temporary help after surgery or who is no longer driving or cooking for themselves. Your parents can't stay healthy if they are eating poorly.

Many companies prepare either heat-and-eat meals or fresh, premade meals you assemble and cook, with all kinds of menu options and diet preferences such as paleo or vegan. **Ask if you have to buy into a plan or sign a contract, and can cancel with no penalty, and if they offer a trial period of some kind.** This will simplify healthy eating and keep your parents well fed! Companies to look up and compare are Home Chef, Factor 75, HelloFresh, Freshly, and more. Search top home food delivery companies to see who has the best reputation in your area.

Other Options

If you are able, you can always cook extra meals and deliver them once a week and put them in the freezer. I have also known acquaintances who pay their mother's neighbors extra money to bring Mom dinner every night. Mom is happy, and the neighbor makes a little extra money.

However, if you see lots of food going bad in Dad's fridge, and he says "There is nothing wrong with that food" because he can't see the mold

---

Meals on Wheels

Meals on Wheels is a national program administered through USAging that has over five thousand local senior nutrition programs in the Unites States and provides over one million meals for free every day to seniors who need them! They deliver to many senior centers, and some programs deliver directly to the senior's home, especially if mobility is limited. If you are told that the program is full and cannot help (often true), call your local USAging office and see if they can help or refer you to another agency that can help provide meals.

growing, you have a problem. Time to get some help in the home and have the home health aide clean the fridge weekly and fix a good lunch or dinner. Ask what would work for them. They might be delighted if dinner was delivered two to three times a week by a local restaurant or delivery service, or a box with pre-assembled ingredients came once a week.

Hiring an Aging Life Care Specialist

Aging life care is the field that used to be known as geriatric case management. The field has grown and now includes those that are senior advocates, educators, planners, as well as those with advanced medical training. Many are Care Manager Certified (CMC) or are a Certified Case Manager (CMM), and have a nursing background. Many have certifications in social work such as Certified Advanced Social Work Care Manager (C-ASWCM). Some Aging Life Care Association members help pay bills and help with insurance claims, take your parents to the doctor, and oversee a care plan. Always call and ask what services an ALCA (Aging Life Care Association) member offers and what they charge.

For example, I specialize in helping people make a plan to age successfully, before a crisis, whether they wish to age in place or find the right senior living community.

If you are having trouble figuring out what your parents need, or need assistance finding the right in-home help, turn to an experienced professional who is not only trained in this area but knows all the local resources to recommend. **I cannot stress enough how much help an aging life care professional can be to a family.**

Look for what you need by visiting the Aging Life Care Association website, aginglifecare.org. Enter your zip code in "Find an Aging Life Care Expert" and likely you will have several candidates to choose from. Because there is so much variety, look for someone who matches your needs. For a parent who has medical issues or requires a lot of help, such as overseeing and coordinating care in the home, look for an ALCA member at the "Advanced Level" who has some kind of care management certification through several national certification associations. Find someone with a social work background if the issues are more emotional or involve difficult family dynamics. Always make sure to ask for references, and ask questions such as:

- What kind of training or education do they have?
- What is their area of expertise?
- How long have they been employed in this field?
- Would they be able to respond in an emergency in the middle of the night?
- Do they charge by the hour, per visit, or require a monthly contract?

Find out the parameters of what they will or won't do, as they vary greatly. The ALCA website is extremely helpful in educating you about how to choose the right member, what questions to ask, and the different levels of membership.

You can expect an initial consultation fee of around $100 to $500 if they are doing an in-person assessment. Most charge hourly and you can expect to pay $80 to $200 an hour depending on location and level of education and experience. **Medicare does not cover these services.** However, think of the potential money you could save by having someone determine your parents' needs, arrange for these services, monitor any staff or agencies, and send you regular reports! Sometimes a one-hour consultation is all you may need. They can make a huge difference in outcomes for you and your parents.

In your absence, an aging life care specialist can:

- Be the communicator between your loved one, the doctor, the hospital, and you;
- Be your eyes and ears and help you keep your sanity;
- Provide some oversight over home care and home healthcare, and report back to you;
- Arrange transportation and accompany your loved one to a doctor's appointment;
- Help you evaluate any aging plans and give you recommendations and referrals;

- Do crisis intervention;
- Pay bills;
- Lead families to "actions and decisions that ensure quality care and an optimal life for those they love, thus reducing worry, stress, and time off work for family caregivers," according to the ALCA website.

No matter what they may be called on to do, they will always look for what is best for the client and try to ensure their well-being, safety, and happiness. ALCA does not allow its members to accept referral fees from facilities so you can count referrals to be unbiased!

When Home Care Is Not Enough

How do you know when home care options aren't working anymore? Usually, it is due to:

- Caregiver burnout
- Increased cognitive decline
- Parent needing a higher degree of nursing or medical attention

Depending on all of the above, you may be looking at either assisted living, memory care, or perhaps even a skilled nursing home. Even with a live-in companion (hired or a family member), there comes a time when higher levels of care and supervision are more than one person can provide. If you have a parent who is now wandering away at night and getting lost, it may be time to consider a secure memory-care neighborhood in an assisted-living environment. If, for example, your parent has multiple complex diagnoses, like advanced congestive heart failure (CHF) or advanced chronic obstructive pulmonary disease (COPD) and is on oxygen, or needs any wound care, this will require a skilled nursing facility, not assisted living. Chapter 13, "Choosing the Best Nursing Home or Skilled Nursing Facility," will provide you with all the information you need about all these higher levels of care, including admission requirements, cost, and how to evaluate any of these facilities.

Chapter 11

The Confusing World of Home Care

Hiring either home care or home healthcare will likely be your first typical solution to helping your parents in their home. It could even be help in *your* home if your parents live with you and you are away at work most of the day. No matter what, you need help navigating this world. Your goal of course is to find a trustworthy, compassionate, and responsible caregiver for your loved one. No matter who you hire, try to interview applicants together with your parents and use the vetting process in this chapter before hiring anyone, either through an agency or privately.

Finding the Right Company

If you have a list, it will help you stay focused. Prioritize the things your parent or parents need assistance with. It could be simple like help with shopping and making meals. It could be help getting out of bed in the morning, getting showered and getting dressed, and taking medications. Knowing this before you contact any kind of company will allow you to call the right company! If a parent needs ongoing wound care, like dressing and changing bandages, shots or IV drugs, or physical, occupational, or speech therapy for any reason, you will be calling home healthcare, *not home care*.

I suggest using the Medicare home health comparison services page at medicare.gov/care-compare/results for finding and researching home health agencies in your area. It is also good for researching any kind of hospital, nursing home or senior care community in the US, and allows you to look up doctors by name, rehab facilities, and more. It is a useful online tool for checking and comparing costs and consumer ratings. There are many companies to choose from, with names like Touching Hearts, Comfort Keepers, Visiting Angels, and plenty more. Just do your home-work first. Here is a helpful hint: the word "agency" (as in nursing agency) usually refers to home healthcare and is not generally applied to a home companion company.

Using a company or an agency does have some advantages, such as pre-screened workers, backup care if a worker becomes sick, and very important, paid-for liability protection. You do not need to worry about payroll taxes or workers' compensation, and complaints can be handled by the agency. However, there are some downsides. You will likely pay more than hiring privately, and you will have to comply with minimum required hours per week, so there's very little flexibility in scheduling.

Hiring Help Privately

If you are not going through an agency, ask friends and neighbors who have employed caregivers for recommendations, names, phone numbers, and hourly rates of those they found to be outstanding. Get specifics. Your neighbors may not have the same needs as you. Here are some suggestions on how to find the right person:

- Consult the community.
- Leave your name and number and the particulars of the job—including needs and hourly wage—with the receptionists at nearby houses of worship, senior centers, local gyms, yoga studios, and community centers.

- **Q** Call your local USAging office and ask if they have recommendations. Local—and sometimes state—employment registries will have lists of available nurses and aides in your area.
- **Q** Call the person directly.

If you live in a small town, and you can find a reliable well-known local person who you think is completely trustworthy, then this is often ideal. They can be more flexible in their work hours and will cost you less per hour.

But beware of the pitfalls of hiring through the community. What is your liability if they are injured on the job? Are they contract labor, self-employed, or will you need to pay and file their taxes? Expect to pay the going market rate for a privately hired helper, perhaps a little less. If you are managing long-distance caregiving, be sure to read Chapter 14 for more tips.

Home Care

The assistants working in home care are usually called PCAs or personal care assistants, or HHAs, home health aides or home care aides. These terms are almost interchangeable. These people are not licensed and have varying levels of experience. Certifications also vary state to state, so ask the company about any certifications or specific training their employees receive. PCAs or HHAs can provide help with everything listed below as part of assistance with ADLs (activities of daily living) or IADLs (instrumental activities of daily living). These services are also referred to as custodial care. Here are the services you can expect from home care, with the key words here being "assistance with":

- **Q** Meal preparation
- **Q** Dressing
- **Q** Bathing
- **Q** Medication reminders
- **Q** Light housekeeping, laundry
- **Q** Shopping
- **Q** Transportation
- **Q** Companionship

If you do not like the HHA assigned to you by a company, it is fine for you to nicely request someone different. However, with the staffing shortages currently being experienced (2022), you may not have much flexibility. I recently worked with a family who lived in a very rural area on a horse farm, and they needed someone unafraid of snakes, horses, dogs, cats, and parrots! The aide was going to be outdoors sometimes, helping the wife, who had cognitive issues but still loved feeding her horses. It took us a while, but we finally found the right person. A company should be willing to work with you to find a good match. It is important to communicate what type of person will likely work best for your loved one. Take the time to write down a good description of your parents' likes and dislikes and preferences, and a general description of who would be compatible. While companies can't discriminate, they are just as eager as you are to find a good match. You should also tell them if your parent smokes, for example, or if you want a nonsmoker, if they have pets, or any other issues that might be problematic.

How Much Does Home Care Cost and Who Pays?

You can view the median hourly wage or annual cost for these types of jobs as well as any home care, home healthcare, or senior living facility anywhere in the United States through the cost of care page at the Genworth website (currently genworth.com/aging-and-you/finances/cost-of-care.html). No matter what, costs are going up due to staffing shortages and so many people leaving the caregiving field after Covid.

The hourly median wage in 2021 for "Homemaker Services" or a "Home Health Aide" is listed as $26–$27 an hour or an average of $4,957–$5,148 a month for a full-time helper. This is typically for more urban areas or high-cost areas. You can expect to pay approximately $18–$20 an hour in most areas, even if hiring someone privately. This is what a home care company will charge you to provide the services listed above, but naturally the worker will get paid less.

I highly recommend the Genworth website, as it will allow you and your family to compare costs from one state to another and even city by city, and they can vary tremendously. This may be a key factor when looking at more than one possible place for your parents to live. The website even has a way to calculate the cost of care in the future with a built-in denominator year over year. Want to see what any kind of long-term care will cost you in twenty years? You'd better be sitting down.

Expect most (not all) companies to have a ***minimum number of hours per day and per week to accept the job.*** Typically, it is four hours a day, and often five days a week. If you call around, you may be able to find a good company (usually not a franchise) that can be more flexible with their policies. Weekend rates or overnight requirements will always be at a higher rate for any home care company, and holidays always cost more.

The Confusion with Medicare

Medicare never pays for nonmedical home care, such as personal care assistants or home health aides. There are many misconceptions around Medicare's benefits for home care because it is so easily confused with Medicaid. Medicare does not pay for nonmedical care, period. This kind of care will *always* be out of pocket, unless there is a long-term care insurance plan that covers these costs, or the current rules change. Not even a Medicare Supplemental insurance plan will cover these services. A good website for looking up information about Medicare versus Medicaid is hhs.gov/answers/medicare-and-medicaid. It gives excellent explanations about who qualifies for Medicaid and Medicare.

Keep reading to find out more about Medicare paying for some *home healthcare and rehabilitation services* after a hospitalization, and my primer on Medicare in Chapter 15.

Medicaid: Clear as Mud

Medicaid will sometimes pay for home care. Be forewarned. Trying to find out if a parent qualifies for Medicaid services is truly daunting. The rules and formulas are so complex and differ so much from state to state that it would be useless for me to give you anything but the most basic information. Funds for Medicaid come from both the federal government and the individual state government. As such, the rules governing Medicaid also come from two sources. The federal government sets certain standards but gives the states flexibility on the services they provide. This is especially true in the area of home care.

Qualifying for Medicaid will open the possibility of Medicaid paying for far more than just home care. Medicaid will pay for some of the following types of care:

- Home care (ADLs and IADLs)
- Home healthcare
- Home modifications
- Adult day care and adult day healthcare
- Therapy services
- Meal delivery
- A personal alert system (PERS—see Chapter 6, "Aging-in-Place Considerations")

Completing all the paperwork and documentation to qualify is very challenging. Seek help if you can. There are some free services to help you through this. Always check with your local USAging office. Another useful website is payingforseniorcare.com. While sponsored by businesses, they have excellent information and a state-by-state guide to Medicaid's home care benefits.

When Medicaid does provide assistance with in-the-home care, it is referred to as "home and community-based services" (HCBS). The most confusing part is that states call this program by all kinds of different names, and each state is responsible for administering and enrolling anyone in these programs. HCBS can be covered under the following possible names: "Regular Medicaid," often called "State Plan Medicaid," or something called "Medicaid Waivers," also called "1915 Waivers" or "HCBS Waivers." A limited number of slots are available and waiting lists are very common.

You can get a list through the state agency administering these programs to find out which companies will even accept Medicaid, as many private companies will not. Expect it will take months to get through the qualifying process, and expect waiting lists, even when your parent is accepted into Medicaid. Medicaid uses a ranking system upon enrollment, and then uses this ranking system to schedule someone in desperate need sooner, placing others on wait lists, sometimes lasting years.

However, as I write this, the current federal administration is proposing a massive nationwide improvement of billions of dollars to home and community-based services. They recognize the desperate need to help elders age in place safely. Only states willing to participate in meeting certain requirements will be eligible. Make sure to check with your local USAging office to see what is currently being offered in your state. They will help guide you through this maze!

Home Healthcare

While home healthcare is associated more with short-term rehabilitation such as after surgery or a hospitalization, companies also provide ongoing longer-term care in the home as well. But there is no question that if your parents need this kind of long-term care, they likely have multiple health issues that place them beyond the services a home care company provides. All home health companies have a full array of licensed, experienced therapists to provide physical, occupational, and speech therapy for their patients. A home healthcare agency also provides licensed nurses, either LPNs (licensed practical nurses) or RNs (registered nurses), as well as CNAs (certified nursing assistants) or LNAs (licensed nursing assistants).

While CNAs may sound like HHAs, they are not. A CNA can take vital signs, set up medical equipment, change dressings, clean catheters, and monitor infections, *as well as help with ADLs*. Licensed nurses do more. They can manage, observe, and evaluate your loved one's care, and can administer IV drugs, tube feedings, and shots, change wound dressings, and provide caregiver education and training. RNs have a nursing diploma, more advanced training, and can assist doctors in medical procedures, as well as all the above.

As a result of the initial assessment of the older person that all home health companies do, they will assign the right helper who not only can provide the care needed but is properly licensed and experienced in doing so.

How Much Does Home Healthcare Cost and Who Pays?

Remember, Medicare *doesn't pay* for an in-home caregiver when custodial care services like housekeeping and personal care are all you need. Medicare *does pay* for home health services like physical, occupational, or speech therapy; skilled nursing care; and social services if you're "homebound" after surgery, an illness, or an injury. Your doctor will need to certify that the services are "medically necessary," and your home health agency must be Medicare certified. Chapter 13 provides more information on these definitions as they apply to short-term rehab care.

If you are hiring home healthcare for *long-term ongoing care*, you will pay out of your pocket. You can expect hourly fees for nurses to range from $25 to $125 an hour, depending on skill, location, and availability. The median hourly wage in 2022 for an LPN was $24.80 according to the US Bureau of Labor Statistics, and $36.80 for an RN. Expect a similar range for any kind of therapy outside of Medicare guidelines. Most home healthcare companies require a minimum number of hours a day and per week to accept assignment. They will not come for an hour a day or one day a week. They need a schedule with enough hours to hire good staff. An excellent web page to check current costs is aarp.org/caregiving/home-care.

The Spencers Need Home Healthcare and Home Care!

Remember I mentioned in Part I that Josie's dad, Bob, had a stroke? What happened? Sally called 911 when she noticed one side of Bob's face drooping and he was having trouble speaking. The EMTs arrived and whisked him to the nearest hospital. Sally followed behind with her copy of his living will and healthcare surrogate forms, plus a list of all his current medications. They ran some tests and the doctor confirmed he'd had a moderately debilitating stroke. Bob was in the hospital for three nights (so most costs were covered by Medicare! See Chapter 15) and was discharged to a rehab facility to begin physical therapy (PT) immediately, since he had right-sided weakness. He was there for one week and discharged to his home. His doctor ordered PT follow-up as well as speech therapy through a home healthcare company three times a week and a nurse to monitor his new medication regimen that included blood thinners. Sally appreciated the occupational therapist (OT) who also came soon after Bob returned home. The OT recommended removing some throw rugs and the kitty litter box, and she tried to "fall proof" the house and showed Bob the safe way to take a shower. She was happy to see they had already added grab bars, a walk-in shower, and a raised toilet! Sally and Bob practiced exactly what he needed to do to get in and out of the shower safely (and the OT showed Sally how she could assist him). During this time, Medicare covered many of these expenses and his supplemental policy covered the rest. After three weeks, he was discharged from home healthcare. Bob was much improved, and with PT he learned the exercises to do at home to keep improving. He was still eligible through Medicare to continue with outpatient PT for several more weeks. However, Sally, who was preparing for the move to Raleigh, and now doing caregiving and all household chores and cooking, was overwhelmed. Josie contacted a home care company and hired a home health aide who helps with chores around the house, makes lunch, and assists Sally with shopping and getting Bob to and from PT and other doctor appointments. The Spencers paid out of pocket for this care.

Key Questions When Hiring a Home Care or Home Healthcare Expert

You should compare and research agencies in your area by using the Medicare guide to hiring an agency, checking with your local USAging office and website, and asking all your friends who they recommend. You can also ask advice from an aging life care specialist, as they will know the community. AARP has a good list of what to look for when hiring any kind of help and is a tremendous resource for senior care issues.

Consider asking the following questions before you sign an agency contract.

Licensing and Business Questions

- How long has the agency been in business?
- Is the business a franchise, and who are the legally listed owners?
- May I see a copy of your contract?
- Is your agency licensed by the state, and if so, what exactly is the license?
- Does your company have a list of references or quality-control reports by an outside agency? Which agency (state or national) oversees you?

Services Provided

- What services do you offer?
- Are services available twenty-four hours a day, seven days a week?
- Who does the *initial* assessment? What are their qualifications? Is there a fee?
- Could you provide a caregiver immediately?
- How often does your company communicate with family members about patient status? Is it written or a phone call?
- How does the agency handle complaints or issues that arise?
- Is there a written plan of care for each patient? (That's more likely with home healthcare.) How often is the plan updated?
- Will you email this plan to us weekly or monthly, whenever it is updated?
- How do you handle a patient emergency? Call 911, the family, etc.?
- Will you honor a DNR (do not resuscitate) or POLST (Physician Orders for Life-Sustaining Treatment), if applicable?

Staffing

- Do you employ RNs, LPNs, physical therapists, occupational therapists? (Home healthcare only.)
- Do you employ home health aides or personal assistants? What training do your home health aides receive?
- What kind of background checks and drug tests do you do?
- Who supervises the staff?
- Are all your workers bonded and insured?
- Does your staff rotate, or can I request the same person or the staff member that my parent prefers?
- What happens if a staff member does not show up?
- Are all employees covered by workers' compensation?
- What benefits do you provide your staff?

Costs

- What are the rates? Is there a minimum number of required hours?
- How do the rates vary depending on time of day or night, or type of staff employed?
- Are rates higher for holidays?
- Can I cancel my contract anytime? Is there a required notification? Is there a cancellation fee of any kind?
- Do you notify me of any rate increases prior this happening?

The questions above are an excellent start to weeding out companies you do not want to work with. Don't forget that any hospital or nursing home discharge planner is a good person to ask about referrals. They won't recommend one company, but they should feel comfortable giving you a list. You can press them on who they would hire for their own mother! Many hospitals have their own skilled nursing agency and may point you in that direction. While it may be the easiest option, it may not be the best choice.

Covid Questions

Since it appears Covid will be with us for the foreseeable future, it is worth including some obvious and not-so-obvious questions to ask. Sadly, I have heard from numerous clients that healthcare workers showed up to care for a loved one without being vaccinated. Make sure to ask if the company *requires vaccinations* for all home care workers. It has cost the lives of several people I know, including a CNA who was not vaccinated and contracted Covid from a family he was caring for.

- What PPE (personal protective equipment) are you using? Do you provide it for all your staff and pay for it?
- How often is staff required to refresh their PPE?
- What infection-control training and policies are you practicing?
- If a staff person tests positive, what is your policy?
- If another patient tests positive who is being cared for by one of your staff, is staff required to test immediately or quarantine?
- What reports are you required to give to your state (or federal) agency and is this information public? Can I have a copy?

Depending on what you learn from the questions above, you can move forward or not with considering this agency.

When Your Parents Need More than Home Care Can Provide

There may come a point when even home care is not enough, no matter how hard you and your family have tried. It can be a very difficult decision emotionally for everyone to come to this determination. But if your situation is destroying your marriage, or your family, all of which I have seen, it may be time to look at other options.

I had a client who had promised her mother, as she was dying, she would never place her father in a nursing home. She moved her father in with her family, but as his dementia worsened, she knew she had to make a change. Even though she had home care during the day while she worked, her father was beginning to wander at night, and no one was getting any sleep. Her teenage children were suffering, her husband was becoming resentful, and her stress level was out of sight. With the help of some counseling and support, she made the decision to move Dad and learned there were other options besides a nursing home. She found out about memory care in assisted living after reading Chapter 12, an option she did not even know existed.

No matter what your situation, most families don't have the time or resources to provide twenty-four-hour care. Rare is the son or daughter who moves across the country to provide this level of care, but bless those willing and able. I have heard from some families that this was impossibly difficult and others who told me it was a spiritual opportunity and a gift. The next few chapters will educate you on the care available within assisted living and skilled nursing care facilities, what to expect as far as cost, and how you can make the wisest choices for your family, whatever they may be, now and for the future.

Avoiding Family Conflict

One of the most frequent family issues that contributes to family conflict is when the primary caregiver involved in the day-to-day care and/or management is judged by the absent family members as somehow not doing the job right. And often, the absent relatives have no hesitation in telling their sibling what they are doing wrong without knowing all the facts. This is so problematic that it is often the first complaint I hear from families.

Here are some basic guidelines for everyone involved that might help avoid this type of conflict:

1. For the caregiver or care manager, Skype, call, or email regularly with family. Keep everyone up to date on your parent's medical condition, test results, etc. Share as much information as possible. Be transparent. Get copies of medical results and scan them so other family members can see all the information you have.

2. If possible, have Mom or Dad Skype with other family members so it is apparent how they are doing, without you needing to describe things. Including your parent as much as possible will keep them feeling part of the decision-making and part of the family.

3. As the caregiver, ask for input. Do not be the only one making decisions, unless it is an emergency and you have no choice.

4. If you are the out-of-town sibling, don't assume that you really know how Mom or Dad is behaving unless you have been with them for a minimum of four to five days *recently*.

5. Trust the caregiver to have the most accurate picture of how your parent is doing. Stay inquisitive and try to avoid making judgmental statements.

6. Be willing to listen to each other. Get together as frequently as possible and compare notes. What did you each observe on the last visit? How has the situation changed?

7. Offer the caregiver respite care on a regular basis. Set up a firm schedule so they will know that they will have down-time once a week, once a month, a week off, etc. If you are *sure* you can't do this yourself because of your job, then offer, if possible, to help pay for some kind of respite care. This may mean using your vacation days or paid time off!

8. If you are the caregiver, no one can take care of you if you won't take care of yourself. Give yourself permission to take time off and to ask for help. Don't suffer in silence. If you end up in the hospital, you will be no help to anyone.

Many long-distance family members feel guilty that they are not there to help, and this often brings out judgment and fear. They criticize because they fantasize they could do a better job. I've witnessed family feuds that result in siblings never talking to each other again. I have also met some very resentful caregivers; but in their defense, they may be exhausted and at the end of their rope. However, being told by out-of-town family that they should be doing things differently never helps. No one appreciates second-guessing or backseat driving. The critical factor is, as usual, open communication and sharing of responsibilities.

Chapter 12

Assisted-Living Facilities (ALFs)

When your family has reached the point that no amount of home care is working, it may be time to consider assisted living. Most families cannot afford 24/7 care, and assisted living offers a more affordable option. Often a loved one can no longer live alone, and their adult children are unable to provide the care they now need. For the vast majority of working families, staying home or relocating to care for a parent is simply not an option. Going back to Principle #1, *helping a parent maintain their independence*, assisted living provides the support and care needed in a far less restrictive environment than skilled nursing, or what used to be known more commonly as a nursing home. The goal of all assisted-living communities is to treat residents with dignity and provide a high quality of life that allows for privacy, choice, and autonomy.

For many years, I did in-home admission assessments as the administrative director of an assisted-living community. I frequently saw lonely elderly widows or widowers in lovely large homes, using only their bedroom, bathroom, and kitchen. When they moved to an assisted-living community, in a small but comfortable apartment (not so different from the actual square footage they utilized at home), they received the help they needed, and they often flourished. Suddenly they had new friends, new stimuli, and new activities, plus assistance.

Ideal Candidates for Assisted Living

The ideal candidate for assisted living is someone who needs help with their ADLs and IADLs or belt buckle. For instance, the ability to bathe and groom oneself independently, toilet independently, dress oneself, and do basic homemaking tasks like prepare meals, manage money, shop, use the telephone, and, most importantly, take medications on schedule.

These are the types of services you can expect from an assisted-living facility. As you can see, none of the tasks listed require twenty-four-hour nursing-level care. Assistance with any of the activities of daily living might allow someone to stay out of a nursing home for several years or altogether if they are lucky!

With this in mind, assisted-living facilities are far "homier" than skilled nursing care. Residents furnish their own apartment, bring personal items, and can hang art on the walls, unlike most nursing homes. Most apartments have kitchenettes with microwaves and refrigerators, but rarely a full kitchen. Three meals a day are provided in a dining room, as well as access to snacks and beverages. More upscale ALFs will have a full menu. Assistance to and from the dining room can be provided if needed. For many seniors, not having to shop and prepare meals is a blessing, and an important part of staying healthy is good nutrition.

All housekeeping is taken care of, and most facilities have laundry rooms allowing residents or caregivers to do personal laundry. A few are pet friendly for smaller dogs and cats.

Residents are not sick or incapable people, and the environment in assisted living is very different than skilled care. They may be a bit frail or even confused, but given the right helping hand, they can do very well on their own for years. Just imagine having someone help you dress (you can't manage a zipper or buttons or fastening your bra because of arthritis or a stroke), shower (you're afraid of falling like the last time), take your meds (you mixed up your meds and ended up in the hospital), and being on call all night if you need help!

Assisted-Living Basics

The first assisted-living community was opened in the late 1970s as an alternative to the hospital-like setting of skilled nursing facilities, aiming for a more homelike residential setting. Assisted living has become one of the fastest-growing long-term care options for seniors in the United States; one, because it is much less expensive than skilled nursing, and two, because it is a much homier option. There are now over 31,000 communities nationwide, serving over one million seniors, and this number is expected to grow.

The industry as a whole has gone through many transformations. Wall Street invested heavily in assisted living from about 1995 through 2000, and assisted living exploded. Buildings became bigger, communities larger, and services and amenities increased. The average community still serves about thirty-five to forty residents, with larger ones serving three hundred or more residents.

Communities vary tremendously from simple mom-and-pop settings with only a few residents to luxurious multistoried buildings. Expect most to offer various apartment floor plans to choose from, such as studio, studio alcove, and one- and two-bedroom apartments. The size of the apartment and apartment features, such as a kitchen or private patio or balcony, factor into the monthly rate, as does the location of the apartment with regard to views and proximity to elevators (a plus for someone with mobility issues) and easily accessed public areas. Trends in 2022 appear to be offering luxury high-end assisted living in urban areas that resemble first-class hotels, for those who can afford it!

The majority of residents in assisted living are in their mid-eighties, and 71 percent are women. There are always more women in almost any retirement community since statistically, women live longer than men. There are usually no age restrictions of any kind in assisted living, and I have seen people in their thirties living in an assisted-living facility due to a serious car accident or chronic condition.

You might be surprised at the differences between facilities, as some cater to more capable independent seniors, and some have a frailer population. Each facility is unique. About 70 percent of residents have some kind of memory impairment, ranging from mild to severe. For what I like to call "the pleasantly confused," basic assisted living is perfect. Someone with MCI or mild cognitive impairment would do well in assisted living.

Expect most assisted-living facilities to have ample public spaces such as living rooms, libraries, meeting rooms, specialized exercise and activity rooms, and nice dining rooms for use by all the residents. There are often many activities/classes to choose from such as exercise, chair yoga, bridge groups, movie nights, and more. Ask to see their activity calendar and which of the staff provides classes/activities. Special activities for those with severe memory impairment are also offered. If this level of care applies to your loved one, ask about what kinds of activities are offered.

You can always get a list of all the licensed ALFs in your area by visiting the USAging website, as well as check up on any facility by visiting seniorliving.org/assisted-living, another excellent resource for any senior issue or concern.

Remember, if you are working with someone from ALCA (Aging Life Care Association), they will know the area and know which facilities to recommend. Members of this association do not accept referral fees, so their advice is based solely on their experience, unlike some of the national referral agencies that depend on large referral fees, and whose opinions might be influenced.

Specialized Memory Care

Many ALFs have specialized memory-care neighborhoods, set apart from other residents, and some ALFs are strictly for those with memory impairment. Generally, these neighborhoods or specialized ALFs cater to a more confused resident who needs a great deal of help and supervision, or who may be at risk for wandering away. The term "secure" is often used for this level of care. Often there is a code to unlock entry doors, and only staff and family are given this code. Residents are not allowed to leave these areas unless they are accompanied by staff or an authorized person so they cannot wander away.

Ideally, look for a memory-care area that offers access to a secure outside space that residents can safely visit but not "escape." These memory-care areas/facilities have higher staffing ratios, specialized training, and ideally the same staff is assigned to this neighborhood without rotation so they can get to know the residents! Specialized memory care will always be more expensive than traditional assisted living, usually about 20 percent to 30 percent more in monthly fees.

Bob and Sally Spencer Revisited

It's been three years since Bob and Sally moved into Maple Village, a full life care community in Raleigh, NC. They are very happy; they love the community, and they have made many wonderful friends. Living near Josie and Dan and the grandchildren has been great. Out of state family John, Sophia, and Wendy enjoy their visits, and they can even stay in the guest rooms at Maple Village or with their parents in their apartment.

But life throws another curveball and Bob has another stroke. He goes to the hospital, followed by rehab for a few weeks, only this time he can utilize the PT on-site at Maple Village, since they offer full rehab services identical to what is described in Chapter 13 on skilled nursing facilities. He recovers enough to return to their apartment in independent living, but he still needs help with things like dressing and showering. Sally is seventy-nine now, and Bob is almost eighty-two, and he needs more help than Sally can provide. Bob and Sally talk it over and decide together that it is time for him to move to a smaller apartment in the assisted-living area at Maple Village where he can get all the help he needs, such as assistance with dressing and bathing, and help at night to get up and go to the bathroom safely. Sally will stay in the apartment in independent living. She can easily walk to his smaller apartment in the assisted-living wing to see Bob. The community helps move some of the Spencers' furniture into his apartment, and he likes having a little kitchenette so he can still eat ice cream every night! Bob can join Sally in their old apartment any time, or she can join him in the assisted-living dining room. He can even spend the night in the apartment on occasion when he feels up to it.

He continues with physical therapy at Maple Village, but he understands he will likely stay in assisted living for the foreseeable future. He is grateful that he and Sally can still be together much of the time, but the burden of care does not fall on either Sally or Josie. And Sally does not need to drive to see him. Sally can sleep at night knowing he is taken care of and she can see him whenever she wants.

Advantages of Assisted Living in a Life Care Community

Despite the fact that the Spencers are living in a life care community, everything about assisted living still applies for our story. You may remember from Chapter 8 that in a life care community, residents start in independent living but have the option of moving into assisted living or skilled nursing care when their needs increase. Even if Bob and Sally were living in their own home, and the same scenario occurred, Bob could move into a stand-alone assisted-living facility to receive the same level of care as he is receiving in Maple Village.

If you are lucky enough to have a life care community nearby, like the fictitious Maple Village in the Spencer story, this could be ideal. Why? Many life care communities offer direct admission into their assisted-living areas, usually without charging any kind of entry fee. An entry fee is typically charged only if a person begins in independent living first and is on a specific contract that often reduces cost of care at higher levels. However, as mentioned earlier, some life care communities have begun charging much lower entry fees for admission into assisted living. A person moving straight into assisted living can access assisted living initially but could move to both memory care and skilled nursing if this becomes necessary. This means your loved one can transfer to a higher level of care *without making an additional move to a new community*. Expect to pay the normal market rate, and just like any ALF, it could be an all-inclusive monthly fee or a fee based on the level of care needed by your loved one.

Cost of Assisted Living: It Can Be Confusing!

In 2022, the national average cost of care in assisted living was $4,300 a month for a small studio-type apartment, usually about five hundred square feet. Costs vary from state to state with Alaska, Delaware, and New Jersey currently the highest, at over $6,000–$7,000 a month, and Missouri at the lowest, charging about $3,000 per month. Keep this in mind if your family is considering several states. Some assisted-living facilities have one inclusive fee for all support services, but many use a model that charges by the services needed, based on an initial assessment prior to admission. These are often referred to as "levels of care" or "tiered services." As you'd expect, the larger the apartment and the more services needed, the higher the monthly fee will be.

The cost of assisted living is not always obvious for families. Don't assume the amount you are quoted on the phone by the marketing office is representative of what you will pay. The financial model most assisted-living facilities use is based on the resident's level-of-care needs. Fees for the basic services are set at a flat rate but go up for any additional services. This flat rate is what you may hear first when you call to inquire. Find out what is and is not included. Basics (or Level 1) may be meals and housekeeping only, but extra services like medication management, or help dressing and bathing, result in additional fees. Some ALFs go up to a Level 6 for those in memory care needing help with everything. For every "extra" service provided, there will be an additional cost added monthly to the flat fee. Keep in mind that a "Level 6" assessment could add another $2,000 a month to the base rate!

Make a list of what your loved one needs in the way of help, and make sure it is realistic! No ALF can admit a person who does not meet the state admission guidelines, so you should anticipate a full assessment in person or virtually. Don't choose a community or base your cost projection on your family member's *current needs*. Take into consideration that these fees will probably go up as a person's needs increase. You don't want to have to move your family member if the cost becomes too high. If your mom or dad is still fairly independent, it makes sense to choose a facility that starts with a base rate. It does not make economic sense to pay for services your parents don't need.

However, if your family member is already frail or has a progressive condition, some people feel it makes more sense to pay more for an all-inclusive approach to services. This means one monthly fee that already includes help with any ADLs. Depending on the age of your family member, do a cost projection and ask the facility about annual increases and factor this in. Ask for a five-year history to get an idea of annual percentage increases.

If your loved one has a long-term care policy, make sure to check and see if it covers assisted living, and what "daily benefit" is allowed for care, which should always be listed on the "schedule of benefits" page. Almost all long-term care policies written in the last twenty years will cover assisted living. An older policy may use words like "custodial care." These policies will reimburse your parent, not pay the facility directly, but the ALF can give you statements to use for reimbursement. Please see Chapter 15, "Medicare, Medicaid, and Paying for Long-Term Care," for more information on long-term care insurance.

Surprise or Additional Costs

Most ALFs charge a "community fee" that is nonrefundable when first applying. These fees are usually about $1,500 to $5,000. I am told they cover the cost of handling an admission, which can be time consuming for the staff. I have never heard of a community waiving this fee, but some are willing to finance it and break it up into two or three amounts over time. This community fee may be on the higher end for placement in a specialized memory-care neighborhood. Also, if a couple is moving in, the community will charge a second community fee for the second person, but usually it is less than the initial full fee.

Expect a separate second-person monthly fee for a couple of any kind. This could be two friends who choose to live together, two sisters, or a traditional or nontraditional couple. For example, if the basic monthly rate for a one-bedroom is $4,300, the second-person fee might be $1,600 and up. Typically, this second-person fee is significantly lower than the first. This fee will include meals, housekeeping, and maybe laundry. Even if the second person is totally independent and just wants to live in the ALF so they can be with their spouse or partner, they are required to complete an admission form. If they do need assistance, they will be assessed separately and charged accordingly.

Always make sure to read the entire contract before signing it or having your parent sign. Ideally, an attorney or someone knowledgeable in the business will read it and can advise you. Most ALFs charge only month to month and not on a lease basis. Sometimes, as a "move-in special," they will offer not to increase the rent for one year. Read the fine print; it will likely show a return in a year to "then current" rents including prior rent increases you avoided because of the special move-in deal. It won't hurt to ask if they have any discount offers or move-in incentives prior to a move, such as first month free.

Here are some additional fees to expect:

- Cable TV and internet, although a few may include these.
- Any supplies like incontinence products.
- Laundry is usually extra if the staff is washing and folding clothes; otherwise, a family usually has access to washing machines and dryers they can use.
- If a community is pet friendly, they will have some kind of additional monthly pet fee plus size limitations or an up-front damage fee.

Paying for Assisted Living

Most people do not realize that typically Medicare *does not cover any costs in assisted living*. You should expect all ALF costs will be out-of-pocket expenses, with very few exceptions. In some states, Medicaid offers what is known as a "Medicaid waiver" program, and it is designed to help those who meet Medicaid low-income guidelines, and who would otherwise be forced to live in a skilled nursing home. The state "waives" their usual non-payment for assisted-living facilities and agrees to pay a set amount toward the cost. States eager to keep long-term care costs down are willing to pay for less expensive care in assisted living, provided this person meets admission guidelines. Many families are forced to place a loved one in skilled nursing care, even though they don't need this level of care, because Medicaid will help pay for this. These waiver programs are limited, but again, don't make assumptions about what your state offers or if your parent qualifies. Seek guidance from your local USAging office or seek the counsel of a Medicaid waiver expert. And of course, you can ask any ALF if they are a Medicaid-certified assisted living facility or if they accept a Medicaid waiver. Many Medicaid-certified facilities aren't allowed to charge more than the federal Supplemental Security Income (SSI) rate plus any state supplement for room and board. (SSI is a federal income supplement program designed to help aging, blind, and disabled people who have little or no income. Check out ssa.gov/ssi for helpful information on the SSI program.) **ALFs are absolutely not required to accept Medicaid waivers, and many do not.** I suggest you go visit ALFs that do accept Medicaid waivers and see what you think. Look for a smaller, more rural setting and you may have some good options.

I recently helped a family decide to move Mom closer to her son in Louisiana when I discovered Louisiana offered assisted-living payments under an expanded Medicaid waiver program. The mom had very few resources and had she stayed in Florida, where this program is very limited, she would have had far fewer options. Check out medicaidwaiver.org or CMS.gov (the online home of the Centers for Medicare and Medicaid Services) to see what programs are offered under the waiver options.

These services also can include home care services and more. Keep in mind that these programs can be funded and unfunded by the government and change all the time, so make sure your information is current. This may be a critical factor in choosing the best place financially for a parental move if paying for assisted living is a concern.

Another good website comparing costs state by state for assisted living (besides the Genworth cost of care survey already mentioned) is consumeraffairs.com/assisted-living/statistics.html.

Licensing and Oversight of Assisted Living

All assisted-living facilities are required to be licensed in the state they operate in. It varies so much that you will have to check with the state. Licensing goes by different names. Just remember that these licenses protect you and your loved one because they hold the ALF accountable. They must comply with state law and provide the staff and services required, and are subject to oversight through the state they operate in.

In Florida, there are four types of licenses:

- Standard, which can provide help with ADLs or activities of daily living;
- Limited nursing or LNS, which can provide a higher level of care discussed below;
- LMH (limited mental health), a license that allows a facility to provide memory care or care for other mental health issues;
- ECC or extended congregate care, which allows for the highest level of care allowed in an ALF in Florida. This license can be of critical importance to you and your family, as you will discover later in the chapter.

I list Florida's licenses because Florida is one of the states with the strictest licenses and admission criteria and will give you a framework to compare. In some states, there is only one license, and regulations are loosely written, but the care allowed may be more minimal. Often states issue licenses based on the allowable number of residents, such as "family care," from one to five residents; "small group," from one to twelve; "large group homes," from thirteen to twenty; and "congregate," twenty-one residents and up. States with large populations of seniors like Florida, New York, and California will have multiple licenses with different names.

It is a good idea for your loved one if an ALF has some kind of "limited nursing services," or something similar. In New York, for example, the similar license is called the "EALR" or "Enhanced Assisted Living Residence" license, and the "SNALR" is the "Special Needs Assisted Living Residence" license required to provide memory care. These licenses will allow a facility to meet the needs of your loved one as their needs increase and change!

With an LNS license, you can ask to see progress reports, scope and outcome of services provided to your family member, and general status of health in a written format.

Larger ALFs, especially those owned by large corporations, will usually have an expanded nursing license so they can keep residents longer as their needs increase. This helps with occupancy (translate: monthly fees) and allows a resident to "age in place" longer. But let me also point out that with staffing shortages and salary increases, a larger number of ALFs are opting for more standard licenses and no nurses on staff, only nursing assistants or personal care aides. The theory is that this will help keep costs down and make ALFs more affordable for more seniors. Should a resident need more help, they could hire home healthcare through Medicare (or private pay), as well as therapy services, and the burden of this cost does not fall on the ALF staff, timewise or costwise. It will be up to you to decide which model you prefer for your loved one.

In Florida, if a small mom-and-pop business has five or fewer residents, they can operate under an "Adult Family Care Home" or AFCH license and can offer personal care on a twenty-four-hour basis to either disabled adults or frail elders who are not relatives. These types of arrangements are more affordable and could be ideal for your loved one. You can get a list of licensed smaller care homes from your local USAging office.

The state agency providing oversight for any ALF varies from state to state, but often it is the Department of Health or Aging or Elder Affairs. Also look for Regulation and Licensing, or Division of Long-Term Care, and many more! In Florida, the Department of Elder Affairs works hand in hand with the Agency for Healthcare Administration (ACHA). All of these agencies are responsible for making sure that assisted-living facilities comply with state guidelines.

These various oversight agencies typically conduct surveys every twelve to twenty-four months to ensure ALFs are complying with the laws that govern these facilities. The agency will look at patient care and well-being, and a host of other criteria. Facilities are scored, deficiencies are noted (some far worse than others), and citation reports are published and submitted to the facility. Facilities must take corrective measures to address anything serious. Look for this kind of information through the agency that oversees the facilities in your state. You can also request this information from any facility, such as "statements of deficiencies" or "regulatory citations."

ALFs are not required to have a medical director/doctor on staff, unless the ALF is part of a life care community that also has a licensed skilled nursing care wing. This is because only a licensed skilled nursing care facility is required to have a doctor on staff due to the more complex care offered. Some smaller ALFs will not employ a nurse at all, as I said, but large ones usually have an LPN or RN as director of nursing (DON) to oversee and manage nursing staff, as well as a licensed administrator who oversees the entire facility. Ideally for larger ALFs, there is an LPN on *each shift* overseeing nursing assistants of some kind, but this is becoming more and more difficult to find.

Why an Extended Care License Could Be Critical

A critical question to ask an ALF is this: Do you have any kind of license that allows you to deliver a higher level of care to your residents? It allows an ALF to meet the medical needs of a person that go beyond the guidelines for just a normal ALF or LNS license as described above. With this type of license, staff can provide "total care" with activities of daily living, not just assistance with personal care. Why might this be very important? Because it could mean you won't have to move your parent if they develop a medical condition that would otherwise require you to transfer them out of the ALF. This alone could save your family thousands of dollars since an ALF is typically less expensive than skilled nursing care, unless your loved one qualifies for Medicaid.

Some ALFs have an extended license so they can keep their occupancy up and allow a resident to age in place longer. Many don't because residents needing more care may require more staff. Without an ECC, you may be shopping for a skilled nursing home sooner rather than later. If your loved one exceeds even the ECC guidelines, then they will have to move to a skilled nursing facility that is prepared to handle a higher level of care, or come up with another option.

Admission Requirements

All licensed ALFs are required to do an initial assessment before accepting any new resident. Any oversight agency wants to be sure the ALF can meet the needs of a new resident and is not accepting someone who needs a higher level of care. However, admission requirements vary from state to state. In Florida a person cannot need help with more than four ADLs, but in some states, it may be limited to help in one or two ADLs.

In Florida, the person's doctor must fill out and sign what is called an 1823 form before an ALF can admit the person. It will likely be called something else in other states, but it is an admission form that is usually several pages long and asks the doctor to evaluate and score the person in their care. Expect most states to use a similar form. Forms will generally ask about the following:

- **Ambulation:** How well does this person walk? Do they use a cane, a walker?
- **Bathing:** Do they bathe independently, or do they need standby or total help?

- **Dressing:** Do they need help with dressing, tying shoes, etc.?
- **Eating:** How well can they feed themselves? (This is not meal prep.)
- **Self-care:** Do they brush their teeth, comb their hair, stay clean?
- **Toileting:** Can they go to the bathroom, or do they need help? Are they incontinent?
- **Transferring and mobility:** Can they easily get up and down from a chair and in and out of bed? Walk to the bathroom safely? Do they use a walker or cane?
- **Diet:** Do they have any special needs like no or low sugar, no or low salt, or an allergy?

In addition, they will also assess how well the person performs IADLs. The Florida form asks a doctor to either check "independent," "needs supervision," or "needs assistance" with the following:

- Preparing meals
- Medication management
- Shopping
- Making phone calls
- Handling personal affairs
- Handling financial affairs

Most forms require the doctor to list all medications, medical history and hospitalizations, allergies, cognitive and behavioral concerns, and any nursing or therapy services needed that might make a person unsuitable for residing in an ALF.

Understand that a higher score often means *a lower level of independence*. The doctor will either recommend placement or they may not. A staff member from the ALF must personally meet the prospective resident and perform their own evaluation. It typically takes several days to go through the admission process. If your loved one cannot do an in-person assessment, the ALF may allow a virtual assessment. An ALF can deny placement to any resident based on their conclusion that they cannot meet the needs of the person, if the person is simply inappropriate for congregate living or if the level of care they require exceeds the ALF's licensing restrictions.

Admission Restrictions

Keep in mind that it is state laws that set admission guidelines for assisted living, not the facility! No one wants an assisted-living facility to accept someone whose needs they can't meet. If a person scores too high on this admission form, or they need help in more than four ADLs, the doctor or the facility may feel the person needs skilled nursing. If your loved one is wheelchair bound, truly bedridden, has any pressure sores, or is unable to transfer without major assistance, they will not be accepted. This list is not meant to be complete, but hopefully, this will give you an idea if your loved one is appropriate for assisted living.

ALFs are usually not equipped to handle psychiatric patients, unless they have their specialty license called the LMHS or limited mental health services. If your loved one has any history of sexual or behavioral issues or could pose a danger to themself or others, they will not be accepted. Have they ever hit a staff person or another resident? Do they have angry outbursts or throw things? Due to the liability and the fear of staff or other residents being injured, the facility won't take the chance. Sometimes these behaviors can be modified through medications and the facility might accept the person if they have the correct license to do so.

Choosing an ALF

Make a list of the communities you are considering and drop in on a weekend first, with no appointment. Talk with several visiting family members, and you will learn a great deal about the facility. If you like what you hear, schedule a formal tour with marketing. Save yourself some time and call first to see what their availability is and how you are treated on the phone. Please note: I have a far more extensive list in the next chapter about choosing a nursing home that is also applicable to assisted living, so be sure to read it. See "Questions to Ask When Touring Any Senior Community or Facility" at starbradbury.com/resources as well.

If you live long distance, consider asking for a virtual tour, since Covid forced all marketing people to develop one. If it is simply impossible for you to visit, consider hiring a geriatric case manager or aging life care consultant to explore your options. You need a local independent expert who can guide you through this process. I do this for families and provide detailed reports for their consideration.

During Covid, almost every state kept current data for Covid cases, and I would advise you to check and see how any facility did. Agencies providing oversight will also have this data. Also, look at the CDC website. As long as Covid remains an issue, expect facilities to require a Covid-free test prior to any move, as well as proof of vaccination in most states. If positive, but without symptoms, expect a fourteen-day quarantine upon move-in and a retest.

According to the Covid Tracking Project, by mid-2021 there had been 418,463 Covid cases and 73,478 deaths nationwide in skilled care and assisted living combined. You want to choose an assisted-living facility and skilled nursing home that has a history of handling Covid with minimal infections, not with a high percentage of deaths for both staff and residents.

I predict many companies will be in financial trouble and may want to get out of the business altogether. They will be required to spend more money to ensure proper staffing, proper training and PPE (personal protection equipment) for staff, increased infection control, and possibly massive remodeling to allow for less crowding. All of this means a volatile senior living industry, and difficulty getting into the better facilities.

Who Owns or Manages the Facility?

Sometimes there are layers of what I will refer to as "responsible parties." I have discovered that a building can be under a management contract, but owned by an REIT, or Real Estate Investment Trust. The REIT is the responsible party for the upkeep and overall maintenance of the building proper, but the staff is hired under the management contract. Some of the largest assisted-living companies in the country have divested themselves of property to try and stay profitable. Large numbers of buildings have been bought up by REITs, which have no interest in staffing or management per se. They will partner with a management company that has a history of running a profitable building. They may be trying to make a building profitable so they can sell it in a few years. Pull back the curtain and take a closer look.

The REIT may be willing to pour money into maintaining the building. I saw this recently when an older ALF bought by a REIT received new carpets, new paint, and remodeled bathrooms, etc. But this particular ALF had changed hands many times in the last five to six years and was not particularly well run. Since this book was written, it has changed yet again. Constant changes in either ownership or management are not good signs. Do some homework and ask the administrator (not necessarily the marketing person) for a six- to eight-year history of both ownership and management contracts or any *third-party agreements*.

I recommend finding a community that has been both owned and operated by the same company for years and has multiple ALFs in several states. This shows stability, commitment, depth of experience, and depth of management. Frankly, these types of companies have more skin in the game. Spend some time looking into the companies behind the sign.

Staffing Questions

For smaller ALFs you will likely meet the two to four people who both own and operate a homelike setting, especially if they are operating under the AFCH or Adult Family Care Home license for five or fewer people. But for larger ALFs, you can expect a nurse administrator or director of nursing whose job it is to hire, oversee, and train staff. Ideally, they should be an RN or have a BSN (bachelor of science in nursing). Since ALFs don't require a medical director, having an RN as the director of nursing means you have a medically qualified person able to notice changes in a resident's health, and they can catch problems before they become serious.

Typically, though, ALFs manage staffing costs by having only one nurse on the main day shift. A really top-notch larger ALF will have one LPN on every shift, even the night shift. Additional staff include CNAs or personal assistants of some kind. With the cost of staff increasing after Covid, many

ALFs are adopting the model that hires no nurses and only personal care assistants. The idea is that a resident can hire more help privately if needed, and perhaps Medicare will pay for some of these costs if they qualify, such as skilled rehab care that is received within the ALF after a hospitalization. (See Chapter 13 on short-term rehab care.) Personally, I recommend having at least one qualified nurse on staff.

Most importantly, ask about the training for the staff and the staffing ratios. Find out the minimum staffing ratios for the state under consideration. ALFs are required to meet these staffing numbers, and remember, these are minimums, never ideal. Obviously, staff numbers will vary based on the size of the facility and level-of-care needs. A good rule of thumb for assisted living is about *one staff member for every six to eight residents for most day shifts*. At night, this ratio will go up to as high as fifteen residents per staff person. I recommend at least two staff people at night to be able to handle any emergency! I have heard horror stories of residents calling for help in the middle of the night and waiting hours. This should never happen!

The term HCA (healthcare administrator) is often found within the skilled facility world, but for ALFs, ask who oversees the entire staff and ask to meet them. They will set the expectations for the staff and demand excellence and compassionate care. That is why you need to meet this person— at least virtually. Look for "Questions to Ask When Touring Any Senior Community or Facility" under "Medical Alert Systems, Medical Affiliations, and Levels of Care Questions" at starbradbury.com/resources.

Is It a Good Fit?

When choosing an ALF community as a future home, the overarching question to ask is (once you have established safety and quality of care): Will it be a good fit? Does this community feel like it could be a place your loved one could be happy . . . or as happy as possible? Once you visit a few ALFs, you will see how varied they can be. Is it too fancy for Mom, who always liked simple and would more comfortable if the place were more down-to-earth? Do they offer the one or two things Dad loves, like walking trails or bridge or poker games? Is there a church service on the premises they can attend, if this is important to them? Look for a good match. Chat with residents and see if they are happy. My strongest advice: Tour any ALF first on your own, before you bring your parent. I am guessing you will eliminate half the ALFs you are considering, and you can save your loved one the disappointment or exhaustion.

Moving into an assisted-living community can be a big relief for a person once they realize the level of help offered. If your parent is older, they may not know that an ALF is not a nursing home, and this may make them very resistant. If they have lived alone for years, they may be lonely, depressed, and isolated. I promise you, I have seen residents blossom and come back to life in the right community!

When Your Parent Needs More than an ALF

When your loved one needs more care, beyond what an assisted-living facility can legally provide under their license, you will have to move your parent. Otherwise, the ALF is at risk for losing their license to operate, and they will not risk this. This means if your loved one exceeds the ALF services, they will be *required to leave.* Now it is time to navigate yet another transition, but this does not mean you can't apply both principles set forth in this book. What options are available to you and your loved one that, no matter what you choose, will maximize their independence? The window of planning (JITSP) has likely become much shorter, but even now, a three- to five-year plan could be appropriate. Time to take a deep breath, look at your parents' current needs, and make a new plan. This will likely mean finding the right skilled nursing care facility, and the next chapter will help you do just that.

Chapter 13

Choosing the Best Nursing Home or Skilled Nursing Care Facility

No one ever wants to place a parent into long-term nursing home care, but sometimes it just can't be avoided. When your parents' needs exceed assisted living, or home care is just too expensive, families often have no choice. If you are trying to work, raise children, and keep your own family together, you may have to look at this option, even if you live nearby your loved one. And unlike assisted living, today's nursing homes for long-term care are usually far more medical and institutional than anyone would like. No one goes to a nursing home because they want to. As hard as this is to accept, by the time your loved one is in this setting, they are well beyond the no-go years I mention in Part One. Even Principle #1 on maximizing their independence gets reduced to far simpler criteria such as making sure they get out once a week (if possible) to see the world outside! It could mean helping them maintain the limited mobility they still have left by considering ongoing physical therapy or participating in chair yoga or exercises. Principle #2 become less applicable as well, since you are generally not trying to plan for a three- to five-year window. The average span of time a frail, unwell elder will spend in long-term care is between two and two and a half years with slight variations for men and women. But keep in mind, I have seen residents who were in skilled care for ten years and longer.

My own mother passed away in a long-term care nursing home. She was young by anyone's standards, only seventy-six. But she had a lifetime of smoking three packs of cigarettes a day, suffered from congestive heart failure and vascular dementia, had trouble walking, and was on oxygen. She needed help in and out of bed and assistance getting to the bathroom. My wonderful stepfather, Bill, who had been caring for her for years, was exhausted and now had serious health problems of his own. I lived over six hours away, still had children at home, and was working full time. When it became clear living at home was no longer working, and Mom fell three times in one day and went to the hospital, my sisters and I knew we had to make a change.

She was too sick to move at that point. We looked at our options and chose a good nursing home that my stepfather could easily get to every day to visit her. We all went to see her as often as possible. She lived about one year longer and was as reasonably happy and well cared for as one could hope. Bill was with her when she drew her last breath. Difficult decision, but the best option at the time.

This chapter is designed to educate you on critical differences in the terms used to describe nursing home care, clear up the confusion on who pays for what, and help you find the right facility.

The Difference Between Nursing Homes and Skilled Nursing Care Facilities

Like most people, you may have thought that nursing homes provided the only option for a family needing care for a loved one who couldn't live at home anymore. And for many years, this was true. Then along came assisted living, and the meaning of nursing homes changed forever. And as people live longer and longer, and medical issues become more complex, the definition of nursing home has changed as well. Now, families have quite a few choices, depending on what level of care their loved one needs and what a family can afford. But in the world of nursing homes, the major distinction is: *Does your loved one need short-term skilled nursing services or long-term custodial care?* The answer will dictate where they receive care and who pays for it.

Short-term skilled care is what you can expect after hospitalization for a complex surgery, a fall, or a debilitating medical condition. While home healthcare and skilled nursing care are very similar, a skilled nursing facility provides all the therapy services within the facility itself, not in the home. It is designed to help someone recover and, hopefully, return to their home and a normal life. As you may know, hospitals no longer let you linger and recover in the hospital. They discharge you as soon as possible to a facility that can provide complex medical care and all the rehabilitation or therapy services needed. These facilities go by a variety of names and differ slightly:

- Skilled nursing facility (SNF)
- Inpatient rehabilitation facility (IRF)
- Acute care rehabilitation center
- Rehabilitation hospital

All of these terms refer basically to the same kind of facility, but the IRF and acute care facilities are generally for more complex issues such as spinal cord injuries or a significant debilitating stroke.

All of the above are required to have a medical director/doctor who oversees medical care and care planning, writes orders, and works as part of the care team. Nurses, RNs, and LPNs provide wound and incision care, handle IV drugs, dispense medications, monitor and oversee care, and more. All provide various therapies.

- Physical therapy is designed to restore function, relieve pain, and retrain any lost or impaired skills needed to live independently.
- Occupational therapy strives to provide patients with the necessary skills for proper self-care, such as dressing, personal hygiene, and cooking—skills that may now be difficult due to surgery, a fall, a stroke.
- Speech therapy is often used to help people who have had a stroke recover or improve their speech, and to help with swallowing difficulties.

Short-term care is goal oriented; a person is given a full range of therapies with the expectation they will improve over a matter of weeks or even
a few months. SNFs can meet the needs of active seniors recovering from
knee, hip, or shoulder replacement, or help your mom or dad recover from
open-heart surgery, a stroke, a broken pelvis, or more.

How well the patient recovers determines what happens next. If, after
time, it is clear the person is not going to be able to recover fully enough to
return to their previous level of independence, a family may have to consider a nursing home or long-term custodial care. It could be the person
has been diagnosed with a chronic or progressive disease such as Parkinson's, or has had such a debilitating stroke that they need twenty-four-hour,
nursing-level help and care. Maybe they live alone or their spouse can no
longer manage. Loved ones who fall into this kind of category not only need
help with their ADLs, but they also need medical and therapeutic services
beyond what assisted living can offer. If they are in a wheelchair or need
help with transferring (in and out of bed, on and off a toilet), they will need
long-term custodial care.

This care is assumed to be indefinite, ongoing, and not short term. The
medical staff needed to provide this level of care is equipped to handle any
serious health issues or know when to send the patient to the hospital. To
be clear, a skilled nursing facility is not a hospital (though some are located
within a hospital), even though the services they provide are close. They
do not perform surgery, and they are not designed to handle emergency
acute medical situations like injuries, accidents, strokes, and heart attacks
in progress.

People staying long term can often bring personal items to decorate their
rooms, but usually they are in a hospital bed. If they can afford it, people
may have a private room, but typically a room is semi-private. Expect a wide
variety of activities, social time, salon services, local transportation, and
more from most long-term facilities. Newer, more upscale nursing homes
are trying to change the culture and environment that have given nursing

homes such a bad name. I have personally seen nursing homes that look very similar to assisted living, with lovely dining rooms, beautiful outdoor spaces, and even good food!

Home or Short-Term Skilled Rehab (SNF)?

While people are often given the option of going home after surgery to receive therapy in their own home, there are plenty of reasons a person should consider facility rehab instead. It is important to ask if your parent has the support system at home to manage on their own—or even with a spouse. How capable is the spouse? Can they help them dress or shower during this recovery time? Can your parent run errands, shop, prepare meals? Would it be wiser to recover in a setting with qualified staff present twenty-four hours a day to help, with three meals a day, and all the therapy and therapy equipment needed? I might also mention that there is always a level of socialization and recreational activities offered, even in this setting.

I worked with a client who had hip replacement surgery. She had the option of returning home or going into an excellent rehab facility. She lived alone, but she missed home so much, that is what she chose. After being home only two days, she fell and broke her wrist! Now she was in a cast, couldn't use the walker she needed to do hip rehab, and she put her recovery back by months. She had no choice but to stay in rehab for a far longer period of time. Help your parent make a wise decision when it comes to rehab. Even if you can be there to help, it may be a smarter decision to recover in an SNF before returning home.

And please, if your parent says, "I don't need any of that therapy stuff," do everything you can to try and convince them. I have seen clients refuse therapy after hip surgery, and their limp and pain prior to surgery never went away! It is hard to unlearn muscle patterns from years of pain or limping without professional help. Therapy offers the increased opportunity to make a full recovery!

Cost of Short-Term Skilled Nursing

First the good news! You can expect Medicare to cover the bulk of any expenses under current Medicare rules if your loved one is in a short-term rehab skilled nursing facility. But first they must meet specific criteria, based solely on your doctor's opinion, such as requiring intensive rehab, continued medical supervision, and coordinated care from your doctors, therapists, and nurses working together. Medicare will cover:

- Therapy services (PT, OT, speech)
- A semi-private room
- All their meals
- Nursing care
- Medications, supplies, and hospital services while in rehab
- Dietary counseling

Medicare does not pay for phone, TV, internet, personal items, or a private room, unless deemed medically necessary. It is safe to anticipate that Medicare will pay all of their costs from *day one through day twenty* in a skilled care facility after meeting a deductible, as discussed in Chapter 15.

From days twenty-one through one hundred, there will be a fee, set by Medicare, that can change from year to year. In 2022 this fee was $194.50 per day. This amount is called "coinsurance," and the patient is fully responsible for this cost unless they have a separate "Medigap" policy they are paying for privately. (See below for information on Medigap policies.)

After one hundred days, they will be charged 100 percent of the daily cost. These formulas change somewhat for in-patient rehab care for an IRF (Inpatient Rehabilitation Facility) or acute rehab center and allow for up to sixty days, not twenty, for a more complex rehab situation. It will all depend on what your loved one is recovering from and what the doctor orders. Please refer to Chapter 15 for more details on some complex rules that govern these payments.

A helpful booklet for checking current Medicare payments for rehab care can be found at medicare.gov. (Scroll down to Take Action and click on

"Find publications." Search for "Medicare Skilled Nursing Facility Care." You can view the PDF or order a print copy. Note that websites frequently change, though.) You can also call 1-800-Medicare or 1-800-633-4227 or your State Health Insurance Assistance Program (SHIP), which is a free and extremely useful resource to help you or your parents with the confusing Medicare Supplemental policy options. Visit shiphelp.org or call 1-800-MEDICARE to get the most up-to-date SHIP phone numbers.

What Are Medigap Policies?

Most older adults who are on what is called "Original Medicare" also buy what is known as a supplemental Medicare insurance policy, or "Medigap" policy, through many different companies such as UnitedHealthcare, Blue Cross Blue Shield, Aetna, Cigna, and others. These policies protect families from the costs of care that Medicare doesn't cover (for skilled rehab care only), and they can vary tremendously. Remember the daily charge listed above after day twenty? This can add up fast, and a good supplemental policy will help pay some of these costs.

First, not every senior I know has one, since they can be expensive. The government requires that Medicare Supplemental insurance policies be standardized to offer the same core benefits, no matter who is the provider. Plans can be as low as $50 a month for lower coverage, and as high as $300+ a month for full coverage. But they could pay thousands in uncovered costs, so many feel they are worth it. Just like any insurance product, the higher the deductible, the lower the premium. (See medicarefaq.com/faqs /top-10-medicare-supplement-insurance-companies to review the top-rated Medicare supplemental insurance companies.)

Many seniors have what is known as a *Medicare Advantage Plan*, which is like an HMO or PPO, and these plans are different from "Original Medicare." While often free or very low cost, coverage can be greater for some things, like prescriptions, and less for others, like rehabilitation. Most of the commercials you see on TV are pushing these advantage plans and because of their low-to-no cost, they are very appealing. But most seniors do not understand that if they should need rehab care after a fall or surgery, these plans pay very little. In fact, some SNFs won't accept Medicare Advantage plans at all! See Chapter 15 for more information on Medicare Advantage plans and what Medicare does and does not pay for. Plans can range by region, even zip code, prior tobacco use, and more. See what is offered in your area and state. SHIP (Seniors Health Insurance Assistance Program, shiphelp.org) and SHINE (Seniors Helping Insurance Needs for the Elderly; each state has their own program, so websites vary) both offer educational resources on plan options and what may work best for your parents. They also offer free unbiased counseling on Medicare supplemental plans.

I suggest you ask your loved ones if they have any kind of supplemental policy, and if they can afford it, encourage them to get *something*, even one with a high deductible that will lessen their risk of large unexpected medical costs in general. Note: No Medigap policy will cover long-term care! These are not and never will be a long-term care insurance policy.

Three-Day Rule!

The three-day rule for Medicare reimbursement takes a lot of people off guard! It requires that a person be admitted to the hospital as an inpatient for at least *three consecutive days* for rehab in a skilled nursing facility to be covered. They must be officially admitted to the hospital by a doctor's order to even be considered an inpatient, so watch out for this rule. Spending the night in the ER, even in a room, will not count. In cases where the three-day rule is not met, do not expect Medicare to pay any of these costs, and of course, neither will a Medicare Supplemental insurance policy!

When the Twenty-Day Rule Won't Apply!

Let me share with you a story about a family I worked with. Lenore was a feisty eighty-year-old who was fiercely independent. After a hospital stay for a fall, she was discharged to a regular skilled care facility to get some physical therapy to gain strength in her legs, improve her balance, and to improve her transfer skills. Her family expected she would be in therapy for at least twenty days, the allowed amount of time Medicare covers. However, Lenore refused to go to therapy after ten days and was promptly discharged, with two days' notice. In fact, she told the therapists to "go to hell." She was not what you would call a patient who complied! No amount of cajoling or reasoning would convince her of the possible benefits. She was not able to live independently anymore, so I helped the family find a long-term care facility near one of the daughters in another state.

Medicare will cover most of your expenses for the first twenty days and some of your expenses up to one hundred days, but only if the patient is *showing continued improvement* and is cooperative with the therapy team. It is considered Medicare fraud to bill for services not received, and facilities are strict about this. Your loved one will be discharged if they are noncompliant or if dementia interferes with retaining any therapy skills.

Cost of Long-Term Care

Now the bad news. When a patient transitions from improving (with physical, speech, or occupational therapy) and needs what is called "custodial care," Medicare stops paying. If your loved one is in this rehab phase, make sure to stay informed about possible discharge dates. You should be developing a plan as soon as possible if they still need care! Have early conversations with both the discharge planner in the hospital and the business/insurance office in the rehab facility. Ask them about the anticipated length of stay based on the care team's assessment. For them to speak with you, make sure you are on the HIPAA list (see Chapter 2 on HIPAA info). If you have medical power of attorney, they will share medical information as well.

Medicaid and Long-Term Care

Medicaid is a totally different and very complex story. If your parents are on Medicaid or you think they will qualify, please read the information included in Chapter 15. But to give you a brief intro, Medicaid can cover both long-term custodial care and what is called "Home and Community Care," which allows a person to receive services in their home instead of having to move to a nursing home. Benefits vary tremendously from state to state, so check to see what is possible for your parents, especially if they live in a different state from you. Relocation for either one of you may be seriously influenced by what they are eligible for. Check out the State Overviews drop-down menu of the medicaid.gov website. Keep in mind that, in many states, waiting lists for these Medicaid-related services can be years long.

Choosing a Skilled Facility

Step 1: Do Your Homework

Who do you think decides where you will go if a hospital says you can't go home? Most people say the following: "I or my family will decide." Not true. About 95 percent of the time, it is not you (or your parent), not the doctor, but the discharge planner or social worker, who is under tremendous pressure to get you out of the hospital bed they need today for another patient. If your loved one's needs are no longer critical and can be met in a rehab facility (or assisted living) of some kind, they will be discharged. Believe me, they will discharge the patient *somewhere*, and usually it is a place with a vacancy or an open bed that will meet your needs. This will be extremely important if you think your parent could be in a facility long term and not just for rehab. You do not want to have to move them again if at all possible!

How much less stressful if you could say to the discharge planner: "What about Sunview Living; I heard they are the best rehab or SNF in town? Do they have a bed available?" If you wait for a crisis like most people, you often have limited options. Find out ahead of the need what SNFs have the best reputation in your parents' hometown. If a facility has a great reputation for skilled care, they likely also will be a good option for custodial long-term care.

However, if a hospital tells you they are moving your loved one to a facility you don't approve of, speak up. They may present this as a done deal, but you can object. This is why it is so important to try to learn ahead of time what facilities you would choose. You may have the option of buying time, as in delaying discharge by a few days, but even this is dicey. Try to work with them if you are negotiating a move to a facility that needs a day or two to accept your loved one. But know this: *Getting into any facility is always easier when being discharged from a hospital instead of from one's home. Hospitals will always have more clout than you do.* Facilities depend on referrals from hospitals, so they try to accommodate them far more readily than an individual family.

Step 2: Get a List and Compare Quality

It is generally a good idea to double-check with insurance plans, especially if your parent is in an HMO (Health Maintenance Organization) or Medicare Advantage plan, to see if the SNF you are considering is in the plan's network. Remember, these plans only help pay for short term, never long term! As I said above, any discharge planner can give you a list of all the options in your area, or go to medicare.gov/nursinghomecompare to find a list of all of the Medicare- and Medicaid-certified nursing homes in your area and general information about every Medicare- and Medicaid-certified nursing home in the country. Nursing Home Compare has information about the quality of care provided by each nursing home. You can look up health inspection results; mandatory survey results, including deficiencies and citations; and what is called "quality care measures," used by the CMS (Centers for Medicare and Medicaid Services), known as the Five-Star Quality Rating System. I have included more information later in this chapter about how reliable the CMS rating system is.

If you don't have access to a computer, your local library or senior center should be able to help you. Call your local USAging office, visit eldercare .gov, or call the Eldercare Locator at 1-800-677-1116 (weekdays 9 AM–8 PM eastern time). They will have all kinds of lists and helpful free information.

Make sure to ask your friends, family, or your aging life care consultant who they recommend. Word of mouth from people you trust is still invaluable!

I also suggest checking with your local ombudsman's office as well. The ombudsman program helps residents of SNFs (and ALFs) solve problems by acting on their behalf. Ombudsmen visit all senior living facilities and speak with residents throughout the year to make sure residents' rights are protected. They're a very good source of general information and can work to solve problems and help resolve complaints. They may be able to help you compare the SNF's strengths and weaknesses. Ask them questions like how many complaints they've gotten about a SNF or ALF, what kind of complaints they were, and if the problems were resolved. Two good websites are acl.gov/programs (click on Protecting Rights and Preventing Abuse) and ltcombudsman.org.

You can always check with a local elder-law attorney, as they will also be able to make recommendations, usually at no cost for this simple question, or with an initial consultation.

Step 3: Ready to Tour and Ask the Right Questions

Your first scheduled visit will be with a marketing or general admissions person. Many of these questions will be more important when vetting a facility for long-term stays, so please keep this in mind. Plan on several visits before choosing, if at all possible. I still recommend a drop-in weekend visit to meet other visiting families so you can pick their brains and ask them questions. First, do residents/patients look happy, clean, and well cared for? Is staff pleasant and responsive? If you hear a call bell, how long before you see a staff person responding? If the answers are positive, then proceed to the categories below.

Building

The first thing to note is the outside and inside of the building itself!

- Is the place spotless? Any odors? Do rooms look clean and neat?
- Grab bars and handrails in halls, bathrooms? Fully handicapped accessible?
- Are there safe outdoor spaces that are wheelchair accessible?

Save yourself a lot of time if your first impression is awful. If it is not clean and odor free, it will be downhill from there. Having worked in a top-notch skilled facility, I know it is possible to meet these criteria. If they pass this test, move on to ask these "first visit questions."

First Visit Questions

- Who owns and operates the facility? Is it part of a corporate chain?
- What state licenses do you have?
- Are you certified for both Medicare and Medicaid?
- What is your CMS rating, and can I see reports from the last few years?
- Who is your medical director, HCA (healthcare administrator), and director of nursing?
- What is your private pay rate for long-term care? Daily rate for rehab care?

They will know you have done your homework with these types of questions, so their responses will tell you a lot. Pay attention. Are they resistant or cooperative? If you have made an appointment, my hope is that they will give you the time you need to make an important decision.

Second Visit Questions

Likely you have eliminated two or three facilities after your first visit and lists of questions. On your second visit, try to schedule time to meet with the healthcare administrator who runs the whole building and/or the director of nursing. The list below is oriented more to these meetings. If you have not had a formal tour of the building, make sure to request this when scheduling.

Staffing and Care

- How long have you worked here? Has there been a lot of turnover among the top administrative or top nursing positions?
- What is the mix of RNs, LPNs, and CNAs, especially at night? What are the staffing ratios?
- Do you have weekly care plan meetings at times I can attend? Do you email care plan reports to family?
- How do you handle people with dementia? Do you have a separate wing? A secure environment?

Activities

A good skilled nursing facility does what it can to provide stimulating activities for the residents. You will notice a wide range of people in skilled care, those who are nearly bedridden and those who are fully ambulatory. Will this facility keep them physically active if possible and mentally engaged and stimulated? Here are some good questions to ask:

- May I have a copy of your activity schedule (movies, singing, chair exercise, walks, outings, arts and crafts)?
- Are there specialized activities for people with dementia?
- How do you celebrate holidays, birthdays, etc.? Can families organize parties for their loved one? Is there a room to use? Access to a kitchen for parties?
- Is there a resident group or family council group? When do they meet?
- Is there a safe and comfortable outside area for families to visit or walk? (This became extremely important during Covid when it was the only visiting option at times.)

A note about the importance of a resident council. Federal and state laws give residents the right to meet as a council and almost all ALFs and SNFs have one. This group is made up of both residents and family members, and they will often act as a collective voice for the welfare and concern of the patients with the administration of any building. They have the right to meet privately, but staff, friends, and relatives may participate at the invitation of a council. Find out if they will allow you to access this group before moving your parent. Talk with whoever is running the group and ask questions. They may have a digital newsletter or Facebook page you can check out or join.

Food

Nursing homes have notoriously bad food, so if it were me, I'd ask to try a meal. There is no getting around the importance of food. This is a huge challenge for any facility, and the larger the number of residents, the harder it is to deliver consistently good food. It is being prepared in an industrial kitchen and then plated and delivered to another floor or neighborhood where it might sit for some time before being served. Really good facilities have satellite kitchens that might bake or assemble or do final prep. Even in skilled care, a top-notch facility will offer a limited menu for some variety. And yes, the food can be good! Ask the following questions:

- How is the food? Are there several options at each meal? Can I see a menu for the week?
- Are snacks accessible and provided? Look for apples or oranges or snack bars in common eating areas.
- Do you accommodate a vegetarian, diabetic, gluten-free, or other specialized or restricted diet?
- Do you help residents to and from the dining room? Do you provide assistance with eating?
- Can I bring food to my loved one? Join them for any meal? What is the cost?

Step 4: Making a Decision

After all this vetting, groundwork, and visiting numerous facilities, be they assisted living, skilled nursing, or long-term care, the hard part is making a final decision. You want your loved one to be happy, to receive the highest quality care, and to be in an environment that allows them to be as independent as possible yet get the services and support they need. They should be treated with respect and dignity by the staff and remain safe from any harm or abuse. In fact, all facilities are required to post a "Patient Bill of Rights," which outlines what a resident should expect if they live in the facility. Ask to see it and use it for talking points with the HCA. We all know this does not always happen, but your goal is to choose the community that will meet the needs of your loved one and give you peace of mind. My hope is that your options are not totally dependent on cost, but if they are, please read Chapter 15 for options on paying for care you may not have thought of. Trust your instincts as well. If the facility is up to your standards, the staff is as well, and residents are happy, then you should feel confident in your choice.

What Is the CMS Five-Star Rating System and How Reliable Is it?

There is a lot of confusion about the Five-Star Quality Rating System, developed by CMS, the Centers for Medicare and Medicaid Services, to evaluate skilled nursing care facilities specifically. It was created to help consumers, their families, and caregivers compare nursing homes more easily and help identify potential problems. They have a recently improved website (cms .gov/Medicare/Provider-Enrollment-and-Certification/Certificationand Complianc/FSQRS) that allows you to find any nursing home in the country and review their ratings. Nursing homes with **five stars** are considered to have the **highest rating**, and nursing homes with **one star** are considered **much below average**.

The system evaluates patient care based on "short stay" and "long stay," as we have already defined. It tracks if patients get pressure ulcers (bedsores), had catheters inserted, were physically restrained, or had urinary tract infections or falls. CMS ratings include health inspections, complaint investigations, and a look at "minimum quality requirements." The most recent survey findings are weighted more than the prior year. They review staffing and look at the number of hours of care provided "on average" to each resident each day by nursing staff. The final category is called "Quality Measures," or QMs, and reviews fifteen different physical and clinical measures

Climate Change and Nursing Homes

Once upon a time, only coastal nursing homes worried about hurricanes. But now, with climate change, and severe flooding and more severe storms affecting wide swaths of our country, take special care to ask to see a facility's official Evacuation Plan. Every single facility (nursing homes, assisted-living facilities, and even life care communities) must have one. Most are inadequate. While residents' abilities vary from facility to facility, nursing home patients are most at risk. They are frailer, sicker, and have more complex medical conditions. Scrutinize the evacuation plan and find out where the facility will move patients, if generators are on-site already, and if there is a kitchen that can provide food and water. Do they have enough buses to safely transport residents, or how are they going to handle this? Once evacuated, can they provide enough bathrooms, food, bedding? If they are part of a corporate chain, ask how many other facilities and residents are using the same evacuation site. Tragic situations and multiple deaths have occurred recently due to poor evacuation plans. The best solution? Evacuate them yourself, if possible, or have a backup plan. If a hurricane or other natural disaster is predicted to hit the facility, plan far in advance if possible, and retrieve your loved one.

for nursing home residents. All of this combined data helps CMS understand how well a nursing home is caring for its patients.

The CMS received some extremely negative feedback in 2021 based on a *New York Times* investigation that uncovered widespread inaccuracies in the data they used for the Five Star rating system. According to the article, the government rarely audits nursing home data, inspectors dismiss serious issues, and much worse. This investigation seriously undermined consumers' faith in the rating system. I include this as a heads-up for anyone relying on this system alone to vet any facility. I still advise any family to review these findings and take them into consideration, but don't rely only on this data.

Ask discharge planners, local area geriatric case managers, social workers who focus on seniors, and even home care and home healthcare companies who are in and out of these facilities all the time.

I also recommend looking at the *US News & World Report* annual ratings book that evaluates nursing homes, assisted living, and dementia-care facilities nationally at health.usnews.com/best-nursing-homes. Facilities are listed by state and zip code, so it is very user friendly.

Nothing will replace your diligent research, your own personal tour, and answers to powerful questions.

Family Oversight and Involvement

I simply cannot stress enough the importance of staying involved and connected to your loved one in a nursing home. If Covid proved anything, it showed us that isolation and loneliness killed almost as many seniors as Covid. With in-person visits banned, and required quarantines in facilities, patients gave up. For those with dementia, it was worse. Try to visit as much as you can, and if you can't, try to arrange for visits from neighbors, friends, other family, or volunteers. Break up the monotony and plan simple things besides watching TV. Read Dad's favorite book out loud. Music is an amazing mental stimulant for anyone but especially for those with dementia. Play the songs they listened to in their youth and young adulthood and watch miracles happen. If you have not watched the movie *Alive Inside: A Story of Music and Memory*, you will be moved to tears as patients with advanced dementia get up and dance. You can watch it for free on YouTube.

Play a board game, play cards, do a puzzle. Buy one of those awesome adult drawing books and bring out the crayons! Take your loved one for an ice cream cone if possible. Get outside if you can, even with a wheelchair. The Japanese call this "forest bathing," and see it as a critical element of staying healthy!

Believe me, the staff knows if you will be there to check up on your loved one. Be friendly to the staff; let them know how much you appreciate what they do for your loved one. Bring them treats every now and then. A staff that feels appreciated will be more attentive, like it or not.

And don't be afraid to speak up if something doesn't seem right. If you believe there is serious abuse, neglect, or exploitation, you should report it immediately by calling ***Eldercare Locator (1-800-677-1116)***; they will refer you to your local abuse hotline. The government website hhs.gov /answers/programs-for-families-and-children/how-do-i-report-elder -abuse can also advise.

If the problem is minor, speak to the DON or HCA. If it is not minor, or you are getting no response from administration, go to the ombudsman representative (mentioned above) and see if they can help you resolve an issue.

Listen, watch, pay attention. You are your loved one's advocate and angel. If you can't be there yourself, the next chapter deals with long-distance caregiving and will give you critical tips you can use immediately to help, no matter what level of care your parents need. Having lost all my parents, I encourage you to do the best you can, and appreciate the time you have left.

Chapter 14

Managing Your Parents' Care Long Distance

The National Alliance for Caregiving (NAC) and AARP (American Association of Retired Persons) published a report in 2020 (caregiving .org/caregiving-in-the-us-2020) about the caregiving facts and trends in our country. This report is updated every five years, and the trends reveal an increase in family caregiving that is eye opening. The total number of caregivers in the US in 2020 was fifty-three million, an increase of 21 percent from 2015. One in five Americans is providing unpaid care to an adult with health or chronic functional needs. By the way, 61 percent of these caregivers are women, 39 percent are men, and 61 percent are still working. When you dig down into the report, you will find that 76 percent live within twenty minutes of the person needing care, 13 percent live up to an hour away, and 11 percent of caregivers live from one to two or more hours away. But 11 percent of fifty-three million still means that 5,830,000 caregivers are trying to provide care to a loved one over an hour or two away. This is a serious challenge. In fact, 26 percent (13,780,000) report having difficulty coordinating care, and a whopping 45 percent report at least "one financial impact."

The report talks at length about the emotional and financial stress of caregiving and the impact on the health of the caregiver, and many reported feeling "they had no choice" when it came to providing care. One could argue that if you were trying to provide care for a loved one only twenty minutes away, on top of working a full-time demanding job and caring for yourself and your own family, twenty minutes could sure feel like hours! Long-distance caregiving may mean your parent lives in their own home but needs help, or perhaps lives in assisted or skilled care already. No matter what the distance or where they live, this chapter will hopefully give you ideas and tips to manage long-distance caregiving.

Plan Your Visit

Regular visits are the most important tool for managing long-distance care. There is no replacing a face-to-face visit for several days to really see how your parent is doing. Parents can seem fine on the phone, but once there, you may notice the stacks of unpaid bills, poor eating or personal hygiene, or more worrisome signs. This is a sure warning that they need more help in their home! If you simply can't visit them due to family responsibilities, your job, or your own health, do what you can to arrange for visits from professionals, volunteers, or friends who can report back to you.

Make sure to try and meet any of the current service providers coming in and out of the home. Do you have all their contact information and cell phone numbers? Don't leave credit cards or statements out in the open where they can be stolen. Same with jewelry, checkbooks, and so on. I am sad to say that most of my mother's jewelry disappeared when caregivers were going in and out of her condo, and both theft and identity theft are a common occurrence with almost any kind of home care. Buy a top-notch home safe, make sure it is as permanently secure as possible, and advise your parents to place any valuables and important financial documents in the safe. Educate them about the high incidence of elder fraud, theft, and exploitation!

Make notes about any house problems and see if you can schedule any repairs. Ask the handyman or repair people to follow up with you, take photos before and after, and verify the work has been done. If there is any kind of neighborhood association where they live or a neighborhood newsletter of any kind, you will often find a list of reliable local repair companies, lawn services, carpenters, roofers, and more.

Some home modifications and repairs are covered under either Medicaid home and community-based Services or veterans' benefits, especially if these modifications allow your loved one to age in place and avoid moving to any kind of facility (see Chapter 6). I'd also ask your local USAging office about state programs that will cover safety modifications like ramps, grab bars, even bathroom changes. Some service clubs and church youth groups look for "senior-friendly" projects they can take on, and some can be significant, such as painting a house, repairing dry wall, or major yard cleanups. Try calling large charitable or religious organizations if you need this kind of help for your parents.

Prioritize what is critical to the well-being and safety of your parent every visit. Decide before every visit who may be able to help you accomplish what needs to be done so you are not doing it all. Ask siblings or other family members, if possible, to take on some of these tasks. If you hope to go with your loved one to a medical appointment, plan far ahead and let your parent know you want to accompany them, if possible.

Remember to try and schedule something fun or relaxing for both (or all) of you. Ask your parent what they would like to do if you have time. Maybe they want to shop for a new dress, eat at a nice restaurant, go for a walk in a lovely park, visit old friends. Try to not make it all business and no play.

Start with the Basics

If you are a long-distance caregiver of any kind, I suggest that you think about this as three different buckets. Doing even a little bit of research will make your life infinitely easier if you know where to find help or who to call ahead of a crisis. As mentioned, it is not *if* your parent will have a crisis, it is *when*. My experience is that there is always more help available than you may think, and some of it is even free!

- **Bucket One:** How prepared are you for an emergency situation? Are critical documents organized and readily accessible, either safely online or in hand? What information would help you if your loved one is rushed to the hospital or has a bad fall? Do you have a list of critical information, similar to the one I provided in Chapters 3 and 4? Review these lists and gather the most important documents for an inevitable emergency.

- **Bucket Two:** How strong is your loved one's existing support network, excluding you? While the solutions may differ depending on if they live alone or already live in a senior community of some kind, they share some commonality. No matter where they live, do they have neighbors, friends, or staff you can call to ask for help, or someone who can check up on them when you are worried and can't be there yourself? Think of this as building your own informal support network, since you, as the caregiver, need one as well!

- **Bucket Three:** Know the local resources you can draw on for help of any kind. Find out ahead of the need or a crisis who to call for home care, home healthcare, local adult day care, and more. Knowing about a terrific local senior center or free Uber rides for your mom or dad could make a huge difference. Have your list handy!

Bucket One: Emergency Situations

Organize Critical Paperwork

I learned a tough lesson in my own life many years ago about not having the information I needed in a family emergency. My stepmother, Patricia, lived in a high-rise in New York City. After my father died, she went downhill. I called her at least once a week to check on her. I lived in Florida, and after being unable to reach her for four or five days, I was frantic. I did not have the names and phone numbers of her neighbors, friends, or the superintendent, so I called the police. When there was no answer, they broke down the door. She had fallen and was unconscious, but alive.

An ambulance took Pat to the hospital, and when the doctors finally reached me, I did not have a copy of her living will. As it turns out, she passed away within forty-eight hours. It was very traumatic for my sister and me. This was years ago, before I had the experience I have now. I didn't have a crisis plan in place, much less critical paperwork, and looking back, I could have been more resourceful. It might not have made a difference, but I would feel less guilty.

- The priority under this category needs to be advance directives such as a living will and healthcare proxy, or medical power of attorney, as discussed in both Chapters 2 and 3 and included in the list below. Make sure these documents are current, have correct contact information, and all the doctors and hospitals have them. See if you can upload medical records to your parents' patient portal. These kinds of documents become even more important when you do not live close by and you get a midnight call from the hospital.

- Very important: Is your name on the HIPAA list with all their doctors and hospitals so they will communicate with you about your loved one's medical situation?

- While not the first thing you would think of during an emergency, if you know your parents have completed a will, make sure you either have a copy, know where one is, or know how to access these documents easily if needed.

- Review the list of critical documents in Chapters 2 and 3: things like medication lists, doctors' names and contact info, emergency contacts, and much more. Make sure this information is easily accessible and *shared with whoever may be responding first to the emergency.* If possible, all these documents should be in digital format, (with paper copies handy if needed), and be easily scanned, etc.

It is not at all unusual for an older person to call an adult child living hours away when they are in trouble. One of my dearest friends, who is a remarkable ninety-two-year-old, told me she called her daughter, who lived two hours away, to come take her to the hospital at three in the morning. She did not feel it was a 911 kind of call, although they did admit her, and she knew her daughter would be a strong advocate for her. If you have been to an ER lately, I would not want to go alone, no matter what my age! You may not be able to jump in a car and help, so you need to have people to call who can get to your loved one quickly. By the way, some certified care mangers will agree to be on call for these kinds of emergencies!

Vial of Life or "Lifesaving Information for Medical Emergencies"

As you learned in Chapter 2, most EMTs are trained to look for what is known as the "vial of life"—lifesaving information for medical emergencies that you can think of as a longer version of a medical ID bracelet. Many seniors place it on a refrigerator in a clear plastic magnetic envelope, usually with a large bright-red sign on the front. It is recommended that your parent keep a copy in their purse or wallet, and even in the glove box of a car. Many of these vial of life kits come with a red decal or a sticker your loved one can place on a front-facing window, or even the front door, so EMS personnel know your parent has one, especially if they live alone. Simple forms can be found online for free, or more complete kits can run about thirty dollars.

The vial of life form includes basic information like date of birth, insurance info, living will, etc., but in addition has a section for allergies, medical conditions, any implanted devices, hearing aids, glasses, and more. Most importantly, it lists if your loved one has a DNR (Do Not Resuscitate) or POLST (Physicians Orders for Life-Sustaining Treatment) on file. Buy a kit for your parent and help them fill it out if needed. It has saved lives.

Facility After-Hours Phone Numbers and Contacts

Remember, most life care communities have 24/7 security people who could go to your parents' home or apartment at any time of the day or night and do a wellness check. Facilities always have a cell phone number to reach security. ALFs and SNFs also have staff twenty-four hours a day, and you need the after-hours phone number to call. Nothing is more frustrating than calling a daytime-only number when you have received a frantic call from your parent in a facility of any kind. Try to get cell phone numbers of night staff if possible.

Bucket #2: Informal Support Network

Procrastination and social hesitancy may prevent you from doing this one simple thing that may turn out to be lifesaving. Don't let it stop you. Make a list of your dad and/or mom's neighbors or friends, even if they live in a senior community.

Maybe they have friends at a senior center or recreational center? Is anyone already helping from a church, synagogue, place of worship, or social club? Are they members of Rotary, Kiwanis, or veterans' clubs? These organizations may have an outreach program for older club members. Get their names and numbers.

Many religious houses of worship have outreach volunteers who would be willing to check on Dad once a week. Call and ask. What types of help could they provide? A meal once a week? An in-home visit? Occasional transportation? These friends may be your first line of defense if you live too far to physically check on your parent. Think of this as building your ERT or emergency response team! At my church, there is both a health ministry team and an outreach team that calls on members who are frail, ill, or disabled. It is becoming more common for large churches with an elderly population to hire a part-time nurse, so check and see what resources might be available.

Share Your Own Information!

Make sure these friends and neighbors have all your and/or your siblings' contact information, including various cell phone numbers and emails, etc. I suggest you create a card or sheet and laminate it, so it won't get lost. I also think that including your parents' primary doctor's information or hospital of choice is important. If an ambulance arrives one night and Mom is unconscious, the neighbor can call you, and the EMTs will have your information as well. Meet the neighbors now if you have not already and ask if you can have their contact info as well. Make sure to keep this information up to date.

If your parents already have friends or neighbors helping, make sure to meet and thank them for all they are doing. Just hearing a sincere thank-you from a daughter or son means a great deal. Share your concern and ask them if they mind if you call them every now and then to check in and get their perspective on how Dad is doing. Don't forget to ask if they have noticed any changes in Mom or Dad's behavior, health, or anything that could be a concern, and to please call you!

Bucket #3: Know Your Parents' Local Resources

Obviously, if you live hours away in another town or another state, you are not going to know who to call if you need more help. For that matter, you may not know what is available in general when it comes to senior services, senior living options, or senior care! These resources can be found anywhere and will be invaluable to you as your parents' needs increase or you are thrust into an emergency situation.

Area Agency on Aging

As mentioned many times, the best place to start is with your local USAging office. Use the national website and the zip code locator to find services in your desired area or you can call 1-800-677-1116 and talk with an elder-care specialist. They will mail you up to five free publications, and have all this information in several languages.

Need legal assistance? They can refer you. Do your parents need help paying for their medications? They can help. Want to know how you can arrange telephone reassurance calls to homebound seniors or disabled persons? How to get Meals on Wheels? Alzheimer's support groups? They will provide information on almost *any* service having to do with elder issues.

Just to be clear, whoever they refer you to will likely charge fees, but the referral service is free. They will refer you to recognized agencies, volunteer groups, and not-for-profit agencies. You will do most of the coordinating of services, but you will know what is offered in your parents' area and who to call. They also have tribal agencies that have programs to meet the needs of rural Native American populations and programs for the LGBT aging senior population.

National Council on Aging

The National Council on Aging (NCOA—ncoa.org) is a not-for-profit advocacy and service organization whose mission is to improve the lives of millions of older adults, especially those who are vulnerable and disadvantaged. They offer a variety of programs that focus on the health, finances, and employment of our senior population. These programs are free, and information is readily available on the NCOA website.

Senior Centers

Find out if there is a city- or county-run senior center near your parents. In addition to offering a social and support network, they may have access to tennis courts, walking trails, wiffle ball, pickleball, and more. Many are free or very low cost, and they may provide rides to and from the centers and various facilities and activities, and perhaps even serve meals.

Volunteer Services for Seniors

Numerous organizations provide services to the elderly, including in-home visits, meals, and transportation to doctors, and they are free. Most have national websites, so you can contact them and ask if they have programs and affiliates where your parents live. Check out Volunteers of America (voa. org), a 125-year-old service organization focused on services and programs that promote health and independence for the elderly, or elderhelpers.org, who claim they have more than 10,000 volunteers who want to give back to the elderly and learn from their wisdom. (Make sure to ask how well they screen their volunteers.)

Local Long-Term Care Ombudsman Program

This agency will be especially important if your parent lives in any kind of senior community, even life care. They will be your go-to option if you wish to make a serious complaint. All long-term care ombudsman programs work to resolve problems related to the health, safety, welfare, and rights of individuals who live in long-term care facilities, such as nursing homes, board-and-care and assisted-living facilities, and other residential care communities. They are part of a federal program, with offices in every state. Check out the website acl.gov (click on Program Areas/Protecting Rights and Preventing Abuse/Long-Term Care Ombudsman).

I recommend having this information ahead of time. It can be useful to know who the local representative is just in case you need support. I would not hesitate to call them and ask them to recommend the best facilities in the area since they handle complaints regularly and will make recommendations.

Local and/or National Veterans' Affairs Benefits Office

The National Association of Veterans & Families (navf.org/benefits) is a wonderful not-for-profit advocacy, support, and educational group for veterans from WWII, Korea, Vietnam, the Gulf Wars, and any current conflicts, and their spouses and families. They help with homelessness, job assistance, healthcare of all kinds, and, most importantly, will "Shepherd the [benefit] application process to completion for all veterans, spouses and families." If your loved one or their spouse (even an ex-spouse) served in the military, they may be eligible for benefits. This website covers information on "aid and attendance," disability compensation, burial benefits, FAQs, and more.

Social Worker in Doctor's Office

As more and more patients need help securing in-home services or care, more physicians are realizing that a case manager/social worker is needed on staff. The doctors and nurses don't have time for these services and often, without a family member to help, the older person with medical needs falls through the cracks. Especially with the increase in telemedicine, physicians will see the need for a case manager/social worker. Physician practices associated with hospitals seem to be more likely to have a full-time staff person to address such issues, especially those practices that focus on senior geriatric health.

Hopefully your parent has already added your name to their HIPAA list so the case worker will feel free to talk with you. If not, I would be honest with your parent and ask them to add you to the list. Tell them you want to introduce yourself to both the doctor and the social worker. I think most parents will appreciate your desire to be prepared and to be ready to help when needed. Introducing yourself to the case manager and making sure they have your information can be a critical part of long-distance care management.

If you have seen changes in your mom's or dad's habits, memory, or health, you should feel free to call the social worker and let them know. Sometimes during a short office visit, the doctor or nurse may not see what you noticed on your last visit, in person or virtually! Social workers are always relieved to know there is an adult child involved who cares, so they want to work with you. Ask them if they will email you information if they see any serious changes in your parents' health. Being informed about diagnoses, anticipated progression of a disease, and what you can expect will make a huge difference, especially if you're managing long-distance caregiving and trying to plan.

My advice? If for any reason your parent must change doctors or is moving, find a primary care physician, preferably a geriatrician, who has a case manager or social worker on staff! Seriously consider hiring an Aging Life Care expert through the Aging Life Care Association (aginglifecare.org). They can be your eyes and ears and help you keep your sanity.

Make Use of Technology

I covered a lot of AgeTech options in Chapter 10 that offer solutions for providing more care in your parents' home, but it is clear that technology is changing the way families support their aging loved ones. Covid changed our culture by showing us how easy it is to stay connected through Zoom, FaceTime, and other apps. These options are a lifesaver for families managing long distance, and I advise setting a weekly time to check on Mom. If the family is spread out, set a weekly or monthly time, and invite all the siblings who want to be involved. Many seniors I know are extremely tech savvy and use Apple watches to replace alert systems, or even Alexa to call their family and stay connected. If your parent(s) are not computer literate, and they are getting help in the home, you can ask a personal assistant to be there to help with Zoom and other issues around tech.

> ♀ Various online scheduling tools can help your family coordinate who is dropping off dinner Wednesday night or driving Auntie to

the doctor Friday, as well as allowing care providers to share information with you and the entire family. (SignUpGenius (signup genius.com) is one of my favorites.)

- Home security systems can be set up to alert your parents and you—even over a distance—to the potential issues that I addressed in Chapter 6 on aging in place safely. The systems vary in cost and complexity, but I recommend any senior who lives alone or a frailer older couple to have a home security system that includes a medical alert option.

- I also covered medication management systems in Chapter 10, apps that would notify your loved one (or you) if a med is missed. Financial and banking apps can help you prevent financial abuse by alerting you about large money transfers or unusual activity in Mom's checking account, and I recommended a few of these in Chapter 10 as well.

Workplace Time-Off Policies

It is a good idea to know your workplace leave policy ahead of a crisis. Ask your HR department if you qualify for time off to provide care under the federal Family and Medical Leave Act. If not, can you work remotely for the time that is needed? Again, if there is anything positive to say about Covid, allowing millions of people to work from home is one of them. Hopefully this will give you some flexibility to handle an emergency when needed.

As employers compete for workers, HR departments are offering more accommodations for aging parents. Be sure to ask before changing jobs or accepting a new job. This might be a crucial factor in your decision.

Be Kind to Yourself

For years I have listened to family members torture themselves with guilt and remorse for what they didn't do, couldn't do, forgot to do, didn't know how to do. Please acknowledge that anything you do for your loved one is better than nothing. With twenty-five years in senior living, I have seen those who have no one, or are just neglected by family. Our lives today are so stressed with work and family obligations that adding the job of caregiving, even for those we love, can be almost too much. I stand in awe of those who manage well. My hope is that this chapter gives you new information to help lift the stress of caring for a loved one long distance.

Chapter 15

Medicare, Medicaid, and Paying for Long-Term Care

If you are wondering if your parents will need long-term care (LTC), here are some startling statistics. According to the US Department of Health & Human Services, someone turning sixty-five today has almost a 70 percent chance of needing some type of long-term care services in their remaining years. Women are predicted to need long-term care an average of 3.7 years and men an average of 2.2 years. The odds are high that your parents will be trying to figure out how to pay for long-term care now or in the future unless they are avoiding this altogether or counting on you. When I worked in the senior living industry and someone used to tell me they were counting on their kids to take care of them, I always inquired, "Have you asked them?" Usually, I was met with silence. Why do you need to address this? Because medical bills and long-term care are one of the main reasons people declare bankruptcy, and they put enormous strain on everyone involved. All financial advisors will tell you to try and plan for the cost of long-term care through some kind of long-term care insurance product or healthcare annuity or savings plan.

Defining Long-Term Care

By now you may be screaming, "Okay we *know* what this means!" But do you? There is so much confusion about this, I think we can summarize to make sure. This term is used by financial planners, medical professionals, doctors, hospitals, senior care facilities all to refer to one thing: *a person who can no longer live independently without help of some kind and is not expected to improve or recover.* It could mean care in the home, but it usually means care in a nursing home for custodial ongoing care (as explained in Chapter 13), and though it usually does not really apply to assisted living, I have heard it applied to that. Hence the confusion. The degree of help needed, and the location of where this help is received, varies, and it will dictate the cost and who pays.

With over 50 percent of people under the misconception that Medicare covers long-term care, let's clear this up. As stated in Chapter 13, Medicare never pays for long-term care, only for short-term rehab care for patients expecting to improve with therapeutic services (physical therapy, occupational therapy) in a licensed Medicare skilled nursing facility. It is designed to help someone recover and, hopefully, return to their home and a normal life. Short-term skilled care is what you can expect after hospitalization for a complex surgery, a fall, or a debilitating medical condition. It requires doctors' orders, and care rarely exceeds ninety or one hundred days, although in complex cases it can go longer. Once a patient is no longer showing improvement, they will be discharged.

But here is a safe assumption: If your loved one does not qualify for Medicaid and is not a veteran or was never married to one, do not expect much help from either state or federal programs to offset the cost of long-term care. And the cost is expensive, as we will look at in this chapter. This is why it is so important to have conversations with your parents many years ahead of the possible (read "probable") need. With some early planning and knowledge, it is possible that you and your parents can develop a plan to address these costs. Just as in Chapter 1, "Get the Ball Rolling," I'd like to encourage you to start a conversation about paying for long-term care. This chapter will give you several ways to approach this topic and what avenues there may be to find help, besides just Medicaid.

Discussing Money Matters

If you think discussing end-of-life issues is difficult with parents, just try talking about money! It can bring out tremendous defensiveness on so many levels. My sister and I tried to talk with my father and stepmother about their plans to pay for possible future care, and if they would move closer to one of us. My dad had already been diagnosed with Parkinson's, so we knew his care needs would increase. We thought it had gone well until we received a poison-pen letter saying we were only interested in their money, and it was none of our business! It took lots of additional conversation to straighten this out. Any kind of stepparent situation can complicate things. So, approach with caution. I suggest starting with some very basic questions/statements.

- Have you thought about what you would do if either one of you needed more care?
- Do you want to stay in your home with care if needed?
- My siblings and I are worried about you both; we think some extra help would make a difference. Can I check with some local companies to see what they offer and how much it costs and then we can talk about it?
- Did you know about the Genworth cost of care website? It is such a great tool to look up the cost of any kind of care anywhere in the US. Can we look at it together?
- Do you know if you qualify for any help with paying for home care? Let's find out together.
- Do you know the cost of long-term care? I was shocked when I looked into this.
- Have you ever thought about buying some kind of long-term care insurance product? There are some new options where all your money comes back to your estate if you never use it!

How you approach this is critical since timing is everything. How soon should you start these conversations? I suggest you start talking while your parents are in their late fifties or early sixties. Why so early? Because if they decide to apply for some kind of long-term care insurance, they want to purchase it before turning sixty or sixty-five, to be sure they can qualify while still able and healthy. Or perhaps they will find out they are eligible through work benefits for some kind of group long-term care insurance plan they could not get otherwise. Maybe now is the time to begin setting aside money for long-term care through a special annuity or insurance vehicle that grows over time? There are lots of reasons to bring this up sooner, not later. If they expect to qualify for Medicaid, planning ahead of time will help with the qualifying process.

Go back to *Principle #1: What decision can you help your parents make that will maximize their independence?* When applied to paying for long-term care, this means making decisions far ahead of the need, which will leave them in control of *where they receive this care, who provides it, and if they can age in place in their home.* Framed like this, they should want to discuss this. This conversation is for their benefit as much as yours. And depending on their age, *Principle #2, JITSP,* will dictate the planning window (three to five years) and the urgency. Do they foresee needing care in three to five years or, if they are sixty, perhaps not for another twenty or twenty-five years? The more lead time, the better.

Median Cost of Long-Term Care

You may be unfamiliar with just how much long-term care costs in the United States. It is worth mentioning again that the best way to look at current costs is the Genworth cost of care survey that has become the industry standard and is updated every few years. The most current is the 2020 version: genworth.com/aging-and-you/finances/cost-of-care.html. It will not only show the median costs of both skilled and assisted living state by state, but it also shows median costs of adult day care, home care, and home healthcare. The median cost of skilled care in the US is $7,756 a month for a semiprivate room and $8,821 a month for a private room. I have recently spoken with several SNFs that charge $12,000 a month for long-term nursing care in a private room.

For assisted living, the median cost is $4,500 a month or $54,000 a year for a typical one-bedroom apartment. I personally think this number is on the low side, or it may reflect the base rate that doesn't include higher levels of care. It certainly does not reflect the median cost of memory care. The website seniorhousingnews.com is excellent for looking at any senior housing information nationally. And seniorliving.org/nursing-homes/state -federal-regulations has a simple but clear comparison between assisted and skilled care's costs, regulations, and more.

Please keep in mind that costs vary tremendously by geographic location and level of care needed. You can expect that high-demand urban areas are more costly, but Alaska may be at the top of the list. Your takeaway needs to be that you can expect to pay around $90,000 and up for a year in skilled care, and these will be out-of-pocket expenses unless you have some kind of long-term care insurance policy or your parents qualify for Medicaid. Full-time home care is far more expensive. Medicare never covers assisted living, as you learned in Chapter 12, and I predict it never will. Medicaid rarely covers assisted living except in states that allow what is called a Medicaid waiver (see page 206) and these funds are historically limited.

What Is Medicare and What Does It Pay for?

I have heard from so many adult children that they are totally confused about Medicare, what it is, and what it pays for, that I am including a basic primer on this to help families understand it. A basic understanding of Medicare benefits will help you navigate costs and estimate what your parents can expect to pay as well.

In 2022, there were thirty-five million seniors enrolled in what is called "Original Medicare." First, almost everyone is eligible for Medicare at age sixty-five, with the exception of some public state or federal employees who may be excluded. One can enroll in Medicare without necessarily being on Social Security yet. These are two different programs with different rules. Social Security funds retirement; Medicare funds medical and related healthcare costs. An older person still working at age sixty-five may enroll in Medicare and also keep their work health insurance, although one of these will be the primary insurer, usually Medicare.

Seniors can enroll three months prior to turning sixty-five, and any time three months after. This is known as the "Medicare Initial Enrollment Period." Seniors can also enroll during the Annual Election Period (AEP), also called Fall Open Enrollment, October 15–December 7 every year, as well as change plans during this period.

Original Medicare falls into categories called Part A, for costs in hospitals and skilled rehab care, and Part B, for costs with doctor's services, tests, outpatient care, home health services, durable medical equipment, and other medical services.

Each year, the Medicare Part B premium, deductible, and coinsurance rates are determined according to the Social Security Act, and they increase annually. The standard monthly premium for Medicare Part B enrollees was $170.10 for 2022 and is deducted from an enrollee's monthly Social Security check. The annual deductible for all Medicare Part B beneficiaries was $233 in 2022.

Most people receive premium-free Part A thanks to paying a sufficient amount of Medicare employment taxes during their working years. If they did not make enough payroll contributions, they may not qualify for free Part A. Check out medicare.gov/what-medicare-covers for more info.

Prescription Drugs: Who Pays?

What about prescription drugs? Original Medicare, Part A and Part B, doesn't include prescription drug coverage, except in certain cases. Part A usually covers medications given as part of your treatment when you're a hospital inpatient. Part B may cover prescription drugs administered to you in an outpatient setting, such as a clinic. But when it comes to medications you take at home, Original Medicare doesn't cover them, in most cases. This is where **Medicare Part D** comes in.

There are two ways to get Medicare prescription drug coverage. Both are available from private, Medicare-approved insurance companies, and costs vary, depending on the plan. Some, but not all, Medicare Advantage plans cover some medications, and expect to pay a coinsurance of some kind. But there is a catch: If you opt out, and don't sign up for Part D at age sixty-five when you are eligible, you will have to pay a "late enrollment fee" at a later date when you do enroll in any plan . . . that will be charged for the rest of one's life. Website for Part D info: medicare.com (click on Medicare Part D).

The famous "donut hole" referring to out-of-pocket expenses for prescription drugs applies to Part D since it has deductibles and various payout limits that change every year and can expose seniors to significant costs for expensive drugs. See healthline.com (and search for "Medicare donut hole") for more info. As I write this, the Inflation Reduction Act was just passed and could be a game changer for millions of seniors, limiting out-of-pocket prescription costs to $2,000 a year and allowing the federal government to negotiate drug prices for the first time. These changes will go into effect in 2023, and all websites should be updated by then to reflect current information.

Medicare Replacement Plans

In 2022, over twenty-nine million seniors were on some kind of Medicare replacement plan, known most often as Medicare Advantage plans (Part C) that are managed-care plans that allow someone to get Medicare coverage from a private health company that contracts with the federal government, but first you must be enrolled in an Original Medicare Part A and B before switching to an Advantage Plan.

Insurance companies are given a set amount of money regardless of the amount of care received, although they are required to offer the same benefits as Original Medicare Parts A and B, but can do so with different costs and coverage restrictions. These include plans known as HMOs, PPOs, and PFFS or private fee-for-service plans.

In 2022, the average Part C–type plan cost $62.66 a month, much less than the $170 deducted for anyone on Original Medicare for Part B. Many seniors have these plans due to the lower cost, the fact that co-pays are generally less expensive, and they cover lots of services.

However, with these types of plans, as I have mentioned, one is exposed to higher costs of medical care, especially for short-term rehab or longer hospital stays, and stricter "in-network" rules. A recent concern (based on new data) is the potential incentive Medicare Advantage plans have to deny access to services and payments to providers in an attempt to increase profits. This is not legal and I believe will become a bigger issue. A great website that sorts all this out is www.medicare.gov; look for "Join, switch, or drop a Medicare Advantage Plan." There is a special "general enrollment period" just for those on any Advantage Plan from January 1–March 31 when any changes can be made, in addition to the fall enrollment period.

What About Hospital Costs and Medicare?

Different rules and formulas apply for in-patient hospital stays under Part A of Original Medicare. You already learned about the mandatory three-day rule for Medicare to pay *any* hospital and sometimes rehab costs (see Chapter 13). This one fact is critical to understand, so make sure to read the following website: hospitalmedicaldirector.com (search "Confusion about Medicare's two 3-day rules"). More and more hospitals and doctors are using a loophole to disqualify coverage. So called "observation days" don't count, even if your parent is in the hospital! Spending the night in the ER also will not count. The clock starts ticking when the doctor formally admits a patient for "inpatient status," and the clock needs to turn past three consecutive midnights to count. If this rule is not met, costs can be in the tens of thousands and will be out of pocket for your loved one.

Keep in mind that one has to meet the Medicare deductible per benefit period before Medicare starts covering any inpatient hospital costs. In 2022, the deductible was $1,556. The benefit period begins the very day you enter a hospital for care or a skilled nursing facility. The benefit period ends when sixty days have passed since you *last received either hospital care or care from a skilled nursing facility.*

Once the deductible is met, Medicare will pay the facility up to $371 (in 2022) per day for days sixty-one through ninety. Over ninety days, the rules change again for what are known as "lifetime reserve days." Medicare Lifetime Reserve Days limit the number of days Medicare Part A will cover expenses for extended hospital stays past ninety days. They are limited to only sixty days over the course of a lifetime. There is a coinsurance associated with these reserve days.

In 2022 the coinsurance was $778 per day. To be clear, this is what is NOT covered by Medicare and is the patient's responsibility. Of course, typically people are not in the hospital for this long, so luckily, this is rare. I include this information to help educate you in general about how Medicare works.

An excellent website to sort this all out is medicareinteractive.org (click on Get Answers/Medicare-Covered Services/Inpatient hospital services/Lifetime reserve days).

Medigap Policies Revisited

If you remember what you learned about Medigap policies in Chapter 13, you will make sure to talk with your parents about signing up for some kind of Medicare Supplemental insurance plan, which generally have a letter designation like Plan A, B, F, N, and so on. With these kinds of co-pays, you can see why medical bills bankrupt seniors.

For example, some Medigap plans also pay for the in-hospital deductible of $1,556 per benefit period. Some more expensive policies add an additional 365 lifetime reserve days. If your parents are on Medicare Advantage plans, they are subject to different costs and different rules and very likely less financial coverage for *any* rehab stay.

Your takeaways for all of this are two things:

- If your parents are in poor health prior to turning sixty-five, and they can afford it, help them get Medigap policies that will protect them financially. Policies can be as low as fifty dollars a month.
- Second, this is such a complicated and stressful topic, so seek out help from the free trained volunteers who are unbiased and not trying to sell a Medigap policy over the phone to your vulnerable parents.

Where to Turn for Free Medicare and Medicaid Insurance Advice

SHIP: State Health Insurance Assistance Program

If your parents are approaching sixty-five and need help sorting out which plan works for them, or if they qualify for Medicare or Medicaid, there is a free organization known as SHIP or State Health Insurance Assistance Program, an extremely helpful resource. From their website:

> SHIP is a national program that offers one-on-one assistance, counseling, and education to Medicare beneficiaries, their families, and caregivers to help them make informed decisions about their care and benefits. SHIP services support people with limited incomes, Medicare beneficiaries under the age of 65 with disabilities, and individuals who are dually eligible for Medicare and Medicaid.

Qualifying for Medicaid

Medicaid was designed to be a program for the poor and medically needy, and, basically, it still is. But the rules for qualifying for Medicaid change regularly and received a major overhaul with the Affordable Care Act. Eligibility can vary state to state depending on how the state applies federal guidelines for eligibility. Although this criterion was supposed to simplify things, qualifying for Medicaid is no longer as straightforward as you may think. While your income plays an obvious role, your eligibility could also depend on your participation in other government-run programs like disability or SSI (Supplemental Security Income). The government no longer disqualifies you from assistance, even if you own a large home or other real estate!

Medicaid eligibility used to be based on how much money you earned and how much you owned, e.g. your income, your assets, and your net worth. After the Affordable Care law was enacted, eligibility was split into two distinct groups. Some people continued to qualify for Medicaid the old-fashioned way (income alone), while others qualify based on their *modified adjusted gross income (MAGI)*. Using MAGI is now the norm in most states, but the formula is complex and can vary. There is a long list of groups or individuals who fall into the criteria requiring the use of MAGI, and those who are considered non-MAGI. Depending on which group you fall into, the government uses different factors to decide if you qualify for Medicaid.

When it comes to Medicaid eligibility, however, MAGI has two components. The first is your household income, and the second is the size of your household. If a parent is alone, on their own, or in a family of two, or in a family of five, they will have different qualifying MAGI levels to become eligible for these programs. Each state will have different MAGI levels depending on whether they enacted Medicaid expansion. Florida, at least so far, has opted out of Medicaid expansion, so double-check about your parents' home state. When it comes to non-MAGI Medicaid eligibility, both one's income and assets come into play. Most of the government programs that qualify someone for Medicaid use an asset test.

Medicaid Asset Limitations

The rules for qualifying for Medicaid to help pay for nursing home care or in-home care are so varied from state to state and so complex that most people need help. Please make sure to go online to medicaidplanning assistance.org (click on Eligibility/Income Eligibility Chart) and look at the state-by-state guide for both income and assets. This site is a tremendous source of information on everything to do with Medicaid. If your loved one has income less than $2,000 a month, you likely don't need a Medicaid professional planner, but if they own real estate and/or have income above this amount, a planner can help you and your family. Compare costs for these planners as they vary and can be even more than an elder-law attorney.

Is your parent single, married? About 50 percent of states allow up to $2,382 a month if single, and up to $4,764 a month for a married couple, as the high end of monthly income to still qualify for Medicaid. But more than thirty states have set limits as low as $1,191 a month for a single person. Candidates can take advantage of spousal protection laws that allow income (or assets) to be allocated to a non-applicant spouse. See what is legal in the state that applies to your family.

Please know that if Medicaid is paying for skilled nursing, most of the person's income, like Social Security, except for a personal needs allowance (which ranges from $30 to $150 a month), must go toward paying for their cost of care. In most cases, their income is allocated directly to the nursing home in which they are reside. Nursing homes often coordinate directly with Social Security, so the person's Social Security check goes straight to the nursing home. The rules change if one is receiving services in home or "in the community." Make sure to ask a professional if your state accepts a Medicaid waiver for home care, day care, or assisted living rather than make assumptions.

You can educate yourself by taking a simple three-minute online test at the website medicaidplanningassistance.org to see if you meet the basic requirements for your state and then proceed to get professional advice.

Should Parents "Spend Down" to Qualify for Medicaid?

Do not let your parents "spend down" or sell a home to qualify for Medicaid! To begin with, most applicants can retain their home and still qualify for Medicaid. There are a variety of factors that determine whether owning a home impacts eligibility, including marital status, type of Medicaid program, home equity value, and state of residence. Medicaid looks at two types of assets, "countable" and "exempt," when judging whether an applicant qualifies. Homes can be in the exempt category, but only under certain conditions that vary from state to state; see your state Medicaid website.

Did you know that retirement assets are not counted when trying to qualify for Medicaid if parents are taking their RMD (retirement minimum distributions) every year? Assets can be moved legally, under current Medicaid rules that allow some assets and funds to be preserved. You could find out that "the spouse" (let's say Mom) is protected from being impoverished under Medicaid rules, allowing her to retain some income even if Dad is on Medicaid and already in skilled care. *Do not even apply for Medicaid without seeking professional advice.* If you do, and your application is disqualified for any reason, Medicaid can formally "disqualify" you from applying again for up to seven years! I highly recommend seeking the advice of an elder-law attorney or Medicaid specialist first.

Still, do not let your parents make high-value gifts or transfers within sixty months of applying for Medicaid without understanding what is legal or not. There are some very arcane rules and exceptions about exempt assets. Be advised that many people still think their parents can simply give their money away to the kids, sell a home for under value, and intentionally impoverish themselves to qualify for Medicaid. This has not been true for many years. Most states look back through tax returns and detailed financial records for at least five years as part of the application process. You do not want to be in a mandatory "payback" situation.

Also, nursing homes have people on staff who will help determine Medicaid eligibility if you are considering placing your parent in the facility, but many will not give you a complete picture of your options. Your local Social Security office can help, and so will the VA if one of your parents is a veteran. Your local USAging office is a tremendous resource for information. I advise you to seek more than one person's opinion, and one of those needs to be an independent expert.

Who Is Required to Accept Medicaid?

All stand-alone licensed skilled nursing homes accepting any federal funds are required to accept Medicaid. Usually, they allocate a certain number of beds for Medicaid, but they are not required to accept all patients. If your family has some money to pay a nursing home, my strong advice is to *move them while they can still pay privately,* but get professional advice first. A facility will likely be more willing to accept your loved one if they can pay privately for a while and then continue to care for them when they transition to Medicaid. SNFs located within a life care community are the exception to this rule and almost never accept Medicaid. Their "beds" must be used to meet the needs of the residents on contracts that already live in the community.

PACE Community Care Programs

PACE (Program of All-Inclusive Care for the Elderly) is a Medicare program and Medicaid state option that provides community-based care to people who otherwise would need nursing-home level of care. Their goal is to allow seniors whenever possible to continue living in their home or community. It is the firm belief of members of this organization that it is better for the well-being of seniors with chronic care needs and their families to be served in the community whenever possible rather than going to a nursing facility. They help develop the most effective plan of care just as a private care manager would. To qualify, one has to be fifty-five years or older and be certified by the state in which they live as needing nursing home care.

PACE provide a vast array of services that surprisingly include home care, therapy, prescription drugs, dentistry, optometry, respite care for caregivers, nursing home care, and more! Sadly, there are only 104 PACE sites in thirty-one states.

If your parent already is on Medicaid, they will not have to pay a monthly premium for the long-term care portion of the PACE benefits. If they are on Medicare, they will be charged a monthly premium of some kind. Visit medicare.gov/sign-up-change-plans/different-types-of-medicare -health-plans/pace or call 1-800-MEDICARE to find the nearest PACE program near you.

Veteran Long-Term Care Benefits

When it comes to residential long-term care options, the VA has its own nursing homes, sometimes called "community living centers." Some states also contract with outside nursing homes to provide care for veterans. Do not make assumptions about what benefits your loved one or their spouse are eligible for! Benefits vary and are based on service-connected status, level of disability, and income. Note: The VA never pays for assisted living, just like Medicare, although sometimes extra nursing services within an ALF may be covered. But the VA will pay for adult day care, respite care, and skilled home healthcare. If your loved one gets their primary healthcare through the VA, they are eligible for all these benefits and more. Of course, this will always depend on availability and services available in your location. Space can be extremely limited, and the VA cannot guarantee a bed in a VA nursing home.

Unlike Medicaid, there are no financial eligibility requirements. If your parent is receiving any kind of VA pension, there are two more additional programs called "aid and attendance" for those who need help with their ADLs, are "partially bedridden," or already in a nursing home. Some home- and community-based services for housebound veterans who may also be covered. Always check with a VA-connected social worker or local VA benefits coordinator. If there are none near you, contact the National Association of Veterans & Families or navf.org for help. Remember, even if a veteran has passed away, their spouse could still be eligible for benefits.

I have a friend, Jennifer, whose father, a veteran, had passed away. Her parents were divorced for many years, but neither had remarried. Mom, now in her nineties, was in assisted living with a high monthly cost. Even though they had been divorced for years, they were married long enough for Mom to qualify for some aid and attendance benefits that would contribute a hefty monthly stipend (well over a thousand a month) that she could use to help pay for the ALF. The stipend was paid directly to her under "survivor benefits" and could have also been used for home care, or for any need she had. This made a huge difference and allowed Mom to live out the rest of her days with peace of mind . . . and Jennifer as well!

Long-Term Care Insurance

If your parents are in their eighties, the cost of standard long-term care insurance is prohibitive, and it is not an option. If they have a health issue, they won't qualify for traditional long-term care insurance, as the criteria for approval are becoming more and more stringent as insurance companies want to reduce their risk. A combination of being overweight, having high blood pressure, or being diabetic means they won't be offered a policy. I recently had a client denied a new policy because she was on antidepressants but otherwise very healthy. Any hint of dementia or past strokes will eliminate them as well. If only one parent can qualify, it could be worth considering. If you are in your late fifties or sixties, read this for yourself!

The time to buy long-term care insurance is when you are in your *early to mid-sixties*. Now, I know there are the naysayers who would prefer to self-insure. These people are so wealthy they can afford it. This does not apply to most people! Make sure to read the section on hybrid policies later in this chapter as an alternative to standard long-term care insurance.

Basic Coverage of a Long-Term Care Policy

This may surprise you, but long-term policies do not start paying from day one of skilled care. Most have a ninety-day exclusion period, which means they do not pay for any long-term care until a person is in skilled nursing/rehab care for *more than* ninety days. You can almost always opt for a shorter exclusion period when first purchasing long-term care insurance, like thirty or sixty days, but every time you do, the cost goes way up. I have seen some "Cadillac policies" with zero exclusionary periods, but they are pricey.

The term "zero exclusionary period" means that from day *one* of care needed in skilled/rehab, the policy will pay the daily benefit. My advice is to stick with the ninety days on the theory (at least so far) that Medicare covers most of the cost of the first ninety to one hundred days.

What can you expect a long-term policy to cover? Ideally, a policy would typically be a three- to five-year plan or have a maximum lifetime payout that would cover most of your expenses for skilled nursing care and assisted living. Most plans have what is called a daily benefit, such as $250 a day, depending on the policy. They also have a maximum payout, for example, of $350,000. At $250 a day, for 365 days, you would use up $91,250.00 a year of the total payout and go through all the $350,000 in about 3.8 years.

All policies should cover these *basics:*

- Home care
- Skilled nursing care
- Assisted living
- Optional inflation rider, usually 5 percent; OR
- Optional COLA (Cost of Living Adjustment) increase

Many people do not realize that long-term care almost always covers home care! This could be everything from an in-home nurse, certified nursing assistant (CNA) or home health aide, to someone trained to provide personal care like help bathing, dressing, making meals, running errands. (See Chapter 11 for full information on the different types of home care and home healthcare.) Often, the home care benefit is less than the daily benefit and may be limited to a specific length of time. This amount should be clearly listed in the policy itself on the *schedule of benefits* page in the front of any long-term care policy. Some policies even allow you to pay a family member to help take care of a parent at home, and sometimes they even cover the cost of training you to provide such care!

Inflation Rider

An inflation rider protects the policyholder from the increasing costs of care over time. It factors in rising costs (inflation) and raises both the daily benefits and therefore the overall maximum payout of the policy. It can be a set amount such as 5 percent or it can be variable.

The younger a person is when taking out a policy, the more crucial it is to pay the extra cost for an inflation rider. It does not make sense to pay for a policy at age sixty and have it remain static for the next twenty years. When you are eighty and need it, the value will have decreased considerably due to inflation and the rising cost of long-term care. What paid most costs in 2025 will pay only a fraction in 2045. Ideally the rider should be based on 5 percent yearly increases, hopefully *compounded*, not simple interest. Sometimes they will call this kind of rider by another name, so always ask how the policy handles inflation. Some policies offer an increase based on COLA, or a cost-of-living rate. This is not as preferable as a true inflation rider.

Do not let your parents drop the inflation rider unless they are close to using the policy and they cannot afford to pay the increased cost. Insurance companies cannot jack up just one policy at a time, but they can increase the cost for an entire "class of policies," affecting everyone who holds this type of plan. I have seen steady increases by all companies, even the best. You can expect the cost to go up, even after you or your parents have purchased a policy. Many companies hoping to contain the rising cost of existing long-term care policies are giving their policyholders options to freeze their inflation riders, decrease length of coverage, or pay a higher premium. This forces policyholders to either devalue the policy they may have had for years, pay more for the exact same policy, or cancel!

Remember, when looking at a policy to determine the current daily benefit, you cannot look at the *original issue date for an accurate amount* if the policy has any kind of inflation rider or COLA increase. Look for the schedule of benefits page to see if an inflation rider of any kind was purchased at the initial contract date. Double-check to see if the inflation rider is based on simple or compounded interest, as this can make a huge difference over time. Insurance companies usually mail a letter annually to the policyholder notifying them of the new increased daily amount, as well as any premium increases. Look for this type of communication from the company.

If you must call, make sure your parent is with you, or they won't speak with you unless you are listed as a contact person and someone they can share information with. I advise you to do this before the crisis and make notes such as: "in 2020 the daily benefit increased to $300 a day." If you can't find the policy and your parent is in the hospital, and the company won't talk to you, it could take weeks to get the information!

What Would Prevent Qualifying for LTC Insurance?

Long-term care (LTC) insurance companies are picky, picky, picky! They don't want to offer coverage if it looks like you may need it! They can't afford to insure everyone, or they would all go bankrupt. This means if you have any kind of neurological, neuromuscular, serious heart or respiratory issues, forget it. If your parent is a smoker, has high blood pressure, is obese, they will not offer coverage. Osteoporosis means falls, possible breaks, and is a red flag for insurance companies. Any kind of mini-stroke or early cognitive impairment are immediate disqualifiers. This is why you must apply *before* you are diagnosed with anything like the above. You can expect either a physical from a company nurse, full access to your medical records, a mini-mental phone interview, or some combination of the above before being offered any coverage. Since they will see all medical records, just ask your insurance representative what diagnosis will disqualify your loved one (or you) from coverage.

How Are the Spencers Paying for Care?

As you may remember, Sally is living in the apartment at Maple Village in independent living, and Bob has recently moved to assisted living within Maple Village, since it is a life care community. Josie discovers her parents had taken out a group LTC plan through Bob's job. She and Sally look up information on the schedule of benefits page and call the insurance company to find out what they will pay for Bob's care. Bob and Sally took the policy out fifteen years ago, and luckily, it had an inflation rider. It turns out Bob's policy will now pay $5,000 a month for his care in assisted living. This is a big help, since Sally is still paying the monthly fee for the apartment.

The policy has a lifetime benefit of $300,000, so will last five years at $60,000 a year. While no one knows how long Bob will live, this relieves some of the financial burden of paying for his care. Sally has her own policy, but of course, it won't pay for her monthly fee since she is still in independent living. If she ever needs assisted living or skilled care, she can use it, and if Bob has to transition into skilled nursing care, he can, too. She has additional peace of mind knowing that should she need some home care while living in her apartment, even at Maple Village, her policy will pay for this as well. The insurance company reminds Sally and Josie to send them a billing statement from Maple Village for Bob's costs so they can reimburse Sally for this amount. LTC companies never pay the facility directly, like Medicaid or Medicare do. They pay the policyholder.

Hybrid LTC Policies

There are some new types of hybrid policies on the market worth considering. The insurance industry is responding to the demand for something besides the standard model. Some see the traditional approach as unsustainable, both for the company and the policyholder. In fact, in April 2019, Genworth, one of the largest underwriters of long-term care insurance, announced that it has stopped selling individual stand-alone coverage and will only sell through employer groups or affinity groups. Dozens of other companies have stopped as well. This will not affect the 1.2 million current policyholders, but it says what the market knows: Long-term care is a risky business for companies. The sale of traditional policies has plummeted as consumers look for alternatives to annual premiums with no guarantee of money back and predictably rising costs.

Companies are now offering a combination of whole life insurance and long-term care in a single policy. You can pay a high lump-sum contribution, like $50,000 or $100,000+, and you're guaranteed to get long-term care benefits with a built-in inflation rider, or, if never used, a death benefit, or a return of your initial payment in full, guaranteed, at any time. The obvious disadvantage is the high upfront cost. The advantage is it shields you from price hikes that will occur in the more traditional policy, and if you never use it for long-term care, your beneficiary gets a life insurance payout when you die. What makes this so appealing is that you have an initial investment of say $100,000 at age sixty, which multiplies over time to a possible $647,000 in long-term care benefits by age eighty, depending on if you chose a 3 percent, 5 percent simple, or 5 percent compounded inflation rider. These policies cover everything that a traditional policy covers, such as home care, assisted living, skilled care, adult day care, care coordination, and more. As of 2021, neither the long-term care benefits nor death payouts of these hybrid policies are taxable.

Another newer option on the market is a **healthcare annuity**. Annuity contracts traditionally provide a guaranteed stream of income over time, until the death of the person or until a final date, whichever comes first. Long-term care annuities offer the added possible benefit of specifically covering long-term care expenses. If your parents already own a deferred annuity, they may be able to exchange it tax-free for a combo annuity healthcare policy. Then the distributions are tax-free if used for long-term care. Again, always seek advice from a professional as you evaluate the best options for paying for long-term care. These kinds of policies are complex and vary tremendously, so do your homework!

Most importantly, *your parent can already have some significant health issues and still get one of these kinds of annuities.* It is easier to qualify for one of these combo options than straight up traditional long-term care plans, so do not make assumptions. All companies will verify health and medical history with doctors, so keep this in mind. Another advantage? Some of these companies offer these plans up to age eighty!

Reverse Mortgages

I want to mention reverse mortgages as a last-ditch effort to pay for long-term care. I am not a fan, but I have seen this save a family's sanity. If your parent owns their home outright or has a lot of equity in the house, they could consider a reverse mortgage to pay for home care.

They can have a lifetime right to stay in the home and have the added income, but when they pass away, the mortgage company receives the value of the home once sold. Do the math before deciding. Make an educated guess about length of life, need for care, and cost of care. If a house is "reverse mortgaged," it can't be sold to pay for long-term care in assisted living or skilled nursing. Make sure to get educated on the pluses and minuses of this option, but the extra income has allowed plenty of seniors to age in place. Beware high interest rates and complex contracts. Have an expert read it first.

HELOC or Home Equity Loans

Sometimes known as a home equity line of credit, this allows seniors to take advantage of the equity in their home in the form of a loan, rather than a reverse mortgage. They retain ownership of the home and borrow against its value. The downside is you have to make payments immediately. Since you can typically repay and borrow against the line of credit as often as you like, these loans are especially appealing for short-term needs. Unlike a reverse mortgage, which requires the borrower or spouse to be living in the home, there's no residency requirement with a home equity loan. You should expect lower fees and interest rates compared to reverse mortgages, in general. There are also no mortgage closing costs. Banks will look at credit scores and credit history to determine eligibility, so not all borrowers will be approved or get favorable terms. This could be an option if adult children want to keep the house in the family and agree to pay the loan.

A National Crisis

As a country, we are facing a crisis. The cost of long-term care is simply unsustainable, but there are no easy solutions. Unless the United States comes up with a better plan to meet the needs of the baby boomers, we are in trouble. After Covid, many people are afraid of long-term care facilities and rightfully so. Our government is only recently looking at ways to help people age in place and fairly compensate healthcare workers and home care givers. I am hoping options for families will improve as our government improves Medicare and Medicaid for poor and middle-class families.

Develop your own plan for yourself and your parents that will, at the least, minimize the risk of financial ruin due to care costs, and, at best, pay for most of the costs. Your goal is to maximize your parents' independence and to provide high-quality care for your loved ones, whether they age in place or move to a community. Try to advocate locally and nationally for policies that help families pay for care and increase wages for healthcare workers. Start contributing to your own health savings account (HSA) tax-free to prepare for your own long-term care costs!

A Prepared Exit Plan

Grief is the last act of love we have to give to those we loved. Where there is deep grief, there was great love.

Author unknown

My motivation for writing this book was to help families navigate the confusing world of senior living and senior care. Sadly, at some point, the next step will be navigating your loved one's end of life, and hopefully, a time for partnering and planning together. And a time for yet more conversation about end-of-life wishes, when to seek or stop treatment, and perhaps how your loved one can live their life fully to conclusion.

As strange as this may seem, you can still apply both Principle #1, maximizing independence for the longest possible time, and Principle #2, "Just in Time" Senior Planning, at this stage. In fact, it is even more critical. From how to have conversations about what a good death might look like for your parents to traditional and nontraditional burial and funeral options and beyond, this section applies the two principles of this book to end-of-life decisions.

Chapter 16

What Is a Good Death?

Having a "good death" requires a lot of forethought and planning. Otherwise, your loved one becomes yet another statistic of someone dying in the hospital when they really wanted to die at home. The truth is, you need a good plan for dying as much as for living, and this section will give your family a lot to talk about as you develop a plan together. The time to talk about this is long before a terminal diagnosis or a trip to the emergency room. Being in control of how one's own death unfolds, to the degree possible, is a form of maximizing one's independence. It preserves your parents' dignity to die in their own bed should they wish, with family present, and not in an institutional setting. "Just in time" planning takes on new meaning when the backdrop is end-of-life planning. Better to assume one has less time than more. Let's start by looking at what a good death might mean.

Slow Medicine

Doctors are trained to save lives and treat symptoms. They don't relish the idea of telling a patient that the procedure they are recommending might only extend Mom's life another three months. And by the way, Mom will be miserable from the effects of chemo in her last three months of life. Typically, families are faced with a medical system that offers up more tests, more chemo, more radiation, more surgery, when perhaps selectively choosing what *not* to do might be better for the patient.

In 2008, Dr. Dennis McCullough published an article in the *Dartmouth Medicine* magazine where he coined the phrase "slow medicine," meaning let's all just slow down and not be rushed into making fast medical decisions with huge implications. His advice? Turn away from "fast medicine" and look slowly and carefully at the medical options offered to aging and sometimes very ill patients. "Nobody seems to know how to put on the brakes. To maximize efficiency, doctors and nurses are always over-scheduled. Taking time for listening and understanding . . . is not paid for and hence not usually undertaken in today's corporate medical environment."

Fast-forward to 2018, and Dr. Samuel Harrington (honors graduate from Harvard and the University of Wisconsin School of Medicine) talks about the same thing in his thoughtful book *At Peace: Choosing a Good Death After a Long Life*. Most people say they would like to die quietly in their home, but often this is not the case. He states that "Overly aggressive medical advice, coupled with an unrealistic sense of invincibility or overconfidence in our health-care system, results in the majority of elderly patients misguidedly dying in institutions. Many undergo painful procedures instead of having the better and more peaceful death they deserve."

What if families put the emphasis on quality of life first, and treatment second, if the treatment will compromise real quality of life? I am sure many of you have watched loved ones opt for aggressive treatment in a terminal situation only to spend the remaining few weeks or months extremely ill. One wonders if they had to do it all over again, would they opt out, preferring to live the best life possible while spending time with their family and loved ones? But "slow medicine" is not just for these types of situations; it can apply conceptually to medical care for any elderly person. Does a ninety-year-old really want a colonoscopy? Yet another prescription drug with some serious side effects? Is the new battery of tests the doctor is recommending really necessary? Maybe yes, maybe no. My goal is to encourage realistic compassionate thinking on this topic. I don't imagine for a second I know what is right for any family or individual. But I do know from my own experience that treatments have side effects that you can't predict.

My beloved elderly stepfather was diagnosed with advanced colon cancer. He opted for surgery and spent the next several years struggling mightily with an ileostomy, a reverse ileostomy, and more. At one point, he had a very minor slip, not even a fall, but he was in terrible pain. The doctor ordered physical therapy and after several weeks of this, his pain was far worse. As it turns out, he had a small fracture in his pelvis. No one thought to look, given that he didn't fall. The therapy was making it worse, not better. The cause? Side effects from the radiation had weakened his bones so much that even a minor slip resulted in a painful pelvic fracture.

You don't know what you don't know, as I am fond of stating. Especially when it comes to unintended consequences from aggressive treatment options. The best way to navigate this territory is to try and encourage your parents to get all the facts before making any decisions. As their advocate, you can assist with this process.

Critical Questions for the Doctor

Here are a few questions specifically focused on end of life that you or your parent can discuss with their healthcare providers, from the helpful Life Course Planning page at floridahealthfinder.gov:

1. Are you comfortable talking openly with me (my parent, etc.) about death and dying?
2. What will happen to me (my parent) as this illness progresses?
3. What are the care options and the benefits and difficulties of these options?
4. What medications will I be taking and how will they affect me (my parent)? What are the worst potential side effects?
5. If I experience pain, how will it be managed?

6. If I want aggressive, limited, or experimental treatment, will you respect my wishes?

7. If I choose only comfort care such as hospice, will you continue to serve as my healthcare provider?

8. What is the range of time I (my parent) might be expected to live?

9. What can I (my parent) expect during the last few weeks or months of my life?

Be specific: What are the advantages and disadvantages of this medication, this surgery, this treatment? What are the side effects, the percent of success or risks for any medical surgery, whether it is an end-of-life issue or not? If there is only a 30 percent chance of success, and the side effects are awful, is it worth it? What other options does your parent have? This is simply not the time to be shy or to care if the doctor likes you. Remain respectful but extremely inquisitive and always doubtful. Insist upon having this kind of conversation in a quiet office space, not in a noisy, rushed environment. If necessary, make an appointment with the doctor for the sole purpose of discussing options and let him/her know why you are coming in with your parent. Ideally, if you are the healthcare surrogate, try to make sure to meet the doctor before a major crisis.

Slow medicine means giving your loved one the time to ponder, weigh, and consider their options very, very carefully. Support them in this. Your job is to slow down, too. No panic and drama, no rushing them or yourself. When I have been in these situations, my mantra is "more listening, less reacting."

Let's say the doctor has just told you and Dad that he is recommending an invasive medical test/treatment that you frankly feel is not in your dad's best interest. You might say (in front of Dad), "Doctor, I'm confused. If my father takes this treatment, how sure are you about a positive outcome? What are the risks? Could it make him feel worse or improve his quality of life?" You don't want to get into a position where you're arguing with the doctor or your dad. Keep this approach going until you are satisfied that you and Dad have all the answers you need to make a good decision.

Make sure your parent has a chance to ask questions, too. If your loved one just got a terrible diagnosis, they will likely not be in a state of mind to ask the right questions. Be sure to take notes, or better yet, record the conversation. This way you can listen to it again. I have walked out of doctors' appointments with a parent, and you would swear we had been in two very different rooms. Sometimes people can only hear what they want to hear, or they literally have trouble hearing. A cell phone recording gives you the option of listening again, together. Plus, you can upload it and share with family if needed.

I recommend always seeking a second medical opinion when it comes to a serious diagnosis or treatment recommendation. You might even go to a different medical system such as two different hospitals or a specialized doctor or hospital that focuses on cancer or the just-diagnosed Parkinson's.

Reminder: It will be far easier to participate in these conversations if you have your parents' medical power of attorney or are their healthcare surrogate/proxy (see page 25). Naturally, any doctor will want to hear directly from your loved one. If they have dementia, then you will need to participate in any medical decision-making.

When to Stop Pursuing Treatment

When to stop pursuing treatment is a difficult decision. I have seen those who never give up, and those who decide long before death is imminent. It is a deeply personal choice that an individual makes. I remind the reader that if you are a healthcare proxy, it is your job to support your loved one's decision in every way you can. Please do not argue or debate or try to talk a person out of their decision. If your loved one is thinking clearly and is not mentally ill, accept their decision. Ultimately, it is the person's or your parent's choice. If they have lost their will to live, and you can clearly see that their quality of life is vastly diminished, they may, for example, opt out of more life-sustaining treatment. I do not judge someone who says they are ready to go.

I knew a woman who simply stopped dialysis, and also stopped eating and drinking any water, but this is an option too difficult for many.

She was ready to go, and her two sons accepted her wishes. Another lovely woman threw herself a wonderful going-away party for all the residents of the community she lived in, and stopped all treatment for terminal cancer. Both these options would be considered passive, meaning death became inevitable due to stopping treatments or no longer eating or drinking water. Because death is fraught with so much anxiety and fear, if your parents practice a faith of any kind, I would ask them if they want to talk this over with their minister, priest, rabbi, or imam. Understand that it may be too difficult to talk this over with their own child, no matter how "grown up" you may be.

Medical Aid in Dying

While a controversial subject, medical aid in dying (MAID) is an option I believe will become more available across the country, and a serious option for many aging baby boomers facing a long, slow, terminal illness. According to one of the leading organizations, Compassion & Choices, "Medical Aid in Dying is a safe and trusted medical practice in which a terminally ill mentally capable adult with a prognosis of six months or less to live may request from his or her doctor a prescription for medication which they can choose to self-ingest to bring about a peaceful death."

Unlike the examples above, this is not a passive option, but an active choice by a person to end their life. It is not considered suicide by the majority of physicians, nor is it called physician-assisted suicide by leading medical organizations. In all states where MAID is legal, the death certificate will say death due to terminal illness and not use the term "suicide." Note: The patient must be able to self-administer the prescription with absolutely no assistance. As many as 33 percent of patients who obtain a legal prescription to end their life never use it. Many say knowing they could, should they choose to, gives them peace of mind.

You might be surprised to learn that the latest 2020 Gallup poll shows that 74 percent of Americans support medical aid in dying, up six points from the May 2018 poll, according to Compassion & Choices. Majority support included every demographic group across gender, race, age, politics, and education. Even the latest polls from Medscape (a medical website for clinicians) show physicians are increasingly open to the option of providing help to patients who choose medical aid in dying. In fact, the American Academy of Family Physicians dropped its opposition to medical aid in dying and adopted a position of "engaged neutrality," hoping to "create change in the best interests of their patients." Whether you believe in the sanctity of life or believe a person should have the autonomy to relieve unremitting suffering for themselves, this option is not going away.

Where Is It Legal?

Medical aid-in-dying laws exist in California, Colorado, the District of Columbia, Hawaii, Oregon, Maine, Montana, New Jersey, New Mexico, Vermont, and Washington as of 2022. Most of the legislation passed requires confirmation by two healthcare providers as to the person's terminal diagnosis, their ability to make a clear and informed decision, and a signed request witnessed by two people (at least one unrelated to the patient).

Expect several mandatory waiting periods, but just recently Oregon waived its waiting-period rules. There are many groups such as Death with Dignity (deathwithdignity.org) and Compassion & Choices (compassionandchoices.org) that are working to get laws passed in other states. By the time this book is published, the number of states allowing MAID will undoubtedly increase, so double-check to see the latest changes and the laws in your state.

If Your Loved One Is Considering MAID

If your loved one is considering MAID, going to a state where active medical aid in dying is legal is a possibility, especially if a sibling or another family member lives in one of the legal states. Check to see if there are residency requirements, waiting periods, or what is required to be deemed a "legal resident."

I would also advise that you speak to your parent's physician if you feel that your parent continues to clearly express their wish to end their life. If nothing else, you will find out their opinion, and they may be able to help your family member accept death in a different way. If hospice can help manage pain or unbearable symptoms, this may be all they need.

What Exactly Is Hospice?

"Hospice is a special kind of care for people with an anticipated life expectancy of 6 months or less, when a cure is not an option, and the focus is on symptom management and quality of life," according to the website hospicefoundation.org (click on About Hospice/What is Hospice).

Hospice takes a holistic, compassionate, person-centered approach to caring for those who are facing serious life-limiting illness and provides expert medical care, pain management, and emotional and spiritual support to the patient and their family. Hospice organizations believe all patients have the right to die pain free and with dignity.

Hospice organizations take a team approach. They will have physicians, nurses, social workers, home health aides, grief counselors, chaplains, and volunteers. This team will develop a personalized plan of care for your loved one. Hospice services are provided:

- In the residential home
- In a facility such as assisted living, nursing home, or a life care community if that is where the patient is living
- In a hospice area within a hospital, or a facility run by the hospice organization
- In a special inpatient facility for a short period of time to manage crisis symptoms or to provide respite for a caregiver

By far, most hospice care is provided in the patient's home, but if home is in a skilled nursing home or community-living arrangement, hospice will provide these services there. Care is not twenty-four hours a day, but you can expect hospice providers to be available by phone twenty-four hours a day, seven days a week.

Care typically includes periodic visits to the patient and family care-givers. Exhausted caregivers, please note that *respite care is part of hospice services.* This means you can receive up to five days respite from caregiving by admitting your loved one to an inpatient hospice facility! Don't wait until you fall apart.

Hospice can also provide any needed medical equipment such as hospital beds, wheelchairs, walkers, oxygen, bandages, and catheters. It will not pay for any treatment or prescription drugs intended to cure a terminal illness.

When Is It Time for Hospice Care?

Too many families wait too long before calling in hospice. A patient does not need to be in their final days (actively dying) to receive hospice care. In fact, calling in hospice much sooner can be a huge benefit to the person and the family. Hospice should be considered when:

- Life expectancy is six months or less, according to physicians;
- There is a noticeable decline in the physical or cognitive status despite medical treatment (things like substantial weight loss, extreme fatigue, shortness of breath, to name a few);
- The patient has decided to forgo treatments aimed at curing a life-threatening illness;
- The patient is in end-stage Alzheimer's or a related dementia.

While 70–75 percent of people using hospice care have a cancer diag-nosis, hospice also cares for end-stage heart patients, Parkinson's patients, patients with lung disease like COPD, end-stage dementia patients, and more. Please keep in mind that many patients live beyond the six-month prognosis. This is simply a guideline, not a prediction.

Instead of being afraid that calling in hospice means your loved one will give up, or that they will die "faster," the truth is that hospice is there to provide help to the family and the patient. Their goal is to make sure your loved one is not in pain and does not suffer needless admissions in and out of a hospital along with treatments that won't help when the diagnosis is terminal.

Hospice in Facilities

Most assisted-living and skilled nursing homes/facilities that provide hospice care have a contract with one hospice company, so you don't get to choose as you would if they were delivering services in your home. Many facilities have a hospice room that allows for both the patient and their spouse and family to be together during this time, some even providing a place for family members to sleep. Once hospice is called into a facility, they become the primary manager for the patient, not the facility. Ideally, they work as a team to coordinate care. Make sure, as your loved one's advocate, to request a meeting with both the facility and hospice care coordinators. Ask them nicely to put in writing what each will provide, now that hospice is part of the picture, such as who is responsible for bathing or medication management. Unfortunately, I have seen some finger-pointing and blaming in these situations. It is always "the other's" fault when care falls through the cracks. Don't hesitate to continue to ask for clarification about who to call when you run into some issues.

Some larger hospitals have hospice-designated rooms or floors. Staff is trained to provide care to the dying and support for the family. They are patient, compassionate, and help educate a family on what to expect and how to manage pain. They are so familiar with the process of dying, they can alert families when death is near and help prepare you about what signs to look for. This is comforting as you face the inevitable yet the unknown.

I recently interviewed a longtime hospice nurse and friend who explained that nursing homes are required by state rules to turn patients, bathe them, get them up to be weighed, make sure they eat, etc. That may be the last thing you want to do when your mom or dad is dying, in pain, or barely conscious! By having hospice become the primary care provider, these requirements are relaxed, and your loved one can rest peacefully and not be disturbed.

How to Qualify and Find Hospice Care

First, talk with your doctor. Let them know that you would like information on your local hospice organizations. They will likely have a recommendation. To qualify for hospice services, a hospice physician and another doctor, often the specialist, must certify that the patient meets the criteria for medical eligibility pertaining to the six-month rule. This may vary depending on the specific diagnosis and the person's condition. But anyone can contact a hospice organization directly and begin the process. All of them will help you and your family with your options and how to initiate services.

Visit medicare.gov/talk-to-someone, or call 1-800-MEDICARE (1-800-633-4227) to find the number for your state hospice organization. Medicare only covers your hospice care if the hospice provider is Medicare approved. Visit medicare.gov/care-compare to find Medicare-approved hospice providers in your area.

In more populated areas, there may be three or more hospice companies to choose from. Some larger areas have hospice centers that can serve the needs of over one hundred patients in one building.

Do your homework. Ask what makes them different from the other local companies, meet with their outreach representatives, and see who you resonate with. Some hospice organizations are not-for-profit and others are for-profit. Some have a religious affiliation. Generally, I recommend a not-for-profit. Find out who has the best reputation and go visit their hospice centers if possible. You can also check with your local USAging office, the American Cancer Society, or a geriatric case manager for a referral. Make sure they are Medicare certified (almost all are) and, ideally, accredited (certified and licensed) by a nationally recognized group such as the Joint Commission, an independent not-for-profit organization that evaluates and accredits healthcare organizations and programs. For extra peace of mind, ask if they have ever been charged with Medicare billing fraud, ever been sued, or under what conditions would they ever "disenroll" or drop a patient.

If you or your parents live in a rural area or receive primary care through a nurse practitioner or physician's assistant, inquire about the possibility of receiving hospice care through them. The Medicare Patient Access to Hospice Act went into effect in January 2019, allowing designated healthcare practitioners with extra training to offer hospice services to rural and underserved communities.

Over the years, I have personally spoken with several distraught family members who felt their parent was overmedicated by hospice. Remember, a hospice's goal is to keep their patient pain-free. Powerful drugs like morphine are regularly used. Make sure you, your parent, and hospice are on the same page, for example if you are waiting for another family member to arrive and are hoping your loved one will be conscious and able to speak or recognize them. Ask about the hospice's standard procedures and medication guidelines early on.

How Is Palliative Care Different from Hospice Care?

There is a lot of confusion about palliative care. There is an incorrect assumption that it is the same as hospice. It's not! *Palliative care is for anyone at any stage of a serious illness who may still be seeking treatment or a cure.* Palliative care specialists are experts in treating physical symptoms like pain and nausea, fatigue and depression. But like hospice, treatment is person-centered and the goal is to offer comfort, education, and supportive decision-making.

It is not necessarily limited to a diagnosis of six months to live or less. Their goal is to provide a person the best quality of life possible given the circumstances the patient is dealing with. To be clear, the person may expect to recover from their illness but is experiencing intense symptoms along the way. Palliative care is for any patient experiencing a decreased quality of life due to symptoms relating to their treatment or illness.

In fact, palliative care can be offered along with curative or long-term medical therapies. Today, 72 percent of hospitals with fifty or more beds have palliative care services. So do some nursing homes and even some out-patient clinics. All hospice organizations offer palliative care as well.

The first thing to do is to talk with your doctor, ask for a consultation, and educate yourself on the options. Some hospice organizations now offer programs that allow the family to benefit from some support and consulting services before reaching the decision to give up treatment.

Who Pays for Hospice Care?

Hospice services are covered by both Medicare and Medicaid, provided care is received in a Medicare-certified hospice. Veterans Health Administration and many other types of health plans, including Medicare Advantage plans, HMOs, PPOs, and other private insurance companies, also cover hospice services. Care that may be unrelated to the terminal illness continues to be covered by Medicare Parts A and B, with all normal rules applying. As of 2022, a co-payment can be expected of up to five dollars per prescription for outpatient prescription drugs for pain and symptom management.

It is always wise to ask if there will be any cost billed to your loved one. For example, hospice does not pay for ambulances, treatment, or prescription drugs used to cure illness, and they do not pay the "room and board" costs of a nursing home.

Perhaps your parent has not reached age sixty-five and is not yet on Medicare? For those not eligible, payment for hospice can come from their own health insurance since these will have a hospice component. Remember that it is generally the philosophy to aid any dying patient regardless of ability to pay, so please don't hesitate to talk openly with any hospice organization.

Often families worry that benefits will "run out" if their loved one lives beyond the six-month life expectancy, but hospice services continue as long as your doctor and the hospice doctor continue to certify that the patient is terminally ill.

By the way, in 2022, Medicare paid an average of about $200 per day for hospice services in the home to the organization providing care. Again, these are reimbursed costs back to hospice, not a cost to the patient. This is why a doctor may recommend hospice or palliative care to a patient because they understand the *potential financial help that comes along with this care.* Check out this booklet: medicare.gov/Pubs/pdf/02154-medicare-hospice -benefits.pdf.

The Best Place to Die

Not everyone can die at home, although this is by far the preference. The latest statistics show that 80 percent of Americans would prefer to die at home, but 60 percent of Americans die in acute care hospitals, 20 percent in nursing homes, and only 20 percent die at home. And yet, a minority use hospice care. If they knew how much hospice could help, they would contact hospice much sooner. But for those with no family, or who may be very sick, they may need a hospital or facility. It takes the worry out of someone being present twenty-four hours a day, needing special equipment, or being afraid or anxious managing a complex medical problem. You may not be able to plan the location of a loved one's death, but if you can, call in hospice long before this time. Listen to what your loved one wants and try to find a way to make this work for them. Hospice has been a godsend to me and my family when we needed it most, both "at home" and in a facility. If you want to die at home and avoid a medicalized death in a hospital, I suggest making a plan and sharing it with your family.

Dr. Harrington's book, *At Peace: Choosing a Good Death After a Long Life*, is so helpful because it is written for "anyone who can look far enough ahead to know that death will arrive and to see that preparing for it in personal terms is better than leaving it completely to chance or in the hands of overly aggressive doctors." It is extremely informative in both clinical terms about specific disease trajectories, what to expect, and at what point it might be wise to opt out of treatment rather than experience a highly medicalized death. He is one of several prominent voices for slow medicine, but he calls it "becoming aggressively passive." The book applies his principles and walks the reader through his own parents' choices and eventual "good deaths."

Even after my twenty-five years in senior living, I found this book to be both informative and invaluable.

Managing Family Conflict at End of Life

One of the most difficult situations is when family members do not agree on end-of-life decisions. Let's face it, families come with a history . . . a history of how each person feels toward the person who is sick, long-standing sibling rivalries, unspoken secrets, or rules about what can be said or what can never be talked about. When the family gathers around a loved one near the end of life, there is likely going to be the potential for serious stress. Concentrate on prioritizing what problems need to be dealt with today and remember that things change very quickly. Always place the focus on the loved one and what their needs are: a peaceful, quiet environment.

It is very difficult for a healthcare surrogate who, acting on behalf of their spouse or parent, disagrees with other siblings or family members on stopping life-saving measures. Watching family members battle over the outcome of a loved one's medical care is a future none of us wants. Here are some things you can do to prevent this from ever happening to your family.

1. Make sure your parents have a living will that truly spells out their wishes and encourage them to have multiple conversations with everyone in the family about exactly what those wishes are.

2. If you know one of your family members will likely disagree with your parent's wishes to opt out of treatment, make sure to request that your parent speak with them one-on-one, write them a letter, email, or make a video!

3. If your parent wants to be an organ donor, make sure to let everyone in the family know and make copies of the organ donor card for your critical medical info file.

4. If your parent is enrolled in hospice care, you can talk with the social worker and ask for their help. They are experts and can make a tremendous difference.

5. If your sibling or parent is upset due to religious beliefs (e.g., stopping treatment is considered a sin), call on the hospital chaplain or your parent's priest, minister, or rabbi, etc.

6. An ounce of prevention can go a long way. This type of situation will rarely play out if the right level of communication has taken place prior to the dying process. Don't wait for a crisis. Go back and read Chapter 2 on having "the Conversation."

7. Consider hiring an end-of-life doula (see below). They are very experienced in helping families cope with all the emotions surrounding death.

End-of-Life Doulas

"Doula" is an ancient Greek term that loosely means a woman helping another woman, and the word has long been associated with the birthing process. It has expanded in recent years to include end-of-life doulas, who provide nonmedical holistic support and comfort to the dying person and their family, according to the International End of Life Doula Association. This "can include education, guidance, as well as emotional, spiritual or practical care, from as early as initial diagnosis through bereavement." Just as a birth doula aids in the ushering in of life, an end-of-life doula provides support for the dying and their family. Their aim is to help families recognize death as a natural and important part of life. The end-of-life doula movement is supported by the National Hospice and Palliative Care Organization.

Doulas can make a big difference in the dying process, as their perspective is a bit different from the hospice role. Please note that a doula does not replace the hospice role but complements it. Hospice is rarely there all the time. A doula has the time to be bedside for as long as the family desires and to stay there for as long as needed. They can even discuss with the patient, prior to death, what the patient considers a good death and how to achieve this. Do they want any rituals of any kind, any religious or cultural considerations prior to or at death? Special music played, prayers said? This would be the natural role of a doula to ask these kinds of questions and to guide the family and friends through the dying process in accordance with the wishes of the patient.

Below is a list of services a doula can provide:

- Facilitate end-of-life planning
- Mediation and advocacy so that the dying person's wishes are honored
- Comfort measures for the dying
- Emotional support
- Life review and legacy project support
- Education, information, and resources
- Respite care for the family
- Logistical and household support
- After-death care

Many doulas have received certification and special training through several national programs, and some come from social work or hospice nurse backgrounds. Currently there is no federal authority or regulatory body that oversees the development of doula training and certification. However, Oregon and a few other states have passed measures to regulate and license the practice of being a "death midwife." Check with the state you reside in to see if they have set up any requirements. For the most part, certification is a voluntary process and is not required to identify as an end-of-life doula.

Here are a few well-regarded programs that offer special training:

- LifespanDoulas program: lifespandoulas.com
- National End-of-Life Doula Alliance certification: nedalliance.org
- INELDA (International End-of-Life Doula Association) certification: inelda.org/
- Conscious Dying Institute in Asheville, North Carolina: conscious dyinginstitute.com

Some progressive hospitals such as NYU Langone Medical Center and Baylor University Medical Center have begun to utilize doulas to work hand in hand with their clinical staff. If your loved one is in a hospital or an inpatient hospice facility, I would encourage you to ask if they have a doula on staff.

Doulas are usually very knowledgeable about their community and can educate a patient or family in any area connected with the dying process. They can help with planning funerals or memorial services, and are generally aware of home funeral and green burial options as discussed in the next chapter. Sometimes referred to as covering the "pan-death spectrum," they really can provide a wide range of services, so be sure to ask what is available.

Some doulas provide respite care and care coordination, and even may help someone write a "life legacy." This could be as simple as a short essay about a person's life values, or, time permitting, more of a life history or life highlights. They might provide light massage, even brush teeth, change clothes and bedding, reposition someone in bed, apply cold compresses, hold hands, and provide comfort. They typically do not change bandages, administer medications, or do any "medical" care. This is what hospice nurses or aides provide.

Who Pays for Doula Services?

While some doulas are strictly volunteers, most are not. A doula's salary varies greatly depending on geographic locations, how much training and experience they have, and how many hours they work for you. You can expect costs to vary between $50 and $100 per hour. Some charge flat rates for initial visits and during a dying patient's final days. Total costs for end-of-life services can range from $800 to $2,500 and as high as $4,000 in some urban areas. None of this will be covered by insurance or Medicare and is all private pay. Some in the industry feel this will change as some insurance companies are now partially reimbursing for birth doulas. Make sure to be clear on any and all fees prior to hiring a doula.

Doulas can make the difference in having a good death and making everyone as comfortable as possible on this journey. Those drawn to this service are usually compassionate, caring individuals who help families honor this sacred space as a loved one dies. If your doula is a volunteer, consider a gratitude gift to the doula or to the hospital or organization they are associated with.

The Spencer Family Journey

Bob is now eighty-five, and he is struggling physically and mentally. He has had another stroke that has left him seriously debilitated with limited mobility. He moved out of assisted living into full-time skilled nursing care at Maple Village, the life care community he lives in that provides higher levels of care. Despite PT and OT, he is not improving. The whole family is worried, especially Sally. They ask for a conference with his doctor, who recommends several possible tests to look at blockages in the arteries like a cerebral angiogram or CT scan, followed by possible surgery if he determines Bob can handle it.

But Bob says no, he does not want these tests. He votes for the slow medicine approach and talks with the family, all of whom are in North Carolina due to his stroke. Bob asks the doctor if he qualifies for hospice care and communicates with the family that he is ready to go. Lots of tears are shed. The doctor agrees to call in hospice and the family supports his decision, even Sally. They accept that their time together is limited, and John, with his wife Sophia and sister Wendy, plan for more frequent visits to Raleigh. Josie and her husband Dan who live in Raleigh understand they will be the primary support for Josie's parents through this end-of-life journey. They talk with Bob and Sally about calling in an end-of-life doula that can help Bob plan a "good death," and he loves the idea. He has always been a planner, and now he understands the value of planning his own death and his own memorial. Josie agrees to find several possible doulas and see who her dad likes the most. They treasure every day together, not knowing how long Bob has.

Your Own Family Journey

While none of us can predict the future, it is a safe assumption that we will all die, even though we all regularly behave as if this is not true! What if we began to view death a bit differently?

The Buddhists say death is your last best friend, the last one to be with you as you exit this life. What can we do to help us make peace with the entire dying process? Whatever your beliefs, I hope this chapter inspires you to talk with your loved ones and encourage them to share their thoughts with you about what a "good death" might look like for them . . . and maybe start you on your own journey as well.

Chapter 17

Funerals, Cremations, Green Burials, and Your Parents' Wishes

Unless your parents are super Type-A personalities, you may be the person planning their funeral. Believe it or not, I have known people who wrote their own obituaries! Now that is planning ahead! But we all know this is rare. The point is, you don't just want to talk with parents about their end-of-life wishes, you want to talk about, and plan ahead for, the kind of funeral they want. This chapter will educate you and your family about both traditional options and options you may not have heard of, as well as giving you an estimate of expenses associated with each.

I'd like to remind you that many elders, knowing full well that death is unavoidable, may appreciate your willingness to bring up this topic. Planning a funeral can give great peace of mind to a person, allowing them to share with family, friends, and loved ones what would be meaningful to them, complete with poems to be read, songs sung, music played, and meaningful words or scripture read. Being involved in a service, religious or not, that calls forth the spirit of the person being remembered allows people the chance to feel their grief, and it can bring a little peace of mind to everyone.

Test the waters. Ask your loved one if they have thought about what they want for any kind of memorial or service. Give them time to respond. Start with questions about music, songs, and, if they practice a faith, religious texts. Some people want more of a wake, a celebration of life, while others prefer quiet reverie or a chapel service of some kind. For those who have a church or religious community, sharing grief through faith can be a powerful experience of affirmation. I've also been to many a graveside where the deceased's favorite alcohol was poured directly on the grave, or shots of vodka were passed around at every toast! You won't know if you don't ask.

Explain your motive for asking: knowing their wishes and being able to carry out those wishes as part of the legacy they leave behind. Save the actual burial questions for last. Maybe there is a family plot, or they want ashes sprinkled in the ocean like three of my loved ones.

Traditional Funerals

For thousands of years, various cultures and religions have buried their dead with respect, honor, and dignity, often following certain rituals and traditions. So, what is a traditional funeral in the United States today? Every family is different, and it is almost impossible to say what is traditional, since funerals can be simple or elaborate, public or private, religious or secular, and may or may not include a viewing or visitation. Are remains going to be buried or cremated? All of this will affect the cost. It is expensive to die, with the average funeral costing between $7,500 to $10,000 depending on what you choose, and surprisingly, on your location.

The website worldpopulationreview.com (click on US States and scroll to the bottom and click on Average Funeral Cost by State) will show you up-to-date funeral costs state by state. In 2022, Hawaii came in as the most expensive at $14,975, New England states in the $10,000+ category, and Florida the lowest, at $5,875. Please note, any veteran is entitled to a free burial in a national cemetery, with some eligible veterans receiving some reimbursement for funeral and burial expenses if buried elsewhere.

Most families today coordinate with some kind of funeral home, perhaps known for serving their community in particular, and most offer a wide variety of options and services to choose from. It can be confusing and daunting, especially following the death of a beloved. Are you holding a full-service traditional funeral, which is a service at the funeral home that includes viewings, visitations, staff as ushers, transportation of the body to the burial site, and more? Or are you looking at a simple, direct burial at graveside with no service or ceremony at the funeral home?

When funeral homes refer to the basic service fees that are common to all funerals, this is what will be covered:

- Funeral planning
- Securing copies of death certificates and burial permits
- Preparing the death notice
- Sheltering the remains
- Coordinating arrangements with the cemetery, crematorium, or other third parties

Note the word "basic." If you choose other services or "merchandise," expect more fees: things like a casket or burial container, holding a ceremony or memorial at the funeral home, transporting remains in a limousine, use of staff at burial site, and more.

Expect a funeral home to request a cash advance if you are ordering flowers or paying for clergy to officiate, or special organists or musicians and singers to perform if they are not volunteers or friends. This is only if they are buying or paying for these things with a third party on your behalf. If you are handling these matters privately, let them know.

The Funeral Rule

It is comforting to know that all licensed funeral homes are required to abide by the Funeral Rule, enforced by the Federal Trade Commission. This law protects you and your family, since it allows you to "choose only those goods and services you want or need and to pay only for those you select, whether you are making arrangements when a death occurs or in advance. The Rule allows you to compare prices among funeral homes and makes it possible for you to select the funeral arrangements you want at the home you use," according to the excellent website consumer.ftc.gov/articles/ftc-funeral-rule.

The Funeral Rule prevents unscrupulous funeral directors from pressuring you at a vulnerable time or overcharging. It allows you to buy only the funeral arrangements you want and not a package deal and requires a good-faith written estimate of all costs, including flowers or less predictable costs. Legally, you can get quotes over the phone, without having to give them your name and personal information! Many funeral homes now list their pricing online.

Do not sign anything without carefully reviewing the contract. Look for incomplete estimates, unusual fees, charges you don't recognize, bundling service fees to hide illegal upcharges. And if you feel you have been misled, contact the Funeral Consumers Alliance (funerals.org) or file a complaint with your state consumer protection agency.

Caskets and Costs

Did you know that studies show that the average casket shopper buys one of the first three caskets shown to them by the funeral home employee? But what you may not know is the funeral director may only show you the most expensive ones. Caskets are often the single most expensive item you will buy. The average cost of a casket is about $2,500, but they can range from $650 for a plain pine casket to well over $10,000 for mahogany, bronze, or copper. To protect you, the Funeral Rule requires the funeral director to show you a list of caskets the company sells, with descriptions and prices, before showing you the caskets. It is in the sellers' best interests to show you the higher-cost models and skip over the lower ones altogether. Don't fall for this. Flat out ask what the lowest-cost options are and to see them. You may never choose them, but you will have a comparison. In some cultures, an expensive casket is a sign of wealth and respect. In other cultures, a plain wooden casket is expected, and an expensive casket is ostentatious. You get to choose! Cremation urns cost as little as fifty dollars, but please read on to learn more about the full cost of cremations or casket alternatives.

It is also possible to buy a casket from a third-party dealer and have it shipped to the funeral home. Walmart sells caskets and cremation urns online and can ship for free anywhere in two days' time! You can even buy simple kits from casketbuildersupply.com and put together your own basic

Embalming

Embalming, used by almost every traditional funeral home, uses formaldehyde-based chemicals to preserve the body. Although it is a naturally occurring chemical used in many preservative materials and construction materials such as particleboard, and is readily biodegradable, it is recognized as a carcinogen by the EPA. The funeral industry itself is starting to make major changes partially due to public pressure and the tremendous interest in a greener approach, not to mention the health of the funeral home employees.

Embalming is rarely required by law, *except if interstate transport of the body is needed* or there was a known highly infectious disease at death. However, if someone is having a funeral where the body will be on display for a viewing, a wake, or an open casket, embalming is often chosen. The average cost of embalming is about $500–$1,000, and it includes other types of preparation such as cosmetics, clothing the body, hairdressing, etc. Keep in mind, this represents a small fraction of the overall cost. A possible alternative to embalming is refrigeration of the body, which all funeral homes offer. Some funeral homes now offer formaldehyde-free embalming fluid, which is often made from biodegradable essential oils. Feel free to ask what your options are and the cost differential.

pine box. A funeral home is not allowed by law to upcharge you for purchasing a casket or urn from a third party.

Prepaid Funeral Plans: Pros and Cons

Also sometimes called a "pre-need" plan, a prepaid funeral plan allows one to arrange for the type of funeral services and products that they want, and to pay for them in one lump sum, in installments, or through a trust. When you prepay for a funeral, you are signing a legally binding contract. Generally, there are two types of prepaid options, known as a guaranteed contract and unguaranteed. A guaranteed contract covers all listed expenses at the current rate, so you are not affected by cost increases in the future. A non-guaranteed contract covers expenses up to the amount you've prepaid, which is considered a deposit to be applied to the final cost. If rates increase (and they will), your family will be required to pay the additional amount.

There are also revocable and irrevocable contracts often called "funeral trusts" or "burial trusts." They are used to prepay funeral costs or make sure they are paid at one's death. The funeral trust is a legal agreement between three parties. These include the individual consumer who creates the funeral trust (the trustor, grantor, or settlor), the trustee (the bank, trust company, or funeral home who manages the funeral trust), and the beneficiary (the funeral home that will benefit from the funeral trust). There are some limitations with most states for a funeral trust, usually from $5,000 to $15,000.

There are pluses and minuses to these two options as well. With an irrevocable funeral trust, the trust account is controlled by the bank, not you. But an advantage is that an irrevocable funeral trust is excluded when counting assets to determine if you qualify for Medicaid coverage, but it must be purchased within five years of applying and qualifying for Medicaid benefits. If you set up a revocable funeral trust, then you retain control of your assets. This allows one to make changes to the contract terms, including dissolving the contract and getting most of your prepaid funds back. However, assets included in a revocable trust have an impact on qualifying for Medicaid coverage and will be counted when looking at asset totals. If you know that qualifying for Medicaid is part of your parents' long-term plan, then an irrevocable trust may be an allowable way to shelter funds. A Medicaid specialist in your state will be familiar with the rules. While you cannot cancel an irrevocable contract, you may be able transfer it to another funeral service provider.

Clearly, if a parent can choose their own funeral details and maybe even their own casket, this is a plus. No mutual mystification! Prepaying, if you are locked in costwise, prevents burdening a family with the high cost of funerals, but there are other considerations.

However, it did not take me long to discover an extensive list of reasons to avoid a prepaid funeral plan. Although this used to be thought of as a great idea and a sign of a thoughtful parent who planned, this option has proved problematic. I read of several instances where "Mom" prepaid the funeral home, never mentioned it to the kids, who paid in full, and only found out after the fact that Mom had a prepaid plan. The kids never did get all their money back! What if the funeral home goes out of business by the time your parents pass away? What if the prepaid funds are embezzled by the funeral home director? All of this has happened.

Another concern is that plans generally cannot be transferred. If Mom and Dad pay their funerals ahead of time, and then relocate or move out of state, they are typically out of luck! Even changing your mind on what cemetery you want to be buried in can void the agreement with no money back. Or if they do allow you to transfer or change some condition, they can charge a penalty fee or administrative fee that can be costly. Who can predict what they will do in ten or twenty years or if they would move if they lost their spouse?

Even worse, prepaid plans cannot be changed. As ridiculous as this sounds, changing a flower arrangement or substituting a more affordable coffin may not be allowed and could be considered a breach of contract. Again, high penalty fees. Not all plans are like this, but beware, some are. If Mom chose a $10,000 casket, you might just have to accept it. Many prepaid plans do not cover all funeral costs such as flowers, clergy, car rentals, and more.

Talk with your parents and have them read up on all the cautionary tales about prepaid plans. They can go ahead and plan, just don't pay for it ahead of time. Keep the money set aside in a special fund if they want to have the peace of mind that the cost is taken care of. A professional, honest funeral director will talk about pre-arranging a funeral without requiring prepayment. Better to be safe than sorry! The emphasis needs to be on preplanning not prepaying.

If your family member has already paid the funeral home, just be sure to read through the contract and know ahead of time what to expect. Don't aggravate your parents by suggesting they made a poor decision if the contract cannot be changed.

Cremation

Cremation is a means of final disposition of a body often through high-intensity heat commonly carried out in a closed furnace called a "cremator." The body is mostly reduced to ash, called "cremains," but will always include small bone fragments. A secondary option also offered in the United States and Canada is called "alkaline hydrolysis," and it uses a water-based dissolution process to reduce the human remains to bone fragments as well. The process involves alkaline chemicals, heat, agitation, and pressure to accelerate natural decomposition. This option is typically only available in a few states, but I expect it will become more available over time, as this option is more environment-friendly. Often, these cremains will be placed in an urn, buried in a memorial or burial site, or sometimes disposed of or scattered in various ways.

The basics for this service are:

- Transportation of the deceased from the place of death to the crematory;
- Secure cold storage of deceased prior to cremations;
- The cremation process itself (requiring a special cremation container that is combustible, nontoxic, and nonmetal);
- Return of the cremated remains to the authorized agent.

The cremation business has had its fair share of bad publicity and has undergone some positive changes in both policies and procedures and documentation requirements. Make sure to ask any company what their chain of identification is from the point of removal of the body to confirming the deceased's identity. Each state has different rules and regulations. Find out the law in your state and ask to see a detailed contract so you know what to expect. An excellent website is cremationassociation.org.

Most websites note that the average basic cremation costs can vary from $800 to $4,000, but this does not include costs for a memorial service, urn, or other optional items. Expect more fees for transporting the body and completing a death certificate. Funeral homes usually have a "package" of some kind, but this can increase costs by the thousands. Again, always ask for a breakdown of costs. You could supply your own urn, choose a biodegradable one for less cost, and select other less expensive options. Typical range is about $2,000 to $10,000 on the high end. You could easily spend as much on cremation as a traditional burial. Costs also vary widely from city to city and can differ by many thousands of dollars. Best to sit down with your parents far in advance and find out what they want and encourage them to have a plan. Maybe they prefer to have their ashes scattered at their favorite location, or kept on a mantel, rather than stored in a mausoleum at a cemetery.

The Cons of Cremation

At one time, cremation was thought to be a relatively eco-friendly alternative to traditional burial. But that is not the current thought today, although it is still regarded as less dangerous to the environment than traditional casket burials. Cremation directly contributes to the release of greenhouse gases as well as vaporizing other chemicals such as mercury (think dental fillings), dioxins, and chlorine.

The cremation industry is working on improving emissions and designing more highly effective crematoriums that are more fuel efficient, such as the alkaline hydrolysis option mentioned above. If cremation is your parents' option, you can ask the crematorium if they have a newer system or anything in place to help filter emissions.

What Is a Green Burial?

The Green Burial Council, one of the best resources on this topic, is a not-for-profit corporation that encourages environmentally sustainable death. A true green burial minimizes negative environmental effects by forgoing the usual embalming and traditional caskets. Green funeral homes now offer biodegradable wood, wicker, and even cardboard caskets, all options being far less costly and resource-heavy than your typical casket.

Some people prefer to skip the casket altogether with the idea of returning to "Mother Earth" as quickly as possible. You can purchase a burial shroud, which is specially made and can come with handles and wood panels for the body to be placed on. There is a wonderful green cemetery in my town, and I have heard of people choosing special material, beautiful saris, or a favorite blanket as a shroud. As long as it is biodegradable, like cotton or silk, the green cemetery will accept it. Green caskets or shrouds won't add toxins to the earth as they decompose, unlike commercially produced caskets.

In a green cemetery, large tombstones, cement or metal burial containers, or crypts are not permitted. Instead, flat stone markers or simple plaques are favored or required. Some green cemeteries are created as part of a conservation trust, and any funds generated help preserve the land in the most natural state. For those aiming for the lightest carbon footprint, only GPS markers are used to locate gravesites; there are not even any names on the small metal markers.

Visiting the green cemetery in my town is like going for a peaceful walk in the woods. Except for small mounds with simple natural decorations, you might see wooden crosses, rocks, or various religious symbols made from biodegradable materials meant to eventually disappear. Only native flowers, plants, or trees can be planted. Some people choose a special tree and plant it near or on the grave as a concrete way to nourish the tree and have it become a symbol of their life. You can also opt to purchase a special "living urn" designed to "grow a beautiful, enduring memory tree, plant or flowers with cremated remains." You can purchase a tree directly from Living Urn (the-livingurn.com) for about $160–$170, or buy your own from a local nursery and only purchase the "Bio-Urn" specially developed soil and root system.

How to Find a Green Funeral Home and Green Cemetery

As of 2022, there were approximately 350 registered green cemeteries in the United States and Canada, with these numbers increasing. Only a few are conservation ground burial sites, which specifically aim to restore a purely natural habitat and consequently will have the strictest rules. A large number are "natural" burial sites, still green but with more flexible rules, and then there are hybrid options, which are existing traditional sites that have usually set aside an area of the cemetery for green burials. Some have a religious affiliation so be sure to ask if this is important to you, but most have none. The website of the Green Burial Council (greenburialcouncil.org) lists options state by state and will have up-to-date information. The website us-funerals.com lists green cemeteries using the conservation, natural, and hybrid categories and includes addresses and phone numbers.

Green burial is legal in all fifty states, but rules and regulations for dealing with human remains must be followed. Call the cemetery you have in mind and inquire about their version of what a green burial means and see if it lines up with your parents' plans.

Cost of a Green Burial

The range for a green burial can be as low as $1,000 but likely closer to $4,000 or $5,000, still well below what you would pay for a traditional funeral. There will usually be a cost for the plot, the burial or internment, and the simple casket or urn. There may be a built-in gift that will go toward land preservation. Any cemetery or funeral home should give you a written list of potential expenses. A favorite blanket or homemade shroud costs nothing. This does not include potential costs around a memorial, clergy, flowers, transporting a body, or marker, if allowed. Many cemeteries have a space for families to rent rooms to gather in or hold a post-funeral reception of some kind. Always tour and meet staff before choosing any location or funeral home.

Home Funerals

With more and more emphasis placed on protecting the environment, green burials will become the norm, not the exception. In fact, this approach is simply a return to the traditional way of being buried before industrialization and commercialization of funerals became the accepted standard. As late as the early 1900s, families tended to the dead themselves, especially in rural communities. They washed the body, built the casket, and held the burial at the local cemetery or on family land. This is exactly why home funerals are gaining acceptance again.

By 1955, the funeral industry had evolved to the point where undertakers were the norm, funeral homes had taken over from the family, and the perception grew that there was a legal requirement to hire professionals after death, and that it was illegal to touch a dead body. This actually started changing back in the 1990s, as more home funeral educators began teaching the old skills and promoting family-led funerals. Just as with green burials, part of this renewed interest was a pushback on the financial cost of dying. A home funeral saves thousands of dollars for a family in what they might feel are unnecessary products and services.

According to Final Friends, a grassroots organization in my hometown, home funerals "empower families in caring for their own at death through compassionate guidance and education." They strive to make this a viable option by providing free education and support for a legal home funeral. Again, this option is for those who find it more meaningful and preferable than turning their loved one's body over to a funeral home. They acknowledge that many people are simply uneasy with the thought of being with or touching a dead body, and our culture certainly does not promote it. However, allowing those to be lovingly present during this profound time of losing a loved one has changed many people's minds. End-of-life doulas are usually knowledgeable and can help you with this option.

If you are planning a home funeral, you can expect to take responsibility for:

- Planning and carrying out after-death rituals and ceremonies
- Preparing the body for burial or cremation by bathing, dressing, and laying out for visitation
- Keeping the body cool with noninvasive techniques such as ice
- Filing the death certificate and obtaining transport and burial permits
- Facilitating the final disposition, such as digging the grave or preparing the gravesite

Families who choose this option report experiencing a sense of completion, a sense of peace, and more connection to family, friends, and community. Sometimes family members feel very disconnected from the whole process of death. This allows for family to gather at a time of sorrow and loss, focus on the task at hand, and participate in what used to be the common bond of family burial. People report that home burials give them time to grieve and say a personal goodbye to their loved one rather than seeing their family member, maybe for the last time, in a hospital setting. The family can decide for themselves how to memorialize, celebrate, and grieve for their deceased loved one. It gives family members a chance to support each other, talk about life and death, and accept and process death in a way a funeral home simply cannot. People feel that this approach is more authentic, affordable, and meaningful, but it is still not the norm for most families.

Keeping or bringing a loved one home from an institution after death is legal in every state for bathing, dressing, private viewing, and any ceremony the family chooses. Every state recognizes the next-of-kin's custody and control of the body that allows for a home vigil. Many people are confused about this issue and think a funeral home must be involved in all aspects of a funeral, but this is absolutely not true.

Refer to the National Home Funeral Alliance website (homefuneral alliance.org) for all the information you could need on a home funeral and any rules or regulations particular to your state. You can also find a local support group that can help you. There are end-of-life forms you will need to get such as a death certificate, body transit permit, and burial permit from your local city and county. Some states also require a form for someone to be the designated or "acting" funeral director; otherwise, a licensed funeral director must sign the form. All of these forms are easily obtainable with a little guidance.

Bob Spencer's Passing

Bob Spencer dies peacefully, surrounded by his whole family, just the way he had planned, with the help of his end-of-life doula. He makes it to his eighty-sixth birthday before he has another stroke, this one fatal. He has his favorite music playing softly, and family members read specific scriptures and some of his favorite poems during his last few days. He has a chance to say his final goodbyes, especially to Sally, his children, and even his grandchildren, who are now in their teens, before he slips into unconsciousness. He had decided on a traditional burial in a lovely hybrid green cemetery near Raleigh that he and Sally had visited when he was still able, and they had picked out side-by-side plots under a beautiful live oak. He opted for a simple pine box, as he was a practical man, and he liked the idea of a smaller carbon footprint.

Bob, Sally, and the end-of-life doula, Shanti, had planned a beautiful ceremony together to be held in the church they had been attending in North Carolina. All his adult children had a role in the service, and all had agreed to his requests. Many of Bob and Sally's friends from Maple Hill came, as well as friends from all over the country. It's everything Bob could have hoped for—a wonderful celebration of his life, full of shared memories, laughter, and tears. This is his final gift to his family.

A Prepared Exit Plan

Losing your parents is a time of tremendous loss and grief for most. You want your focus to be on this time of final farewell with a plan that reflects your parents' and your family's wishes. Ideally, funerals should be a time of gathering loved ones to remember the passing of someone important in their lives, not scrambling and guessing what the person wanted. As I suggested in the first section of the book, you can safely bring this up by applying this to yourself. If you like the idea of a green burial for yourself one day, share this with your parents. Talk about it as it applies to you and your peace of mind. Knowing that you love them and care enough about them to have this conversation will mean everything to them . . . and to you.

Chapter 18

Practical Guidelines for the Aftermath: What's Next?

Hopefully you have been able to discuss with your parents what they think is a good death, and what kind of funeral/burial they want as well. But even after they pass away, there is yet more planning to do. The truth is, despite the grief and stress of losing a parent, this period of time demands that you pay attention to an array of legal and financial matters. If you happen to be the executor or personal representative, this is even more true. Hopefully your parent was well organized, and if so, you can be very grateful. This chapter will provide both a basic timeline and some guidelines for handling the aftermath of a loved one's death.

But first, let's acknowledge the grief. The loss of a parent is traumatic, no matter what your relationship was like with your mother or father or stepparent. For those of you fortunate enough to have a wonderful, close, loving relationship, it is tremendously difficult. And it can be equally hard to lose someone who you had difficulty with or worse. There is a finality in death that forever freezes all the memories and inevitably, it brings up a lot of emotions. Be kind to yourself and your extended family as they process their grief in their own way, and for as long as needed.

There is some good news. I am 100 percent certain that if you have been able to gather all the medical and financial information mentioned in Chapters 2 and 3, you will be far more prepared for the aftermath of losing a parent. Ideally, the best time to review the lists in these previous chapters to see what you may be missing is before a parent's death. Remember, you may be notifying all kinds of companies about the death of a loved one, and you will need account numbers, passwords, and more. Trying to find critical documents after the fact is far more difficult.

The First Few Days After

Planning a Funeral

- Make a list of all the friends and family you need to contact who should be notified of the death. If possible, ask other family members to help you with this difficult task.
- Choose a date for any services and reserve any church space, reception halls, or contact any catering services if needed.
- If your parents belonged to a place of worship, you may already know who to ask to officiate at the funeral. If not, decide if this will be a family member, if they agree, or an old friend.
- Always ask other family members if they would like to speak at the funeral so they have time to decide and prepare if needed. It might be that only a few family members are present at the funeral and a memorial is held at a later date.

The important thing to remember is communicating about your intentions and arrangements, whatever they are, so people can plan ahead. It may be that far-flung family attends via Zoom. Many families pay for long-distance family members to travel to the funeral using estate funds, if possible.

If you hired an experienced funeral director, they will be able to walk you through some of the most immediate needs. Are you ordering flowers, or are they? Will staff be ushering or will friends and family? Is the service in a house of worship or in the funeral home? Is there a reception after the service and where is it being held? Are friends bringing food or do you need a catering service? Is everyone invited to the graveside (or actual burial) or only immediate family? There are lots of funeral details they can remind you of: who will speak, what might be read, what music played, poems recited, songs sung, flowers ordered.

Many families now put together a digital slideshow that brings back wonderful memories and can be shown while people are first arriving or again at a reception. This is a great task for a tech-savvy family member. The funeral home or place of worship will have ideas on a program and may even print it for you. Think about any Bible verses, religious scriptures, or meaningful words that could be included. Even if family cannot be present for this preplanning, try to include them via Zoom or FaceTime so no one is left out.

Plan on at least ten copies or more of the death certificate, usually provided by the funeral director. If you are doing a home funeral, you may be responsible for getting one from your local city or county. They will be required by all insurance companies, banks, Social Security, the IRS, and more. Most of these entities want certified copies. Death certificates vary from state to state and usually cost from ten to twenty-five dollars for the first one, and then much less for more copies.

The funeral director can help you choose a casket or urn or tell you the rules of a green cemetery if applicable. Please, reread the previous chapter on funerals and caskets before purchasing one so you don't get scammed.

If your loved one was active on social media, it is a good idea to let their friends know on this platform. It can come as a terrible shock for people who don't know, so be as thoughtful as possible about how news is posted and when.

Writing an Obituary

An obituary is an announcement of a person's death and often includes information about where the person was born, grew up, went to school, their college, career, or military service, and more. Generally, it lists surviving spouse, children, grandchildren, and other family members as well as details about the funeral, memorial, and location, etc. Sometimes working on an obituary together with other family members can provide together time to share memories and history.

Think about any other organizations that would want to know, so members could possibly attend a funeral or memorial.

In the obituary, don't forget to list any charitable organizations you wish to receive a memorial donation in lieu of flowers. You can easily go online to see what information is usually included in an obituary. A very helpful website is legacy.com for all kinds of information about obits and funerals nationally. You can search funeral homes by keywords or zip codes, order flowers, and search for any obituary. The cost of a print newspaper obituary can vary greatly, from approximately $100 for basic information to over $1,000 if lengthy and including a photo. Do a little research on your options, and consider if posting online or through the funeral home is enough.

The First Few Weeks

If You Are the Personal Representative

With the funeral service behind you, you can try and shift your focus to the tedious but absolutely necessary tasks at hand. Most of the tasks I list are carried out by the personal representative, the person your deceased loved one chose to carry out these duties and named in the will or trust. If they chose you, they trusted you, and you must accept this big responsibility.

By this time, you have notified your parent's attorney, located the will, and confirmed you are, indeed, the personal representative. If there was no attorney, you may be looking for a will in a safe deposit box—or even a shoebox on top of mom or dad's closet! My prayer is that you are not guessing where the will is, as you should either have a copy or know precisely who does if you have followed the advice in this book. If your parent did not have a lawyer, you may be hiring one now. I highly recommend getting an attorney's advice if your parents had any assets at all. If there is truly no will, and no attorney, the estate will be handled by the state your parent resided in at death.

I have been the personal representative for three estates. It was far more responsibility than I had imagined, and in one case lasted years. I can tell you that the state of New York has both complex and convoluted laws, so don't die in New York!

You can always ask other friends or family members to help you with these tasks to lessen the burden, provided you know they will accomplish these duties in a timely fashion and report back to you. Start with these tasks first:

- Contact your parents' lawyer, financial planner, and accountant.
- Check to make sure you have a copy of the latest will/trust and so does the attorney.
- Contact your parents' bank(s) to inform them of the death.
- Check for safety deposit boxes and/or keys.
- Notify all insurance companies (life, health, auto, more).
- Check to see if the death affects any health insurance or pension income for the surviving spouse.
- Collect any critical documents such as Social Security cards, driver's license, birth and marriage certificates.
- Notify the Social Security office, the Veterans Affairs office, and return any checks that arrive after the date shown on the death certificate. However, find out if there are any death benefits to cover funeral costs.
- Determine if a surviving spouse is eligible to switch to a higher Social Security amount with the death of their spouse.

Keep in mind that many of these companies will want some kind of proof about who you are as well as a certified copy of a death certificate, not a scanned copy. It is easier to order more than you need than to run out.

Avoiding Scams

One of the reasons that it is important you handle this in a timely fashion has to do with scams. Criminals read the obituaries and sometimes target susceptible spouses or try to hack accounts or worse! Notifying the proper institutions sooner can add a layer of safety and peace of mind for you and your surviving parent. Thieves have even been known to break into a home during a funeral if they think it will be vacant! Ask friends, neighbors, or even the police to keep an eye on things.

The First Few Months

Make a List of All Assets and Debts

As personal representative, now that you have the first line of critical tasks done, you can begin to move on to the other ones. This may take no time at all—or be the heaviest burden on your time. It depends on how many assets your parents had, and if all assets revert to the surviving spouse and thus are not getting distributed at all. Did they bank in multiple locations, have investment accounts with numerous companies, own property in more than one state . . . or country? The more complicated their finances, the longer this will take. In some cases, this process of gathering assets can take years. A lot will depend on the instructions of the will or the trusts. Is property being sold and the money being split between siblings or others? Are other assets, like a business, being sold as well? A second home? If a will or trust is well written, there should be no guessing. If there is no will, then much of this will be put in probate and decided by the court and the state laws. As the personal representative, here is another list of important issues to follow up on:

- Make a list of all assets (titles, deeds, investments, property, IRAs, savings, checking accounts, stocks, bonds, cars, boats, jewelry, etc.).
- Get appraisals of property if needed.

- ♀ Make a list of remaining debts and current bills and pay these out of the estate.
- ♀ Cancel all credit cards as soon as possible or drop/add names if needed and pay balances out of the estate.
- ♀ Obtain copies of the most recent tax returns.
- ♀ If your parent was still employed, check to see if there is any pension plan, or benefits yet to be paid, or unpaid salary.
- ♀ If they owned a business or were part of a partnership, see if you can find the corporate documents and be sure to consult an attorney.

I had a good friend who died very suddenly a few days after he turned seventy and left his lovely wife behind. Despite having a will, his business was not listed as part of his estate, as this was a fairly new endeavor. Both he and his partner invested heavily in the business together, and it was taking off. The end result was unfortunate. The wife was not listed as a beneficiary in any way for the business, nor was she on any corporate paperwork as a shareholder. The partner was uncooperative and basically walked away with the business because he could.

Taxes

You will want to get professional advice on paying necessary taxes, including estate and inheritance taxes. Look to the attorney or accountant to advise you. You cannot procrastinate with the IRS on unpaid or back taxes or you will face serious penalties and interest fees.

Surviving Spouse

Make sure to talk with the surviving spouse about updating their will, as well as any insurance policies. Check to see if any beneficiary information needs updating. Anything owned or held jointly will need to be changed.

Avoiding Family Conflict

Being a personal representative can be very stressful. Ideally, the will and/or trust are documents shared with all parties involved. Try to reassure anxious family members that you are doing your best. Ask your attorney if they can help you with some of the tasks, if possible. Communication is key, especially with difficult family or stepfamily members. Some wills allow for a personal representative to be paid. If so, be transparent about this.

- Send out weekly or monthly emails updating involved family members.
- Show official reports, receipts, or legal documents to verify information.
- Ask the attorney to be present at these meetings to answer any questions.
- Hire a professional mediator for very difficult situations.
- Postpone disbursement of personal belongings and family heirlooms until three months after the death.

Dividing Family Possessions: When Is the Right Time?

Dividing possessions can be a real minefield for families. It could happen right away, or months after a death. Most experts will advise that it is best to postpone this ritual of dividing possessions for months if possible. Waiting for the wave of grief to subside and emotions to settle down is a good idea. The important thing is to have a system or method for distribution. Talk to others who have been through this for suggestions. Whoever is the executor/personal representative gets to have the final say, like it or not. Some families will hire a mediator, friend, or aging life care specialist to help with this if they anticipate problems. If you already know that some relationships are strained, set some firm rules. You can even set up a random system, like drawing straws, where family members take turns choosing one item until everything is taken.

Special things like Mom's rings or Dad's tools may be wanted by multiple family members if they have not been designated yet, so have a plan to address this. One idea is to ask family members to list several of their most wanted items, and have an independent person try to evenly distribute them. If you are lucky, your parents made clear lists of who is getting what, but inevitably someone's feelings are hurt. Most wills usually make general statements such as "property divided equally" among children. Trying to divide items that hold a sentimental value or are perceived as family heirlooms is problematic for even the most loving families.

I have seen families at their worst during this time, and it can scar families for life. If there are items of great value, maybe your parent has indicated who will inherit it or if this item should be sold with all monies going back to the trust. No matter what, handle this situation with the utmost care. My own mother wrote endless "codicils" or additions to the will that listed item after item and who would get what. In the end, this was helpful and left little to decide. My three sisters and I put our relationships first, possessions second, so it all worked out. Ask yourself if losing a relationship with a sister is worth the set of Grandma's china.

One thought is to encourage your parents to give things away while they are very much alive. My older sister knew she did not have long, and at what turned out to be our last visit, she gave away all her jewelry to her daughter, daughter-in-law, and her sisters. She got so much enjoyment from sharing this experience with all of us, and we all felt a bond of love by being together at this time.

If family is too spread out, you can consider taking photos of all major items and posting them online with descriptions and general value. If there are lots of things that no one wants, it may be time to bring in a company that will either have an estate sale or work with you to sell items online or donate them to a charitable organization. They will all charge a fee for these services, and I suggest vetting them carefully. I knew one company that shipped a piano to Australia, so anything is possible, if you can handle the cost.

Heads-up: It can be very emotional to see family items being casually looked at by strangers, so I advise not being present at this type of sale. Hire someone you trust and ask some friends to help oversee this type of estate sale. Spare yourself this kind of upset. On top of the grief, you don't need it.

If you are selling a home, some top-notch companies handle not only an estate sale but full cleanup as well. I have a realtor friend who focuses on helping seniors and their families, even when the senior is moving into a retirement community or assisted-living facility. She will take on all aspects of staging a home to get it ready to sell. She also will coordinate any repairs or simple remodeling to maximize the sale price. Look for a certified "senior move specialist" as they will be more likely to help you or know who can.

A Final Goodbye to the Spencers

After her dad's funeral, Josie's priority is her mom, Sally. It is difficult for both of them, losing a husband of sixty-one years and a beloved father. They support each other through this period of grief. Sally realizes that she and Bob made the right decision years ago to move from New Jersey to North Carolina to be closer to Josie and Dan. If she were still in their old house alone and far from family, she would be facing a different life now with Bob gone. Being closer to family has made a huge difference to both her and Bob over these last difficult years.

Living at Maple Hill has given Sally the support network she needed, and Josie is grateful her parents had decided to move closer to her and build their own life before the "slow-go" and "no-go" years set in. It gives Josie great peace of mind to know that her parents have completed all their advance directives, financial planning, and estate planning. It takes Sally some time after Bob's death to reengage, but she does. Josie and Sally plan to give treasured items that Bob had designated in his gift list to family members at their upcoming family reunion, three months after the funeral.

Sally decides to give away many of her treasured items at the reunion as well, while she can enjoy it. Josie and Sally work together over the next year to wrap up all Bob's business involvements and details. They go through my list and contact the insurance companies, banks, etc., and opt to switch Sally to Bob's Social Security since it is so much higher than hers. The Spencers had already sold their home in New Jersey, so there was no property to sell. Sally decides she wants to move to a smaller apartment at Maple Hill with a lower monthly fee, and she chooses a one-bedroom-and-den apartment she loves.

Josie finds a quiet moment to sit down with her mother and ask her: *"What do you want out of the next three to five years of your life?"* Sally says she wants to be as prepared as her husband was to face her own death. But in the meanwhile, she is planning on living to at least ninety-five and maybe even one hundred! She knows she has the support she needs from her family and from her community *to maintain her independence for the longest possible time!* Her goal? To enjoy life and to be a great grandmother.

Moving Forward

My hope is that when the funeral is over, you will be able to come up for air. I can tell you that even when the business part is settled, the grief will last for years. I still find myself crying unexpectedly as I remember losing the ones I loved. Everyone processes grief in their own way. No matter what kind of relationship you had with a parent, losing one is a momentous sea change. Please be kind and patient with yourself and your family members. Get help if you need it. A grief support group may be a lifeline for you or a surviving parent. There is no perfect time period to process grief, and a wide range of feelings are all normal, including relief, anger, guilt, sadness, and great sorrow. Although I lost all my parents many years ago, I have a tradition of lighting a candle on the anniversaries of their deaths and placing a photo of them by the candle. I honor their memory and practice gratitude for all they gave me during their lifetime. I consciously try to focus on the positives and let go of the negatives.

Hopefully, my book has given you a framework to use with your loved ones: making decisions that will maximize your parents' independence and develop flexible resilient plans. No matter what your age or stage in life, you, too, have the opportunity to look ahead and plan for yourself.

> Do not complain about growing old. It is a privilege denied to many.
>
> **Mark Twain**

Conclusion

Long-term planning is not about making long-term decisions; it is about understanding the consequences of today's decisions. What decisions can you and your parents make now that are within your control, that will have great impact on your future and theirs? Instead of "plan for the worst, and hope for the best," my hope is that this book will help you both *plan for the best and be prepared for the worst*. Accepting that it is not *if*, but **when**, your parents will need your help, will hopefully give you the motivation to get the ball rolling, as Chapter 1 advises. Below is an outline that loosely follows the book that will serve as a general guide for you as you help develop a plan with your parents. I will reference pertinent chapters in each step so you can go back and review for more in-depth information.

Keep in mind that your future may be intricately entwined with your parents or loved ones. According to the latest AARP poll, the responsibility of caregiving is now affecting over 16.8 percent of the US population—an estimated 41.8 million people. Being prepared will help you all. Any plan is better than no plan, and my book provides you with the education and the tools you need to navigate these waters successfully.

Step #1: Get the Ball Rolling

Assess your parents' situation. Are they in the go-go, slow-go, or no-go years? This will help you determine your priorities, but don't get too complacent, as life inevitably throws curveballs. Apply the two basic principles from Chapter 1 that you can use as a framework moving forward for years to come:

- ♀ Principle #1: Maximizing and prolonging your parents' independence
- ♀ Principle #2: Applying the JITSP ("just in time" senior planning) concept

Take a team approach, involve other family members if possible, and start with gentle questions about your parents' plans, hopes, and desires for their future years. Review the Five Pillars of Aging Successfully in Chapter 1 and take a realistic look at what needs to come first.

Step #2: Complete and Organize Important Medical and Financial Documents

Don't wait for a crisis! Find out if your parents have completed the critical medical documents such as a living will or healthcare proxy forms, collectively known as advance directives. Chapter 2 explains what these documents are and why they are so important, as well as other vitally important forms and suggestions. Chapter 3 explains the importance of a will and who needs one, the importance of assigning a power of attorney, and more. Ask your parents if they have completed a will or trust and where they keep all their important documents including insurance policies, deeds, investment accounts, safe deposit box information, etc. Remind them that you *are not asking to see all these documents*, just where they can be found, or information about their attorney or accountant who handles their business. If they share their documents, for instance, uploading everything to Dropbox or any cloud format, make sure you, your parent, and at least one other person know the password! Make sure they review these documents every few years, especially after a divorce, remarriage, death of one parent, or anyone appointed as HCS (healthcare surrogate) or POA (Power of Attorney) becoming unable to carry out their responsibilities. Consider a video summarizing your parents' end-of-life wishes and other critical information. Remember, though, a video is not a replacement for the actual documents. Ask your parents to introduce you to their financial planner, attorney, and accountant, or simply ask if you can call and introduce yourself. Don't be a complete stranger to these key people. It is likely you will need their help at some point.

Step #3: Plan for the Next Step: Aging in Place, Relocation, Downsizing?

Should your parents move closer to you, stay in their home, consider a senior community of some kind? Part Two looks at all the options and helps you and your parents review their plan based on helpful criteria. If your parents are aging in place or this is the plan for the future, assess their home and prioritize what to do first based on the information in Chapter 6. Review current technology and see what you can practically utilize to help maximize your parents' independence and safety. Is it the latest security system, medical alert system, medication organizer?

Make a list of the possible senior communities in their area or the other cities they may move to and begin investigating and touring these options years ahead of any possible move. Wait lists for very successful communities can be years! Review Chapter 7 to learn the best way to tour and ask the right questions, and view and download the full list of questions at starbradbury .com/resources.

Do your parents know about life care communities (Chapter 8)? Is this an option they will consider? What other possibilities are there that are more affordable (Chapter 9)? Senior roommates, tiny house options, NORCs (naturally occurring retirement communities)? Get creative about your options.

Step #4: Planning for Dementia

If there is dementia in your family (and this does not mean it will happen to you), make sure to reread Chapter 4 and take all the steps listed to be prepared for the worst. Remember that many other things contribute to cognitive impairment, so be sure your loved one has a full professional assessment from a trained neurologist, geriatrician, or geriatric psychiatrist. Talk with their attorney about pre-need guardianship if you feel a power of attorney may not be enough. It is critical that any medical advance directives and legal financial documents are completely in order before the disease progresses to the point where your loved one can no longer make their wishes known, or no attorney will accept their signature or any changes to documents.

Step #5: Educate Yourself on Options for Increased Care

Again, don't wait for a crisis! Find out what your local USAging office offers in the way of free classes, services, and workshops. Ask for lists of local senior retirement communities, senior housing, and assisted-living communities as well. I recommend this even if you don't think they need this level of care. It is helpful to know what is available . . . for a future possibility! Go visit nearby retirement communities, assisted living, and if you're ambitious, skilled nursing facilities, especially if your parents are in the slow-go years and already have any kind of serious health issues. Go with a sibling, a friend, and check these out. Older friends of mine just told me they were on a wait list for ten years for a retirement community to get the apartment they wanted! Find out if your parents have a relationship with a home care or home healthcare company (Chapter 10), and explore what reputable companies operate in the area your parents live. Consider yourself part of your parents' healthcare team: your parents, you as advocates, and their medical professionals.

Step #6: What Is the Strength of Your Parents' Support Team?

Do your parents have at least four or five good friends who can help them out in an emergency? Are they still socially connected to their community, such as being involved with a senior center, a religious organization, a service club, or sorority or fraternal organization? Data shows that they will age successfully based primarily on the strength of their support network. Get the names and contact information for all their neighbors and friends they (and you) could rely on in an emergency, especially if you are a long-distance caregiver (Chapter 14).

If you have siblings or extended family, get them involved at the beginning. Call a family meeting and see if you and your parents and the whole family can sit down and talk about various future options. Better to see what conflict might come up before a crisis and iron out some issues now if needed. Review Chapter 1 on developing a plan emphasizing independence and the JIT three- to five-year window. Follow the lead of our pretend family, the Spencers and divvy up assignments to willing parties. If you're in this alone, build your own support team with friends who are willing to help you. Consider hiring a specialist or professional from ALCA, the Aging Life Care Association, to help you.

Step #7: Plan for the Cost of Long-Term Care

The old expression "forewarned is forearmed" is true. You have learned from Chapter 15 that Medicare does not pay for long-term care. While this may change if our government decides to structure a national approach for long-term care, I would not plan on it. If your parents are still in their late sixties, talk with them now, and ask them how they are planning on paying for long-term care of any kind, such as care in their own home with home care, home healthcare, or private care if ever needed in the future. Do they know the cost of home care, assisted living, or skilled care? Help educate them: make sure to visit the Genworth cost of care survey and sit down and show them current costs and the cost calculator predicting future costs. Review Part Three for details on this topic.

If you think your parents will qualify for Medicaid, or this *is* the plan, remember it can take a long time and lots of paperwork to qualify. Do not make assumptions; get expert advice. Spend the money to hire an elder-law attorney or a Medicaid application specialist. It will be worth it. Some work on a sliding scale!

Step #8: Open the Discussion with Your Parents About End-of-Life Care, Services, Wishes

It is hard enough to lose a parent or loved one, without adding the stress of wondering what they truly wanted at the end of their life. Don't be afraid to open this discussion—many families that lost loved ones during Covid wished they had. Your parents will appreciate your willingness to ask and your desire to know. They are likely more practical about their own death than you are as the adult "child." This is not the time for what I call "mutual mystification." What would constitute "a good death," for your loved one? Even if you are not their healthcare proxy, you may still be able to support the person they have chosen for this role. It will help if you know for yourself if they want the "slow medicine" approach (see Chapter 16) or all possible procedures and life-saving measures. Have they planned for a funeral or a special memorial? What would they like? A green burial (Chapter 17)? If you still don't know where their important legal documents are, make sure to ask. Don't wait until it is too late, and you can't find a will at all, as happened to me!

Step #9: Check-In Time: What Applies to You?

If you are one of the likely readers whose parent(s) is in their nineties or one hundred or more, then by all means use this book to plan for yourself. Even if you are in your thirties or forties, you could start a tax-free health savings account! Long-term care is not ever going to go away, and the cost will always go up. Currently this cost is estimated to be increasing at 7 percent a year. After Covid, staffing shortages, and the crisis in all areas of medical and long-term care, I expect the perfect storm. It is not too soon to plan for yourself. Apply everything you have already learned, and you will be far more able to maximize your own independence and age successfully. If you have children, they will be ever so grateful to know you are developing a plan and would like their assistance.

Step #10: Stay Flexible

Recognize that there is no such thing as a perfect plan. Or perfect parents, or perfect children, or perfect caregiving. Life is likely going to throw us all curveballs. Most of us never thought a worldwide pandemic would disrupt our lives for years. And during this time, we all had to adjust, like it or not. Do the best you can and accept that it still might not be enough. Be patient with yourself, be kind, repeat. For the many years I worked in senior living, I always reminded the caregivers that if they did not take care of themselves, they would not be there to take care of anyone. It is OK to say no, it is OK to say you can't do any more, it is OK to say you need a break. Boundaries are healthy and work both ways. Whether you are caregiving out of love or obligation, it is stressful. Use the framework of Principles #1 and #2 to guide your decisions, keep "Plan B" going for the inevitable, and *stay flexible*. The best possible gift you can give your parents is your time and energy helping them develop a plan to age successfully!

Acknowledgments

Considering this book was a process that unfolded over years, please forgive me if I left out your name!

I'd like to start with my wonderful agent, Wendy Keller, who believed in me and whipped me into shape. She taught me what it means to write a top-notch book proposal, and best of all, sold my book! I am forever grateful she took a chance on me and guided and supported me all along the way.

I also want to thank:

BenBella Books and my senior editor, Leah Wilson, who saw the book's potential in her own life, with her own parents, and knew my book could help many other families. Her suggestions were always thoughtful and incisive and helped me write a better book! And thanks to Joe Rhatigan, who also assisted in artfully editing my book without losing sight of my vision.

My many friends who reside at Oak Hammock at the University of Florida, and all the seniors I have met throughout my career who modeled what it means to age successfully and accept life's next adventures.

Special thanks to my friend Shirley Bloodworth, who at ninety-plus is still going strong and working to make a difference for her entire community. Her enthusiasm for life and her support of me has been an invaluable source of inspiration. I am also grateful to Dr. Leilani Mangerian Doty for her years of encouragement and support, and to Dr. Golant for his organizational guidance early in my book writing process.

My coach, Nelson Logan, who always provided sage advice and wisdom, and challenged me not to give up, and my entire Mastermind coaching group, who encouraged me over the years.

Landmark Education, which inspired me to make a difference, and Della McMillan, who told me I needed to write a book to help adult children who, she said, "need more help than our parents!"

My professional colleagues and past coworkers, who have provided inspiration and guidance in the field of senior living and eldercare. To all the senior advocacy groups I have been involved with for years, including my church community, thank you for your encouragement.

Special thanks to my dear friend of many years, Chris Takashima, who provided her expert advice in too many areas to list, as well as countless hours of both professional and emotional support! I am truly grateful for our decades-long friendship.

Thanks as well to my husband, Mitchell—who was endlessly patient, made sure I came up for air occasionally, fed me great dinners night after night, and gave me years of unwavering support—and to my sisters, Robin and Andrea, for their endless patience, and my children, Daniel, Alison, and Jake, who sometimes watched me write during family vacations and never complained. Special shout-out to Jake, who helped with video creations, writing support, and more.

If not for the endless encouragement from my community, dear friends, and family to keep writing through deaths of parents, in-laws, sisters, cousins, and good friends, not to mention Covid, I would not have finished this book. I am grateful to all of you.

Commonly Used Terms in Senior Healthcare and Senior Living

Senior Healthcare, Facility Terminology, and Oversight Agency Acronyms

AAA: Area Agencies on Aging

ACHA: Agency for Healthcare Administration (in Florida)

AD: Advance directive

AD: Alzheimer's disease

ADA: Americans with Disabilities Act

ADLs: Activities of daily living

ADC: Adult day care

AIP: Aging in place

ALCM: Aging life care manager

AL: Assisted living

ALF: Assisted-living facility

AND: Allow natural death (similar to DNR)

AOA: Administration on Aging

APS: Adult Protective Services

CARF: Commission on Accreditation of Rehabilitation Facilities

CCRC: Continuing Care Retirement Community

CCM: Certified care manager

CGCM: Certified geriatric care manager

CMS: Centers for Medicare and Medicaid Services

DNR: Do not resuscitate (end-of-life directive)

ECC: Extended congregate care

EHR: Electronic health record

EMR: Electronic medical record

GCM: Geriatric care manager or case manager

HHA: Home health agency; alternately, home health aide

HHC: Home healthcare

IADL: Instrumental activities of daily living

IC: Intensive care

ICF: Intermediate care facility

ICU: Intensive care unit

IL: Independent living

IRF: Inpatient rehab facility

LCC: Life care community (also known as a CCRC)

LCRC: Life care retirement community (same as CCRC)

LPC: Life plan community (same as CCRC)

LMH: Limited Mental Health license (referring to a level of certification for group living or assisted living)

LTC: Long-term care

LTCI: Long-term care insurance

MCO: Managed-care organization

MC: Memory care

NCC: Nursing care center

NIA: National Institute on Aging (with Dept. of Health & Human Services)

NH: Nursing home

OTC: Over the counter (medications)

PCA: Personal care assistant

PCP: Primary care provider or physician

PCAL Person-centered approach, or PPC, person-centered care

PERS: Personal Emergency Response Systems

PHI: Protected health information

PPO: Preferred provider organization

SNU: Skilled nursing unit

SNF: Skilled nursing facility

UBRC: University-based retirement community (usually a life care community as well)

Medical Acronyms

ARNP: Advanced registered nurse practitioner

BID: From the Latin phrase "bis in die," meaning two times a day, as in a dose of medication

CAT or CT scan: Computerized axial tomography scan

CNA: Certified nursing assistant

CHF: Congestive heart failure

COPD: Chronic obstructive pulmonary disease

DNR: Do not resuscitate

DME: Durable medical equipment

EMS: Emergency medical services

EMT: Emergency medical technician

ER: Emergency room

HHA: Home health aide

HCP: Healthcare proxy

HCS: Healthcare surrogate

HCBS: Home and community-based services

HIPAA: Health Insurance Portability and Accountability Act

HMO: Health maintenance organization

HSA: Health spending account

LPN: Licensed practical nurse

MAP: Medicare Advantage plan

MD: Medical doctor

MRI: Magnetic resonance imaging

NP: Nurse practitioner

OT: Occupational therapist

PA: Physician's assistant

PACE: Program of All-Inclusive Care for the Elderly

PCP: Primary care provider

POLST: Physician Orders for Life-Sustaining Treatment

PT: Physical therapist

QID: From the Latin phrase "quater in die," meaning four times a day, as in dosage for medications

RC: Respite care or short-term care provided by a facility to give the caregiver a break

RN: Registered nurse

RT: Respiratory therapy

ST: Speech therapy

TID: From the Latin phrase "ter in die," meaning three times a day, as in dosage for medications

Online Resources

For the following information and other helpful resources, see
https://starbradbury.com/resources/.

Useful Websites

Tools, educational materials, and more on . . .

- ♀ General support for seniors and their families
- ♀ Home safety and aging in place, including AgeTech
- ♀ Retirement communities, life care communities, and creative living options
- ♀ Home care, adult day care, assisted living, rehab care, and skilled care (including how to find and compare ratings and survey information)
- ♀ Medicare, Medicaid, and other ways of paying for long-term care
- ♀ Dementia, hospice, and end of life care
- ♀ Funerals, cremations, and green burials (including advance planning tools)

List of Critical Medical and Financial Documents

Questions to Ask When Touring Any Senior Community or Care Facility

My free, easy-to-print list of the crucial questions to ask when touring any senior community or facility (PDF download), plus what to ask when:

- Hiring a home health care or home care company
- Shopping for medical alert systems or medication reminders
- Shopping for long-term care insurance
- Getting on facility wait lists
- And more

Index

About the Author

As a senior living expert, Star Bradbury has helped thousands of families make educated and informed decisions as they navigate the world of senior living and senior healthcare. She has twenty-five years' experience in the industry and is the founder of Senior Living Strategies, LLC, a consulting firm focused on helping seniors and their families develop a plan to age successfully.

Star is a member of the Aging Life Care Association and the American Society on Aging and is a regular contributor to her local *USA Today* newspaper writing on topics of interest to seniors and their families. She also speaks and presents at various events and conferences.

You can find Star's articles, helpful videos, and lists of resources on her website, www.starbradbury.com.

She lives in Gainesville, Florida, with her husband.